THE WASTED AMERICANS

THE WASTED AMERICANS

Cost of Our Welfare Dilemma

BY EDGAR MAY

HARPER & ROW, PUBLISHERS New York, Evanston, and London

LIBRARY OF CONGRESS CATALOG CARD NUMBER: 63-20325

To Gaston Bloch and his daughters

. . . in part payment for a great heritage

CONTENTS

Preface ix
1. Go to the Ant, Thou Sluggard . . . 1
2. Newburgh: The Catalyst 17
3. The Shadow Children 38
4. The Obsolete Young 60
5. 65 Plus 85
6. The Turnstile Guardians 104
7. Pay to the Order of . . . 122
8. A Whispered Solution 144
9. The Welfare Curtain 170
10. Whose Welfare? 189
Notes 209
Index 221

PREFACE

Although I did not know it at the time, this book was begun the day the Welfare Department in Buffalo, New York, hired me as a caseworker. When I started that job in January 1960, I was simply a newspaper reporter masquerading as a welfare worker. (The Erie County Department of Social Welfare was unaware that I was conducting an investigation for a newspaper series.) Even though my real identity remained undetected until the first article appeared more than six months later, the fake-caseworker role wore off in the early weeks. The need to consciously pretend disappeared. I fully became a caseworker. I found myself thinking like a caseworker. I became annoyed and angry like a caseworker, often about decisions and policies that would go into effect long after I knew I would be back at my reporter's desk. It was a welfare coworker, quoted later in this book, who made me first aware of my commitment:

"I used to be just like you are," she said. "But I learned . . . you can't beat the system. If you try it, you'll crack up. You see things that are all wrong, but if you get excited about them, you'll wear yourself out."

This book is an effort to contradict that statement. It is an attempt to get Americans excited about a large group of their fellow citizens who are unknown to some and who may have been overlooked by others. This book is not a historical or clinical discussion of the government's public welfare program. Rather, it is about people receiving public welfare. And it is about many other people who, unknown to themselves, are drifting toward the relief rolls.

The original newspaper series prompted the curiosity and anger that led to the writing of this book. The articles, however, are not its substance. As a layman, I have tried to educate myself not simply by reading the voluminous studies and reports, but by interviewing scores of caseworkers, welfare and political officials, who daily grapple with the problem. I have taken my tape recorder into the slums of big cities to record the difficulties of poverty with the help of those who know it best—the poor. Their candor, not only about their problems, but about their shortcomings as well, has helped to account for any breath of reality these pages might have. I am particularly indebted to them.

I am indebted also to a host of workers and officials in welfare departments throughout the nation and to many others laboring with the allied problems of housing, youth, unemployment, the aged, automation, and education. They all had a part in the making of this book.

I am grateful to Alfred H. Kirchhofer, the editor of *The Buffalo Evening News,* for originally approving an unorthodox approach to this problem and for the generous time allowed for its investigation. I am indebted to Paul E. Neville, the newspaper's managing editor, whose editing and encouragement improved the newspaper series.

I am particularly appreciative of the support of the Field Foundation whose assistance permitted the major share of research for this book. It is significant that at no time did the foundation request or receive any outline or portion of the manuscript either during its planning or during its preparation. I am deeply grateful for this editorial freedom.

Men and women from a variety of disciplines who were particularly helpful to me include: George M. Cohen, Loula Dunn, John H. McMahon, Mrs. Ellen MacQuarrie, Mrs. Ellen Perkins, Gordon

Brown, Lowell Iberg, Paul F. Burke, Arthur Greenleigh, Mrs. Florence Conkling, Ollie Randall, and Raymond Hilliard. I am specially grateful to P.B. for the kindness and understanding that helped begin this work and continued with me to its completion.

EDGAR MAY

New York
August 1, 1963

1

GO TO THE ANT, THOU SLUGGARD . . .

"About welfare? What do I think about the welfare?" the taxi driver asked. "It ought to be cut back. The goddamn people sit around when they should be working and then they're having illegitimate kids to get more money. You know, their morals are different. They don't give a damn."

The cab moved down Chicago's Outer Drive, then westward past irregular brick factory buildings and into the neighborhoods where red and gray stone tenements seemed to be fastened together by back-alley fire escapes and clotheslines.

"Stop it. That's what I say. These people they don't work. They don't pay taxes. One illegitimate child, maybe—but three or four and five, unh-uh."

My cab ride was in Chicago. It might have been in Cleveland or in Pittsburgh, in Los Angeles, in New York; the conversation most likely would have been the same. I heard those angry words when I worked as a welfare caseworker. I heard them while covering welfare problems as a newspaper reporter, and I have listened to them many times over while doing the research for this book.

Remove the expletives from the cab driver's phrases and you

have a complaint that fits a large group, if not the majority, of Americans. The complaint is about the high cost of poverty. It is an old complaint.

Specifically, the dissatisfaction is over the government's multibillion-dollar attempts to relieve poverty. It, too, is a lingering dissatisfaction.

This government struggle with poverty is called public welfare. It is large-scale government charity which in 1962 dispensed almost $5 billion throughout every community in the nation. It provided what one welfare recipient described as "eatin' and roofin' " for more than 7.5 million Americans.* For millions of other more affluent Americans it provided perplexity, anger, and controversy. Some defined it as "that gravy train," and others called it "that meager subsistence allowance." Among the many phrases there are two which may mark the boundaries of the welfare dispute. Both come from the document that persistently turns man's attention to poverty—the Bible:

Go to the ant, thou sluggard, consider her ways and be wise. —PROVERBS, 6:6

And if thy brother be waxen poor and fallen in decay with thee, then thou shalt relieve him. Yea, though he be a stranger or a sojourner, that he may live with thee.—LEVITICUS, 25:35

Throughout the history of charity—first motivated by man's desire to receive the grace of God—it is the first of these Biblical quotations which most often has prevailed. It was the philosophical base on which the earliest government welfare programs were built. "Go to the ant, thou sluggard" was the unwritten exhortation in the English Reformation Statute of 1536 which provided

* The total number of impoverished Americans is higher than this. Estimates vary widely. One of the most carefully considered is found in Leon H. Keyserling's study, *Poverty and Deprivation in the United States*. Based on 1960 figures, the report considered poor Americans to include almost 10.5 million multiple-person families with annual incomes under $4,000 and almost 4 million unattached individuals with incomes under $2,000. A total number of 38 million Americans was estimated to be living in poverty, or more than one-fifth of the nation.[1]

that country with its first public relief program.* Its proposals hardly would charm a contemporary social worker. While the law required each parish to maintain the poor; it insisted on three years of residence before a pauper could be registered, and also specified that all able-bodied persons—"sturdy beggars"—had to work. Children between the ages of five and fourteen were to be taken away from their parents and indentured.**

Also in the sixteenth century, dissatisfaction over providing "relief checks" was recorded. Spanish philosopher Juan Luis Vives designed a relief program for the consuls and senate of the city of Bruges, in Flanders. Although it was not put into practice, University of California professor Walter A. Friedlander described it as providing "for aid through vocational training, employment, and rehabilitation, instead of the customary distribution of alms."[3]

Two centuries later, Thomas Malthus, whose *Essay on Population* became part of the world's economic literature, frowned on poor relief because it encouraged paupers to have more children in order to get relief for them.

The "Go-to-the-ant" school received major assistance in the nineteenth century—fragments of which still remain—when Charles Darwin sped across the thought horizon. In his *The Descent of Man* he provided much of the prose that was to feed some of the fiery disciples of social Darwinism in Europe and the United States.†

* In 1961, "Go to the ant, thou sluggard" was a favorite Biblical quote of Joseph McD. Mitchell, city manager of Newburgh, New York. The small Hudson River city made nationwide headlines with its so-called "relief revolt."[2]

** This stringent tone was a part of the many English Poor Laws which followed. It was included in the Elizabethan Poor Law of 1601 and was embodied in the New Poor Law of 1834, which pushed all able-bodied persons into the workhouses. Benjamin Disraeli observed that, with the passage of the New Poor Law, it was a crime to be poor in England.

† The most outspoken disciple of Darwin in the United States was William Graham Sumner of Yale. In *Social Darwinism in American Thought,* Richard Hofstadter pointed out that Sumner opposed all

> We civilized men . . . do our utmost to check the process of elimination; we build asylums for the imbecile, the maimed, and the sick; we institute poor-laws; and our medical men exert their utmost skill to save the life of every one to the last moment. . . . Thus the weak members of civilized society propagate their kind. No one who has attended to the breeding of domestic animals will doubt that this must be highly injurious to the race of man.[5]

Even some of those who wanted to relieve poverty railed against the nineteenth-century poor laws. Thomas Chalmers, a Scottish clergyman, who established the germ of modern-day social casework when he insisted that each pauper's needs be individually investigated, described the existing poverty program in these words:

> We have set up a system of routine, under whose "heartless generalities" an equal measure is meted out to claimants of every kind, without room for generosity on the one side or gratitude on the other. In the place of personal intercourse between man and man, we have the decisions of a "stately and elevated Board"; instead of "living sympathy" there is the grant of "naked provender."[6]

In the early history of this country, "Go to the ant, thou sluggard" was also the philosophical shadow of poor relief. It was applied with particular zest by the Puritans, who abhorred idleness and were convinced that poverty itself was proof enough of moral bankruptcy. The colonists imported the ideas if not the letters of the stringent Elizabethan poor laws and added a few local inventive variations of their own. Paupers in Pennsylvania, for example, had the shoulder of their right sleeve adorned with the letter "P." Elsewhere, the poor often were "warned out," a descriptive phrase that meant they were forcefully sent packing. In some communities they were spurred onward after being "stripped naked from the middle upward, be openly whipt on his or her naked body, not exceeding the number of fifteen stripes."[7]

---

poor laws and institutions designed to relieve poverty because their expense lowered the general standard of living and made it easier for the poor to live. "A plan for nourishing the unfittest and yet advancing in civilization," Sumner said, "no man will ever find."[4]

Local control over the problems of poverty was continued from the time the colonists first formed a nation until that nation nearly sank into bankruptcy in the Great Depression. Relief policies varied widely, frequently were embroiled in political patronage, and most often were accompanied by public grumbling over the tax dollars they required.* Welfare troubles in the 1820's prompted both the Massachusetts and the New York state legislatures to conduct relief investigations—the first of many to follow. The almshouse and the workhouse became the storage bins of the poor.

The conditions of the almshouses were exposed by the nineteenth-century reformers who founded many of the charities that exist today. While prodding city officials and legislators for poor law reforms, many of these charities gave their own assistance to the impoverished. But the confused patchwork of state and local relief policies remained until the decade when Franklin Delano Roosevelt somberly told Americans, "I see one-third of the nation ill housed, ill clad, ill nourished."[9] As the last private and public charity dollars dribbled out of the treasuries, the national govern-

* The political profiteers of poverty were the targets of relief critics. Lewis B. Gunckel of Dayton, Ohio, in an 1897 issue of the *Charities Review,* wrote about Ohio relief:

"Some of the disclosures are disgraceful to the state. Of the money collected from the people by taxation for the benefit of the poor last year, $130,145.95—about one-fourth of the whole amount—was paid to physicians, ostensibly for medical services, but really for political influence and party work. These physicians are not, as a rule, selected because of their learning or experience, but because they are skillful in running the party machine. This will explain some marvelous details found in the official reports.

"In Washington Township, Clermont County, they had $366.47 and only one pauper; they gave him $3.75 for food and $4.22 for clothing, and nothing for fuel, but gave the doctor $135 and kept $150 for themselves. The poor fellow for whom the money was taken from the taxpayers got less than one-twelfth of what was raised. If these outrages are to continue, why not change the title of the statute to 'An act to tax the people to support poor doctors who run the party machine.' "[8]

ment picked up the near bankrupt pieces of poor relief.

The Federal Emergency Relief Act of 1933 provided the states with some of the money to shorten the breadlines. Two years later, on August 14, 1935, America's first permanent national welfare program, the Social Security Act, became law. It provided not only a social insurance program for American workers, but it firmly established the federal government as the fountainhead of public welfare. The relief portion of the act provided for grants to the states for child welfare services and for the needy aged, children, the blind, and, subsequently, the disabled, and the medically indigent over sixty-five.*

The new public welfare system, in tandem with federal public works projects, aimed to salvage an idle nation. For once the persistent tax grumblings were muffled. The standees in the breadlines and the corner apple salesmen required no social worker to tell Americans they were there. They were uncomfortably visible and, further, too many Americans were among them.

Today the scourge of massive unemployment is gone, but the relief problem remains. Programs have expanded and the number in need continues to increase. Since 1953 expenditures for public assistance almost doubled and the number of recipients rose about 40 per cent. Families in trouble have paced that increase. They have taken over the No. 1 relief spot from the aged.** When I was employed as a caseworker in Buffalo's Erie County, the relief budget pushed past the total amount of money needed to educate

* The categories of public assistance are: Old Age Assistance, Aid to Dependent Children, Aid to the Blind, Aid to the Permanently and Totally Disabled (added in 1950), and Medical Aid to the Aged (added in 1960). Besides the federal categories, most communities provide some General Relief, supported by either state or local funds, or both, for persons who do not qualify for any federal category.

** In 1940 almost 62 per cent of all welfare recipients were on Old Age Assistance and 36 per cent were receiving Aid to Dependent Children funds. Twenty-two years later the percentages almost were reversed. The aged represented 33 per cent of all relief recipients and 57 per cent were on ADC.

every child in the city's public schools. It has been ahead ever since.

Once more, the admonition "Go to the ant, thou sluggard" is audible, while its louder proponents are carrying on a resurrected flirtation with social Darwinism.

"Relief is gradually becoming an honorable career in America," Jenkin Lloyd Jones, nationally syndicated editor of the *Tulsa* (Okla.) *Tribune,* told members of the Inland Daily Press Association. "It is a pretty fair life, if you have neither conscience nor pride. The politicians will weep over you. The state will give a mother a bonus for her illegitimate children, and if she neglects them sufficiently she can save enough of her ADC payments to keep herself and her boy friend in wine and gin. Nothing is your fault. And when the city fathers of a harassed community like Newburgh suggest that able-bodied welfare clients might sweep the streets the 'liberal' editorialists arise as one man and denounce them for their medieval cruelty. I don't know how long Americans can stand this erosion of principle."[10]

Amid the dialogue of dissent, the change in American poverty has slipped from view. We have a new poor today but they are dressed in old images. Most Americans clothe them with the Depression characteristics of an impoverished middle class. In the thirties, in addition to factory workers, there were storekeepers, writers, foremen, college professors—if not in the soup lines—certainly on the roster of public works projects. The poor man spanned a wide occupational horizon, and he lacked one major ingredient, money, and the opportunity to earn it.

The national portrait of the pauper erroneously still pictures a middle-class individual—lacking money. But the list of lacks has grown much longer. "The reasons [for poverty] are often more social than economic, more often subtle than simple," President Kennedy said in his 1962 public welfare message.[11]

The welfare departments in the United States have become the funnel of failure—a failure which belongs both to the individuals concerned and to the communities in which they are located. The names on the relief rolls include the unskilled whose job opportunities are shrinking daily; they include the de-skilled whose jobs have been absorbed, and they include those who never have been motivated sufficiently to look for a job where tenure is measured in more than days or weeks.

They, their children, and their women are the flesh and blood behind today's potpourri of domestic problem phrases. They are the people behind studies about school drop-outs, automation, illegitimacy, race prejudice, illiteracy, and many others. They are the wasted Americans; and they are everywhere.

Frequently they are camouflaged by the impressive economic reports of a nation that takes pride in calling itself the affluent society. They are obscured by the press releases that announce record car sales, rising family income, new housing starts, and scores of other benchmarks of what we loosely call progress. Only occasionally are they plucked out of anonymity.

This happens when television cameras roam through a troubled mining town in Kentucky, or when a Presidential candidate brings the campaign press corps into the idle hill towns of West Virginia. It is then that the bleak prose of poverty, buttressed by the dreary statistics of surplus food programs, relief rolls, and unemployment checks, uncovers the shadows left over from a Depression America. Poverty in these towns is no sometime thing. Too many of the citizens have had a part in it for too long a time.

Southern Illinois' Pulaski County contains some of these towns. Its industries were built around the sprawling yards of the Illinois Central Railroad, which operated one of the line's main terminals in Mounds. The county's agriculture developed around the hand-cultivated berry, vegetable, and tree-fruit farms. The industrial base first cracked in the late twenties and early thirties when the railroad pulled out its terminal. Some of the plants held on during the Depression—a box and lumber company at Karnak, another at Ullin, two fuller's-earth processing plants at Olmsted, a veneering plant, a stave mill, a canning factory and a shipyard at Mount City, and a sugar and banana shed at Mounds.

Today all of these plants are shut except for one box and lumber company and the shipyard. There is R. Lowenbaum Manufacturing Company at Mounds, which employs about seventy women, and Star Enterprises at Olmsted, which employs about thirty men. Otherwise, there are no large plants to replace those which closed or moved.

The fertile soil that formerly was used to grow fruit and vegetables is planted with row crops that are cultivated and harvested with modern farm machinery. Strawberries, once shipped out by the trainload, are now handled by a few trucks. The plentiful farm jobs and the town factory work have disappeared.

The largest single "payroll" is made up by the bookkeepers of the Pulaski County Department of Public Aid. One of every five county residents is on relief. In 1961 public assistance payments were more than $1 million in a county whose 10,489 population is less than the work force in the Empire State Building. In the ten-year period between the census, Pulaski County's population dropped 23 per cent. In ten years, too, its public welfare bill increased 66 per cent.

The Labor Department would describe the county as a depressed area. One expects to find the wasted Americans there. But the distinction of Pulaski County is not one of kind, but only one of degree. No county—no matter how wealthy—has been able to exclude the wasted Americans, and few have been able to stem the upward trend of their cost.

For example, New York State's Westchester County is considered the most affluent county in the nation. (In 1962 average annual buying income was more than $12,000 per household.) The post-office addresses of Purchase and Scarsdale are at the apex of New York City's most fashionable bedroom communities. But interspersed among the manicured estates and the ranch-style homes are the slum pockets in White Plains, Yonkers, Mount Vernon, and Peekskill. In affluent Westchester one finds the wasted Americans as well.

If you exclude New York City, the county of Westchester has the third largest welfare operation in the state. In five years, from

1958 to 1962, public welfare costs increased 35 per cent to a record $16.8 million a year. In the same period the average monthly number of recipients increased 12 per cent to 14,300. But unlike Pulaski County, only 1.7 of every 100 Westchester residents was on relief.

Both counties offer the statistics of extreme. They record some of the highs and lows on the national graph of poverty. Neither shows the core of today's public welfare controversy. This is located in the nation's cities. The fastest growing welfare problem, the Aid to Dependent Children program, is a creature of the tenements. It incubates and festers there, fed by a host of social ills that have clung to the walk-ups through successive generations of immigrants.

The adjectives of size and power abound in the cities. Amid the bigness of success is the enormity of failure. For it is in the city that man has found a summary word for poverty. He calls it a slum.

In the central cities of the United States, one out of sixteen children under the age of eighteen is supported by relief checks. This is four times the rate found in the suburbs and about twice the rate in the rural parts of America.*

These are not merely numbers of children in need of public charity. They are numbers of family failures that led to the need for this charity. And it is in the cities where most of America's failing families live. About 58 per cent of all ADC families live in one of the standard metropolitan statistical areas. The largest single group, 44 per cent, live in the central city. More and more are crowding in every day, while in the same twenty-four-hour segments, the middle-class exodus moves at an equal—if not sometimes accelerated—pace. It is this imbalance that is the root of what we call "the urban problem." The shrinking city tax base, the deteriorating neighborhoods and spiraling crime rates are the

* The aged poor, however, are more often found in the rural parts of the nation. In the urban areas one out of nine persons aged sixty-five and over is on relief, while in the rural areas one out of six is on relief. The one exception is the aged in the northeastern and western states. There, more of the aged poor are in the cities than in the country.

social penalties of this inward and outward migration.

The city's history is one of host to immigrants. It sheltered (albeit not too well) waves of German, Irish, Jewish, and eastern European peasants, until the immigration quotas strangled the influx. But there were no immigration laws for the last of the city's newcomers. They were native Americans, distinguishable only by their color. They were as impoverished as their predecessors. But unlike their predecessors, they have failed to discard that poverty.

The Negro's dual trek—both out of the South and into the city—has been one of the largest migrations in American history. Eight of ten Negroes in 1910 lived in the South. Today about half live outside of it. At the turn of the century three-fourths of the Negroes lived in rural areas. Today almost three-fourths live in the cities. The most dramatic effect of this population shift centered in the dozen largest cities of the United States. In the last decade more than 2 million whites left those cities while almost 2 million non-whites replaced them.

The cities have become the new containers of Negro poverty and there is very little leakage. The twin forces of economics and residential segregation are keeping it that way. Peter Marris, a British sociologist studying American urban renewal, warned about a form of political and residential *apartheid*. His speculation of the central city as an enormous ghetto—"a black neck in a white noose" —is fortified by each new population count.[12]

Unlike other immigrants to the city, the Negro has yet to move successfully from the lower to the middle class. Even the most cursory glance at the American economy will show that he has come at the worst time. The footholds offered his predecessors are gone. There is little need for road- and rail-building gangs, for the nimble fingers of sweatshop needle workers, for the muscle that built and fed the open hearth furnaces. The machine, and man's ability to adapt it, is banishing the unskilled from the labor scene.

The Negro's plight usually is discussed with the word "lag." There is the broad opportunity lag and there are more specific educational, cultural, and vocational lags. They are reflected by the content of the pay envelope. In 1961 the median annual income for Negro male workers was $3,883, while it was $5,880 for the white male worker. Since the end of the Korean War this gap has not been materially narrowed. Furthermore, the unemployment rate for Negroes has been rising at a faster pace than for whites. In 1962 the jobless rate—11 per cent—for colored workers was twice that of whites. The total dollar loss to the nation for racial discrimination was placed at $28 billion a year by the National Urban League.

These discouraging calculations are directly connected to the problems of public welfare. For today a disproportionate number of the wasted Americans have skins that are black.

The high cost of public welfare in large measure is the high cost of prejudice. The bill for inferior Negro education, poor Negro housing, job discrimination, and many of the other race problems, is rendered and paid for in the public welfare departments throughout the nation.

In some Negro neighborhoods one out of four children is supported not by his father, but by the government program of ADC. In Chicago, which has the second largest Negro population of any city in the nation, 27 per cent of the nearly 900,000 Negroes were on relief early in 1963.

Nationally, the proportion of Negroes receiving ADC is four times greater than the proportion of Negroes in the total population. The Department of Health, Education, and Welfare estimated that about 44 per cent of all ADC recipients are Negro.* There are indications that Negroes would be the majority of ADC recipients if it were not for restrictive relief policies in some southern states that help to keep them off the rolls. In the larger cities they are more often the majority than not. In at least ten cities Negroes make up more than four-fifths of the ADC program. In Washington it is almost 93 per cent. In some of the nation's larger cities the percentage of Negroes in the population contrasts with the percentage of Negroes on ADC like this:

* The total percentage of Negroes is an estimate because several states do not provide detailed racial breakdowns.

TABLE 1

Percentage of Negroes in Population Compared with Percentage of Negroes Among Families Receiving Aid to Dependent Children (ADC): 1960, 1961

	Per Cent Negro	
City	*Total Population 1960*	*ADC Families 1961*
Atlanta, Ga.	38.1	66.3
Baltimore, Md.	34.7	82.8
Birmingham, Ala.	39.6	86.3
Chicago, Ill.	22.9	87.5
Cleveland–Cincinnati, Ohio[a]	26.1	80.4
Denver, Colo.	6.1	26.0
Detroit, Mich.	28.9	84.2
Indianapolis, Ind.	20.5	75.7
Kansas City, Mo.	28.6	86.3
Louisville, Ky.	17.9	63.6
Memphis, Tenn.	37.0	84.1
Milwaukee, Wisc.	8.4	52.5
Minneapolis–St. Paul, Minn.	2.5	16.7
Newark–Jersey City, N.J.	25.6	78.5
New York–Buffalo, N.Y.[b]	13.9	50.0
Norfolk, Va.	25.9	83.1
Oklahoma City, Okla.	10.2	67.3
Omaha, Nebr.	8.4	56.1
Philadelphia–Pittsburgh, Pa.	24.2	76.2
St. Louis, Mo.	28.6	86.3
Seattle, Wash.	4.7	31.9
Washington, D.C.	53.9	92.9
Wichita, Kan.	7.8	52.6

SOURCE: prepared for the author by the Bureau of Family Services, Division of Program Statistics and Analysis, Department of Health, Education, and Welfare.

[a] Several cities in the same state are lumped together when they fall into the same population category. For example, when there are two cities in one state with populations of 500,000 or more the data are combined.

[b] The New York statistics fail to differentiate between Negro Puerto Ricans and white Puerto Ricans.

These lopsided proportions are not restricted to the cities. Mississippi, for example, has more than four times as many Negro children on ADC as white children. This imbalance is used to adorn the segregation argument. Mississippi State Welfare Commissioner Fred A. Ross is fond of using the statistics himself when he warns against "racial amalgamation."

"The question arises," he told a 1962 State Conference on Social Welfare, "as to how much longer the white population of Mississippi will consent to be taxed and drained of its substance for the benefit of a race, and a nation, which shows no appreciation for their sacrifices."*[13]

But Mr. Ross did more than just pronounce some of the sentiment of the deep South. He verbalized the unspoken accusations in welfare problem areas far from Dixie. The racial factor was a prominent issue in the nationally publicized relief revolt of Newburgh, New York. It hovered in the background of the more recent welfare fight in Illinois, and it accompanied the Louisiana legislators when they threw 22,500 children off the relief rolls because they did not approve of their parents' behavior.

The fact is that public welfare is controversial partly because of its color.

However, the motivation behind the louder demands of "Go to the ant, thou sluggard" lie deeper than that. At the root of the problem is the fact that poverty and its dependence on government charity collides head-on with the folk tales epitomized by Horatio Alger. Every high school student is saturated with the national success stories, be they about the robber barons upon whom a kindly historian may have put a halo, or the Mike Finks or Daniel Boones whose frontier enterprise has been enhanced by

* In September, 1962 the average monthly grant for each of the 50,770 Negro and 11,842 white children on ADC in Mississippi was $11.57. It was the lowest average grant per child in the nation. More than $9.00 came from federal taxpayers. The state receives one of the highest ratios of federal aid. For every dollar it puts up, it collects $4.66 from the national treasury.

the mortality rate of television Indians. Almost daily our newspapers will have a story that begins: "Ephraim Jones, a former $12-a-week clerk, today was named chairman of the board of the multimillion dollar . . ." The pull-yourself-up-by-your-bootstraps school is a national shrine. The collective success stories are the historical pegs of a prosperous nation. And the image has gone far beyond Brooklyn or the San Francisco waterfront. Ask the European immigrant what he heard of this country before he embarked in his home port, and he'll tell you about an uncle or brother who arrived a decade or two earlier and now drives the latest model from Detroit.

We seek out these stories and we are encouraged by them. We will tolerate the occasional exception. It serves as a warning and might even make a good contrast against the accepted image—like an occasional rainy day in Florida. But when the now-and-then failures are lumped together in a ragged governmental bundle called public welfare, we may become irritated because the collection is soiling the image. During the Depression, when the public welfare laws were written, there was no such problem.

Today we are annoyed that both the laws and the need for them remain. We quarrel with them and often insist that they make moral judgments between the "deserving poor" and the "undeserving poor," between the lazy and the industrious. But the law dictates that the criterion is need—do you meet our requirements for assistance? The federal statute books display no moral judgments, even though state and local interpreters occasionally do.

Furthermore, a relatively new professional group, the social workers, tell us there is no difference between the needs of the widow woman and the unwed tramp. It is only a question of circumstances and not one of morality. Both situations have their causes and they should be understood. But they are not. Americans today do not fully support the law or heed the sermons of the social workers.

At the same time, the law and the social workers frequently have been unable to meet the needs of the wasted Americans. These needs have changed but the machinery to meet them has changed too slowly, and, until a few years ago, not at all.

The relief check has only stalled poverty. It has not eliminated it.

This is the dilemma of the wasted Americans. It is the dilemma of the most prosperous nation on earth.

2

NEWBURGH: THE CATALYST

Newburgh, New York: Population 31,000
Noted for: Relief revolt

No road signs give the motorist this message but it is here that a welfare squabble, helped by the midwives of frustration, ignorance, and oratory, was fired into a national debate. And it was here for the first time on a major scale that public welfare really became public. Newburgh became the stage and, like the old vaudeville variety show, there was something for everybody.

There were vignettes for the bigots, the liberals, the conservatives, the alarm viewers, and the point-with-priders, the antis and the pros, those with conscience and the conscienceless, the courageous and the cowards. Their activities brought an outpouring of words that dwarfed any previous public welfare issue. The dispute inked across the front pages of America, blared from radios, and flickered on the television screen. Public welfare, frequently secluded nationally in the sterile statistical summaries of the Department of Health, Education, and Welfare, emerged either as a brazen tramp or shivering waif, depending upon your point of view.

What happened in Newburgh mirrored what might have occurred in scores of other cities of the United States. The chemicals of social unrest were waiting to be triggered. The ingredients were varied and complicated.

What were some of them?

A city whose economy was weakening. The flourishing river trade that had led to its birth had been reduced to a classroom history lesson. The unstable needle trade and pocketbook industry, a mainstay of unskilled labor employment, was slowing. The federal government classified it as a "smaller area of labor surplus." For every relief recipient Newburgh had at least two other persons collecting unemployment insurance benefits.

A city where racial problems fermented beneath the surface. In the last decade the white population of the city decreased, while the Negro population increased sharply from 6.4 per cent to 16.6 per cent.

A city where the most apparent symptom was urban geriatrics. The wide main thoroughfare of Broadway cutting down to the Hudson provided an impression of a dated television movie. Many of its painted brick buildings held cornerstones with dates of the preceding century. In the Water Street river-edge slums, where the weeds fringed the cobblestone streets, housing violations by the score plagued tenants and building inspectors alike.

Over the years this background had helped to build the frustration that was turned on public welfare. And the echoes of irritation reverberated across the country.

There are two stories here and possibly two questions. What did this do to Newburgh? And what did it do to government charity in the nation? Many of the answers to both questions come from a detailed review of the record. It is an angry account with angry words.

In mid-October 1960, a thirty-nine-year-old career government worker began a new job as city manager of Newburgh. His name was Joseph McDowell Mitchell. He was chosen from seventy applicants by the city council, where he received the strongest endorsement from Councilman George F. McKneally—described later as the man who made the snowballs that Mr. Mitchell threw. The following month, at the suggestion of Councilman McKneally, a three-man committee was formed by the city manager to study public welfare operations. It was a move that had been made by dozens of other cities. In fact, only a year earlier in Newburgh the previous city manager formed a committee to find out if Newburgh's welfare department should be merged with that of Orange County, in which the city is located.[1] That report was affirmative.

In the early days of 1961 the welfare issue was confined to an occasional local headline. There was a brief flurry of publicity in February, when the council and Mr. Mitchell proposed sharp cuts in welfare checks of Aid to Dependent Children and Home Relief families to pay for costly snow removal. The plan was dropped after the State Department of Social Welfare said it was illegal. However, the dispute marked the beginning for City Manager Mitchell to become a critic of public welfare.

On February 25, 1961, he wrote a press release for Welfare Commissioner John J. O'Donnell, and instructed him to issue it to the local press. The release recited the increased cost of welfare, the problems of blight, and the attitudes of some relief recipients who supposedly viewed welfare simply as a method whereby they could get money from the state and federal government. It said that the welfare commissioner would submit monthly reports to the city council of the situation as it developed.

"I am convinced that there are many factors contributing to the problems of the city which have been so eloquently revealed by the City Manager. It is my intention to prevent the exploitation of the welfare program by individuals in a manner which would make it contribute to further or existing blight."[2]

Gradually, welfare was becoming a major conversation piece for Mr. Mitchell. Early in March he appeared before the Newburgh Optimist Club for an address called "No Others Need Apply." The city manager said that the very principles of welfare were being violated "by this horde of incoming humanity which makes the solving of one case a joke, in view of the effect on the community as a whole, of this never-ending pilgrimage from North Carolina to New York. We have reason to believe that much of the movement of these migrants is deliberate. They are aware of the security offered by the welfare program."[3]

This theme was repeated again and again. The argument was that the influx of migrants now required Newburgh to apportion about one-third of its city budget for welfare to support 1,382 persons at an annual cost of $983,000 in local, state, and federal funds.*

During the same month the State Department of Social Welfare examined thirty Home Relief and Aid to Dependent Children cases that had been closed in the city of Newburgh in February. They found that of twenty-three ADC cases, twenty families had resided in Newburgh three years or more, and eleven of these were natives of that city. Only three resided in Newburgh less than three years. Of the seven Home Relief cases closed, six had lived in Newburgh more than five years, and one more than three. The results of this survey remained quietly in the files of the State De-

* The city appropriated $423,810 in local taxes as its share of the annual total. The New York State Department of Social Welfare later accused the city of padding its appropriation and asking for welfare tax money it did not need. A report by the State Department's Bureau of Research and Statistics indicated this was done to fan the controversy and to permit subsequent claims of tax savings by showing the savings between actual expenditures and earlier appropriations. The statisticians said in their report:

"The $423,810 appropriation for 1961 was unjustifiably high considering recent past experience. At the time this budget was prepared, it was known to city officials that costs in 1959 were $337,000 and that costs in 1960 were running at less than $30,000 monthly. The total for 1960 was $338,000. The City Manager exploited this $424,000 budget to the full, arousing taxpayer groups to the consequences of increased welfare appropriations. When 1961 ended, it was discovered that City costs for that year were but $315,000. City officials claimed that this was due to economies. Nothing could be further from the truth. Total public welfare expenditures rose slightly between 1960 and 1961 from $897,000 to $905,000—therefore there was no economy. The city share declined from $338,000 to $315,000 due largely to a windfall from the federal government. Federal aid increased from 1960 to 1961 by $43,000 from $263,000 to $306,000 in 1961. State aid went down $12,500."[4]

partment of Social Welfare while Mr. Mitchell continued speaking.

Two months later Newburgh made a few national news ripples. On April 28, Mr. Mitchell handed his welfare commissioner a copy of a mimeographed slip and told him that it would be mailed in the envelopes that normally carried the welfare checks for May. The letter said:

> Your welfare check is being held for you at the Police Department. Please report to the Police Department and pick up your check there. This procedure is effective for this check only. Future checks will be mailed to you as in the past.
>
> JOHN J. O'DONNELL, *Commissioner*
> Department of Public Welfare
>
> April 28, 1961

Commissioner O'Donnell protested. Mr. Mitchell said the letter was going out. The following Monday, Commissioner O'Donnell would answer only "No comment" to the questions of reporters asking him his opinion about the police muster. The welfare department's staff, through Commissioner O'Donnell's deputy, personally protested to Mr. Mitchell. The next day the *Newburgh News* included these paragraphs about the muster:

> At 2:15 P.M. yesterday there were approximately fifty persons standing in a Y-shaped line at Police Headquarters waiting for their checks.
>
> They were interrogated in a small drab back room which ordinarily serves as Communications Center and finger printing room.
>
> The line did not move rapidly.
>
> There were many elderly people waiting. Canes were also in evidence.
>
> The majority of the applicants were women, it was observed during one hour of the day. Quite a few carried infants in their arms.
>
> A short, white haired woman said she had been waiting on line for one and one-half hours. She was seventy-one years old.
>
> When Mr. Mitchell was informed of this he immediately rushed her into the interrogation room.[5]

The muster, which Mr. Mitchell said was simply an accounting procedure, was viewed by some as an effort to snare chiselers. None was found.

Within a week the forty-six-page report of the Committee to Study Welfare Operations was submitted to the city council.[6] Mr. Mitchell, as secretary to the group, prepared the report. A covering letter carried the signatures of Ray Boyea, a theatre manager; Frank Konysz, an accountant, and Irving Weiner, a physician.

The committee blamed much of the problem on "a steady influx of outsiders principally from Southern states. These newcomers, the committee feels, while coming to the city seeking a better way of life, are the underlying causes in the steadily mounting welfare costs. . . . The committee finds the accessibility to slum housing and the accessibility to welfare payments to be the incentives for the influx of people from out of state, who will eventually contribute to high caseloads and costs."[7]

To even the most casual reader the report appeared to use the word "newcomer" as a euphemism for Negro. For example, the committee said that it found "an absolute distinction between the long term or 'original' residents of this city and the newcomers.

> The committee feels that the "original" residents are being harmed by the conduct, behavior and moral values of the newcomers, and that these "original" residents' reputation is affected by the newcomers. These natives deplore the mass migration to our city and seem powerless to exert any influence on the newcomers. These newcomers apparently have no desire to take root and become part of community life.[8]

Meanwhile, in the files of the State Department of Social Welfare there was more information available that might have contradicted the migrants–equals–relief costs claim. It stayed there until July 7 when it was officially revealed in a public investigation of what by that time had become a national controversy. William H. Kaufman, the department's senior research analyst, was on the witness stand. He was being interrogated by Irving Kirschenbaum, a member of the State Board of Social Welfare. The following exchange took place:

Mr. Kirschenbaum: What led you to believe that there were no newcomers? [on the relief rolls]

Mr. Kaufman: The state provides for one hundred per cent reimbursement for any person on the welfare rolls who has not resided in the state for one year. Now it is logical to expect that the district would claim that additional money, and they have claimed but a trivial amount; that is, in 1960 about $205, which would mean that there was a non-resident on the rolls—we have to approximate one family for two months. That is all the $205 would cover.

Mr. Kirschenbaum: Out of how many families?

Mr. Kaufman: Well, say 100.[9]

But three months earlier, while the migrant case was building up, this information was not used.

Meanwhile, the Newburgh city council received a letter from the Newburgh Ministerial Association objecting to the methods of the muster "which degrades the innocent and guilty alike. We hope any further investigation will not be dependent upon the muster procedure which includes the use of the Police Station, but rather employs principles and tactics which uphold the dignity of man." The letter was signed by Rabbi Norman Kahan, the Reverend David Aaronson, and the Reverend Sidney Parker.

"The letter is out of order," Councilman William E. Doulin said, in a motion to reject it. Councilman McKneally observed:

"The letter represents tax exempt properties, not the taxpayer. If the Ministerial Association wants to do good, let them go into the welfare area and instill some morality into the people who are running up these costs."[10]

Twenty-one days later the city council, by a four to one vote, rejected once more three letters written individually by Protestant ministers. (The dissenter and lone Democrat was Mayor William Ryan who consistently opposed the city manager's relief policies.) One of the clergymen's letters reportedly supported the council's stand. "These opinions are outside the province of ministers. They are out of order. I move these letters be declared out of order," Councilman McKneally said.[11]

Meanwhile, on May 25, Monsignor James T. McDonnell, Co-director, Family Service Office, Catholic Charities, met with Mr. Mitchell and Councilman McKneally in the city manager's office, to protest the muster on behalf of Catholic Charities. Monsignor McDonnell was criticized for injecting himself into the issue. After learning that the priest had visited Mayor Ryan at home, Councilman McKneally called the director of Catholic Charities of the Archdiocese of New York, to complain.

Three major religions had been dismissed from the argument.

Mr. Mitchell's speeches reflected the increased animosity of the welfare campaign. On June 19 the *Newburgh News*' report of his speech before the seventeenth annual communion breakfast of the Newburgh Area Protestant Men's League included these two paragraphs:

> The city manager claimed the roots of the welfare state go back to the doctrines of men like Sigmund Freud, who denied, he said, that the individual has much responsibility before God or man for his conduct. He said this was the defense in the famed Leopold-Loeb case.
>
> "Since then," he continued, "criminal lawyers and all the mushy rabble of do-gooders and bleeding hearts in society and politics have marched under the Freudian flag toward the omnipotent State of Karl Marx."*[12]

Until now the oratory concerned itself with the "why" of the relief battle. The "how" was to come when Mr. Mitchell issued the controversial thirteen-point, get-tough reforms. Unreported

* Fifteen months later, after the controversy had receded in the memory of the public, Mr. Mitchell was a witness before Governor Nelson Rockefeller's Moreland Commission on Welfare, an inquiry which largely owed its birth to the Newburgh revolt. The city manager, on September 12, 1962, filed a statement with the commissioners that said in part:

"I recognize the dedication of those in the welfare field, I salute their sincerity, I sympathize with their problems, I understand the complexities facing them. The many barbs and darts hurled at these public servants as a group, such as 'do-gooders,' 'bleeding hearts,' and similar epithets, are undeserved, and show a callous misunderstanding of the problems extant in welfare today."[13]

was that the baker's dozen was part of an original twenty-two-point offering. These were whittled down to thirteen at a closed meeting between Mr. Mitchell and the four Republican councilmen.

Among the unreported proposals were these:

All applicants for relief shall be photographed and a thumbprint taken prior to the issuance of relief, for the purpose of establishing positive identification.*

The names, addresses, relief category, and amount paid of each recipient shall be made public by publication in the *Newburgh News* and posted on a bulletin board for the purpose of providing constructive help by citizens who are unaware of the plight of these people, and for the purpose of cross checking the validity of these cases through public knowledge.

The Republican councilmen balked at these proposals and cut the list down to thirteen points.**

* A portion of this proposal later was carried out. It is detailed on subsequent pages.

** The June 20 memorandum from Mr. Mitchell to the welfare commissioner included these thirteen points:

1. All cash payments which can be converted to food, clothing and rent vouchers and the like without basic harm to the intent of the aid shall be issued in voucher form henceforth.

2. All able-bodied adult males on relief of any kind who are capable of working are to be assigned to the chief of building maintenance for work assignment on a 40-hour week.

3. All recipients physically capable of and available for private employment who are offered a job but refuse it, regardless of the type of employment involved, are to be denied relief.

4. All mothers of illegitimate children are to be advised that should they have any more children out of wedlock, they shall be denied relief.

5. All applicants for relief who have left a job voluntarily, i.e., who have not been fired or layed-off, shall be denied relief.

6. The allotment for any one family unit shall not exceed the take-home pay of the lowest paid city employee with a family of comparable size. Also, no relief shall be granted to any family whose income is in excess of the latter figure.

But the answers to the "migrant problem" that Mr. Mitchell had repeatedly stressed from the podium and in press releases now had been given. This problem-solution relationship was nowhere better portrayed than in the story in the *Newburgh News* which began like this:

Newburgh's standing as a welfare haven is due to come to a sudden halt on July 15, the effective date of the sweeping re-organization of the Welfare Department ordered by the City Council last week.

Under the new procedure, outlined today by City Manager Joseph McDowell Mitchell in a memorandum to Commissioner of Public Welfare, John O'Donnell, anyone coming to Newburgh in search of welfare had best conduct the search elsewhere.[15]

---

7. All files of all Aid to Dependent Children cases are to be brought to the office of the corporation counsel for review monthly. All new cases of any kind will be referred to the corporation counsel prior to certification of payment.

8. All applicants for relief who are new to the city must show evidence that their plans in coming to the city involved a concrete offer of employment, similar to that required for foreign immigrants. All such persons shall be limited to two weeks of relief. Those who cannot show evidence shall be limited to one week of relief.

9. Aid to persons except the aged, blind and disabled shall be limited to three months in any one year—this is a feature similar to the present policies on unemployment benefits.

10. All recipients who are not disabled, blind, or otherwise incapacitated, shall report to the Department of Public Welfare monthly for a conference regarding the status of their case.

11. Once the budget for the fiscal year is approved by the Council, it shall not be exceeded by the Welfare Department unless approved by Council by supplemental appropriation.

12. There shall be a monthly expenditure limit on all categories of Welfare Aid. This monthly expenditure limit shall be established by the Department of Public Welfare at the time of presenting its budget, and shall take into account seasonal variations.

13. Prior to certifying or continuing any more aid to Dependent Children cases, a determination shall be made as to the home environment. If the home environment is not satisfactory, the children in that home shall be placed in foster care in lieu of Welfare aid to the family adults.[14]

What had begun as a charge was now a fact. What had been a legitimate viewpoint in the editorials of the *Newburgh News* was now an illegitimate assertion in its news columns.

But the firmly established "fact" was not to be confined to Newburgh. On June 26 the Associated Press furnished a membership enterprise story to its clients especially written for it by Joseph Ritz, a reporter for the *Newburgh News.* The wire service permitted this lead paragraph to go out over its teletype network: "Newburgh, N.Y., June 26 (AP)—This city nestled in the Hudson Highlands is determined to rid itself of its reputation as a welfare resort."[16]

The editorials in and out of New York state began to mount. What particularly intrigued editorial writers was Mr. Mitchell's determination to make able-bodied relief recipients work for their checks. Forgotten was the fact that the Hudson River city had a work-for-relief program before the new city manager arrived—a program that faltered because there were not enough able-bodied men to put to work. Forgotten, too, was the fact that during the previous summer there were 1,176 recipients in fifty work relief projects in fifteen counties in New York State.

By the time the state welfare department's public hearing on Newburgh began July 7, national publicity firmly established the little city as the underdog hero. The members of the state board were aware of their public image as prosecutors. And Newburgh Welfare Commissioner John J. O'Donnell, who until now had kept silent about the validity of the celebrated thirteen points, was aware of his role as the man in between the major adversaries. The nervous commissioner was forced over each of the thirteen hurdles by Felix Infausto, counsel for the state board. Every phrase was explored and placed against existing law. Repeatedly the testimony was pin-pointed like this:

Mr. Infausto: I repeat my question. Can you implement the manager's directive No. 1 with respect to this program in view of the language [the law] you just read?
Mr. O'Donnell: No, I do not believe I could.[17]

After this testimony, Mr. Mitchell told reporters his commissioner was "a turncoat." Three days later John J. O'Donnell resigned his job because he said he could not violate the oath he took to uphold the laws of the state of New York.

The hearing ended in a near name-calling flurry when the board insisted that Mr. Mitchell and the city councilmen would be heard only if they confined themselves to the thirteen points.

Mr. Mitchell: You mean you deny me the opportunity to make a statement.

Mr. Infausto: I object. You were told at the beginning of this inquiry that questions and answers would be asked pertaining to the legality of the 13 points. You love publicity. You were addressing yourself to the press.[18]

The final dramatic round became the main news story and the early, careful, legal documentation was lost. By denying the Newburghers a chance to say their piece, the state board had enhanced the martyr image.

Meanwhile, Mr. Mitchell's image as the embattled David fighting the state and federal welfare Goliath received a powerful national boost from the spokesman of the conservative Republican wing. He received this letter:

Reading the account of your stand on welfarisms in this week's *Life* magazine was as refreshing as breathing the clean air of my native Arizona.

This took courage on your part, but it is the kind of courage that must be displayed across this nation if we are to survive.

The abuses in the welfare field are mounting and the only way to curtail them are the steps which you have already taken.

My thanks to you as an American for this act and more power to you.

Sincerely,
SENATOR BARRY GOLDWATER[19]

A few weeks later, when Mr. Mitchell was summoned to Washington by his congresswoman, Katherine St. George, for a highly publicized round of introductions to Senate and House of Representatives conservatives, Senator Goldwater told reporters: "I'd like to see the Newburgh plan in every city of America."[20] The senator denied that his praise might have been motivated by politics—the fact that the welfare revolt was on the home ground of Senator Goldwater's principal rival for a Republican Presidential nomination.

The home forces, on the other hand, did not quite share the senator's claim that the issue was outside the sphere of politics. Governor Rockefeller's staff was concerned over the possible political implications of a dispute that was attracting Republican conservatives. A private poll conducted for the governor by the Political Analysis Associates of Princeton, New Jersey, showed that there was ample reason for concern. People of voting age throughout New York state were interviewed. About one-third of those interviewed believed 40 per cent or more of all welfare recipients were chiselers. Almost another third believed that chiseling ranged between 11 and 39 per cent of those receiving welfare.[21]

In Newburgh's gray city hall, fan mail was flowing in by the bundles. Among the letters were the printed hate sheets that social controversy seems to lure out from under the damp rocks.* The words "black bastards" were so prevalent that city hall secretaries joked about it. Many of the letters carried the notation: "This is a Republic, not a Democracy. Let's keep it that way."

"Don't let the bleeding hearts and eggheads of the social welfare bluff you out of the finest ideas espoused in a long, long time," said one.

"Fight this relief to bums, bastards and dope fiends," said another.[23]

* One of these publications was an anti-Negro, anti-Semitic sheet called *The Truth Seeker* produced by the Truth Seeker Company, Inc., New York City. The headlines over editor Charles Smith's two-page article read:

NEGRO-BREEDING DOOMS NEWBURGH
Stupidity, Fertility, and Fornication:
Victorious Virtues Under Need[22]

By mid-July secretaries were spending hours sorting, tabulating and answering this roll call of protest. Later, cartons filled with 5,000 to 7,000 letters were delivered by the Newburgh city dog catcher, on instructions from the city manager to Marvin Liebman Associates, a New York City public relations firm. The letters were used to compile a list of names for Young Americans for Freedom, a conservative political group.

By mid-July, too, Mr. Mitchell's own public relations was about to suffer its first major setback. Radio, television, and newspaper reporters crowded into city hall on July 17, the day the "get tough" program was to be implemented. All able-bodied men had been ordered to report for work. Television cameras and floodlights were ready to catch the lineup. Hour after hour it was postponed. But the newspaper stories summed up the day in their opening paragraphs:

"This city scanned its relief roll today and found only one man on it able to work—and even that case has yet to be fully appraised." The headline over that *Herald Tribune* story read: "In Newburgh's Net—One."[24]

The New York *Daily News,* not known for its motherly outlook on public welfare, printed a dispatch by its reporter Robert McCarthy that began: "With the bravado of an elephant stomping on an ant, city fathers of this Hudson Valley community of 30,000 today launched their controversial 13-point program to stamp out welfare chiseling."[25]

The next day, the state board of social welfare, badgered by reporters for a definitive statement about Newburgh, finally issued a point by point rebuttal of the city's claim. Chairman Amend summarized his side in this paragraph: "In the light of the facts we find no justification whatever for the measures Newburgh proposes to adopt. Some of them are inhuman and indecent, most of them are illegal, and the others are unnecessary."[26]

During this period Newburgh was without a welfare commissioner. On a warm Sunday afternoon in July, former City Manager Albert J. Abrams took Councilmen Green and McIntyre to the

Jewish Community Center for a Turkish bath. A stocky, muscular man was giving them a rubdown when he mentioned that he wanted to make a switch from his full-time physical education teaching job. He worked at the center Sundays to supplement his income. Councilman McIntyre told the others that here was a young man with education who was a local boy. "He's the type of person we ought to do something for," he said. The teacher's name was Peter Z. Petrillo, Jr. Within two weeks, at the suggestion of Councilman McIntyre, he was named the new welfare commissioner of Newburgh.

Although equipped with a new welfare commissioner who accepted his views, Mr. Mitchell's campaign began to lose forward motion. The "one man able to work" episode had been a bad experience. Reporters journeying to Newburgh to record the drama increasingly placed the weight of statistical evidence against the fragile claims. In August a key descriptive phrase by the city manager caused a major editorial shift away from his program.

The relief revolt spokesman told reporters that he wanted welfare workers whose outlook was attuned to the philosophy of the city rather than to the ideology of the state welfare people. He hoped to convert the existing staff by "thought control." The phrase clashed with the image of an underdog. It grated on the ears of editorial writers who had employed it and its counterpart, "brain washing," in campaigns against dictatorships.

The third major setback came much later. It was the television portrait of events in the National Broadcasting Company's White Paper No. 9 *The Battle of Newburgh.*[27] The hour-long network show flailed Mr. Mitchell and his program. Although the intensity of the whipping pushed some viewers farther into the city manager's camp, a large number, nevertheless, turned against the city's relief solutions. Amid threatened lawsuits and charges of rigged films, Newburgh merchants found their credit ratings questioned. "After that show I used to say I was from West Point whenever I was out of town," a Newburgh college student told me. "They thought our whole city was a slum and all of us were on relief."

In Florida, when a baseball player was introduced to the fans as hailing from Newburgh, the fans shouted: "Welfare, welfare."

In August too a New York State Supreme Court justice issued a temporary injunction against the controversial welfare plan. Later twelve of the thirteen points were declared illegal. Justice John P. Donohue included in his official opinion a single sentence that somehow had been lost since the emotion-charged campaign began:

"If the defendents feel that the welfare laws of the State of New York are inadequate to accomplish their purposes, their recourse is to the New York State Legislature which has created these laws."[28]

In Newburgh, however, a large part of the public still was behind the city manager. The occasional bad press had been akin to rallying the fans behind a football star who dropped a pass in the last game. Resentment in a few quarters was mounting.

Miss Marie C. Murray, a senior welfare representative, sent to the city by the state department of social welfare as an observer, described one of her experiences while walking from Hotel Newburgh to the local welfare office:

"I was walking east and the sun was in my eyes and I was shading them when this man approached me and said: 'You don't have to cover your face. You're doing enough damage.' And then he spit on the sidewalk next to me."

However, the Newburgh Chamber of Commerce now was not too sure that all the oratory and acclaim was going to bring any new industrial dollars to a city that acutely needed them. Early in September the chamber—which had endorsed Mr. Mitchell's proposals—hired Ralph R. Gardner, a New York public relations man, to work on the city's image. The chamber placed the price at $2,500, but Councilman McKneally said it was $50,000 and a waste of money. "Our image was never better," he said.[29]

But whatever the state of the image, those who helped make it—the communications media—were beginning to tire. The crowded press conferences were thinning just to the local reporters. Occasionally, there would be a smattering of national publicity. When Newburgh ordered Home Relief and Aid to Dependent Children recipients photographed, there were a few headlines. A welfare worker described the scene to me this way:

"A white sheet was tacked up in a small room in the welfare department. It was about 90 degrees. Commissioner Petrillo couldn't stand it and had to go out once in a while. Some came holding their children. One woman cried and cried, and another said 'If you want to make a model out of me you can take my picture.' A number—from 1 to 60—was tacked on the sheet behind each client."

A few days before the November election, a headline in the *New York Herald Tribune* read: "City manager to quit if Newburgh GOP loses."[30] Mr. Mitchell had placed himself foursquare behind Republican Councilmen Doulin and McIntyre in their reelection effort. The move brought the ire of the International Association of City Managers down on Mr. Mitchell, and on election night came within a few hundred votes of losing him his job. The two councilmen, running actively on the welfare issue, won by fewer votes than in their 1957 effort. "I think we got a machine vote against us," Mr. Mitchell told me six months later. "I don't think we got a true assessment."*

But what of the millions of words, the statements and counterstatements, the charges and the denials? Did Newburgh have a welfare case and what did it accomplish?

Increasing governmental costs obviously are a legitimate concern of a community. Public welfare ranks high among those rising costs. Even though Newburgh's relief rate was lower than that of four other comparable New York cities, there still was valid cause for concern. But the form of that concern—the inauguration of a poverty penal system—was wrong. A protest turned into an organized policy to harass and punish relief recipients off the welfare rolls.

* Mr. Mitchell announced his resignation as city manager on July 8, 1963.

The announced struggle of political philosophies—home rule vs. federal and state control—in too many quarters was a cover for a racial conflict. "If the persons had been white there never would be a thirteen-point program," the Reverend William D. Burton, Negro clergyman told me. The rapidly increasing Negro population and the corresponding shrinkage among the whites were making the majority uneasy.

A surprising 1959 speech by Councilman McKneally, which emphasized Newburgh's Negro problem, was still smarting in the memories of its colored citizens. Mr. McKneally's words were prompted by a report that a gang of colored girls was attacking individuals or small groups of girls from another school. The *Newburgh News* of March 24 quoted him this way at a city council meeting:

> The colored people of this city are our biggest police problem, our biggest sanitation problem and our biggest health problem. They constitute the largest percentage of people needing treatment at Odell Tuberculosis Sanitarium.
>
> We cannot put up with their behavior any longer. We have been too lenient with them. They must be made to adhere to the standards of the rest of the community. If necessary we will enforce our own ideas on them.

How the Negroes felt was made clear later when a parade was held to honor the councilman's brother, Martin B. McKneally, when he was elected National Commander of the American Legion. Negroes planned to picket the Legion building and only last-minute negotiations by then City Manager Abrams avoided a scene. "We were a whisk away from another Little Rock," he told me. The Newburgh welfare controversy, in short, frequently was a disguise for the Newburgh race controversy.*

Mr. Abrams, who was the immediate predecessor of Joseph

* Ironically, as National Commander, Martin McKneally won the plaudits of national Negro groups when he cut off the "40 & 8" society from the American Legion because its members refused to admit Negroes.

Mitchell and who now holds the influential post of secretary to the Senate of the state of New York, probably was closer to the multi-faceted relief revolt than any other non-participant. This is how he summarized for me what happened to and in his city:

> To me this was a great moral issue confronting 31,000 people in the community—a moral issue far more basic than welfare.
>
> The reason the community is in trouble is because it hasn't been true to itself, because it gave in to its basic weaknesses—because it ran frightened and cowered in a corner because of a few blow-hards.
>
> There is no doubt that fear stalked the main streets here.
>
> The businessmen were exploited, with their own prejudices used against them. The small home owner readily joined the emotional binge.
>
> It was a microscopic example of the deterioration of the German middle class under Hitler.
>
> "Will it help us?"
>
> "Should we go along?"
>
> These were the questions asked by the Germans. In Newburgh they were just rephrased.
>
> "He's trying to help our town, isn't he?"
>
> "He's trying to get rid of the colored and chiselers."
>
> If I can express your fears, hopes and aspirations so that I can identify myself with your longings and prejudices, then I've got you hooked.
>
> The role of the politician is often one that requires him to express publicly what the people fear privately. Often it's a play-back of their own voices in louder decibels—and that's what happened in Germany and in Newburgh, except in this case the question was to keep the city from going colored.
>
> These are fears easily exploited when the main population consists of women garment workers, pocketbook workers and factory workers, each earning a minimum wage.
>
> These people never had education to protect themselves against the subtleties of the professional politician.
>
> The only saving thing I saw was that these guys didn't have the know-how to become small-time neo-Hitlerites.

But what made this a story far beyond the city limits?

News of conflict often generates more conflict and, in turn, more news. The momentum of the welfare revolt was aided by a portion of the press whose editors and readers wanted to believe that welfare chiselers were overrunning a little city. The facts to contradict those beliefs for too long were in the role of the tortoise pursuing the hare. Charles Collingwood, in his analysis of Newburgh press coverage over New York's WCBS-TV put it succinctly: "The issues involved are real enough. The argument over the proper administration of welfare will go on, and so will Newburgh's special problems. But there is a moral to all this—before you pick a symbol, make sure that it really symbolizes what you mean it to."[31]

But there were other forces that aided the cause to national prominence. For several months Mr. Mitchell virtually had the podium to himself. While he was making his explosive statements, evidence to the contrary was in the hands of the state department of social welfare. The city manager was a talented communicator. He always was available to all journalistic comers and, unlike his angry statements, was a calm conversationalist. I enjoyed every interview I ever had with him and often wondered if there really were not two Mitchells: the soft-spoken individual and the bombastic creator of press releases and lectern statements. A fact-laden point-by-point denial of his charges against the state was months too late.

The absence of an immediate and effective counterattack was apparent in other quarters, too. After the clergymen were told collectively and individually that it was none of their business, there was no concentrated effort to fight the rebuff. There were a few sporadic individual attempts and that was all. Although Newburgh is predominantly Catholic, protests were restricted to the local director of Catholic Charities, his regional director and one parish curate. They received no support from the Newburgh Catholic clergy or higher church administration—even when Catholic Charities and its director were personally attacked by Mr. Mitchell.

Meanwhile, the private welfare agencies, many of them with national headquarters in nearby New York City, were collecting

Newburgh clippings in their bulging files. Few leaped into the fray and most of those came too late.

But what did Newburgh contribute to the nation?

It became the catalyst for welfare discussion in scores of social work forums, in hundreds of political arenas, from city councils to state legislatures, and, finally, in the taverns and living rooms of these United States. It caused a long needed and sometimes uncomfortable look at poverty—not in the teeming streets of India, but next door. Newspapers turned to their files to see when they last examined welfare in their own back yards, and produced series like that in the *San Francisco Chronicle* where the headline read: "San Francisco Welfare Tough, But No Newburgh."[32]

In the succeeding months President Kennedy became the first chief executive to issue a special public welfare message to Congress, and that body passed a package of laws designed to remove people from the relief rolls and back to productivity. Mr. Mitchell guardedly claimed part of the credit and even his sharpest critic should not deny him a percentage for generating the discussion.

The Newburgh story—nurtured by misunderstanding and propelled by demagoguery—bluntly told the nation that most Americans had yet to comprehend or even accept the idea that billions must be spent every year to support citizens who cannot provide for themselves.

3

THE SHADOW CHILDREN

Amid the abbreviated jargon of social work no three letters carry more public irritation than ADC. In recent years the Aid to Dependent Children program has become the fastest rising welfare expenditure of most communities. It is the hardy perennial among government investigations that crop up in county, state, and federal committees with a regularity that once was reserved for the Saturday night bath. Those who damn it and those who defend it have agreed on a generality to describe it. They call it a scandal.

One side points to a federal investigation in the nation's capital where 59 per cent of a sample group of ADC mothers was found to be receiving tax dollars contrary to the law.* The other

* The Washington survey was conducted jointly in 1961–1962 by the city's welfare department and government investigators from the Office of Investigations and Collections and the General Accounting Office. Five per cent of the city's ADC caseload was reviewed. Actual cases investigated numbered 236, of which 141 were closed because of ineligibility.[1]

The extremely high ineligibility rate startled welfare officials throughout the nation, even though Washington was known for some of the most restrictive relief regulations in the country. (The city is not permitted to provide relief to a family if the mother is considered employable—whether she can find a job or not.) Armed with these surprising ineligibility figures, U.S. Senator Robert C. Byrd of West Virginia, chairman of the Senate Appropriations Sub-committee that controls the rails against the law which in Louisiana willy-nilly cut 22,500 children off the rolls because the state's legislators disapproved of their parents' conduct.

In the debate ADC has become like a snarled ball of yarn. Caught in the tangle are cultural differences, race prejudices, varying sex mores, and, most frequently, hefty moral judgments. The word "chiseler" is prominent in the public discussion of ADC. It is a key motivator of the many investigations and it is unlikely to be put to rest by the recent national eligibility survey that showed relatively little chiseling.*

Amid the furor the minority has eclipsed the majority. ADC is a program for children. But ADC is embattled because of its adults. The unwed mother, the divorcee, and the runaway father are in the vortex of controversy. Their progeny have become the shadow children of these United States.

There are nearly 3 million children in almost a million American families on ADC.** Both their number and especially the

---

Washington city budget, demanded a national eligibility review.

* The survey was conducted by the Department of Health, Education, and Welfare at the request of the United States Senate Committee on Appropriations. It showed that one out of twenty ADC families in a national sample was receiving aid when it was not eligible for it. However, the major cause of this ineligibility was due to faulty welfare administration rather than to chiseling. Nine states—Connecticut, Delaware, Georgia, Kentucky, Mississippi, Nevada, South Carolina, Tennessee, and West Virginia—had 10 per cent or more of the ADC families ineligible. West Virginia led the list with 17.3 per cent. However, when confined to suspected chiseling as a cause of ineligibility, the national review showed that thirty-four states had less than 2 per cent. The highest chiseling rate was found in Delaware and Nevada where it was 7.4 per cent in each.[2]

The chiseling statistics cheered the ADC defenders and left its critics skeptical. The latter downgraded its value with the charge that welfare was investigating itself.

** In March 1963 there were 2,984,000 ADC children in 975,600 ADC families. In 1962 the program was renamed Aid and Services to Needy Families with Children.

expenditures for them have been spiraling from decade to decade. Since 1940 the total number of ADC children has increased by 175 per cent and the cost of the program has jumped almost 700 per cent. The following chart shows the separate ten-year increases:

TABLE 2

Total ADC Payments: 1940, 1950, 1960

December of Year	*Number of Children Receiving Aid*	*Total Payments*
1940	865,300	$ 11,718,000
1950	1,661,500 (92 per cent increase)	47,207,000 (303 per cent increase)
1960	2,377,400 (43 per cent increase)	92,609,000 (96 per cent increase)

SOURCE: Prepared for the author by the Bureau of Family Services, Division of Program Statistics and Analysis, Department of Health, Education, and Welfare.

The common bond of these youngsters is the lack of a common figure—the absence of a personal provider that has made them quasi-government wards from the shacks of Alabama to the walk-up tenements of New York. But frequently forgotten has been the fact that this is a program for children and not a vehicle for punishing their parents. Overshadowed too has been the fact that in some parts of our country we provide less than fifty cents a day to feed, clothe, and house American children; that only eighteen states give their families enough money to meet minimum standards of health and decency, that many youngsters rarely, if ever, see a doctor, not because they are immune to illness, but because there is no money to pay the bill. The fact that these children exist is the first issue of ADC and somebody has to take care of them.

But there is a second issue too. If large segments of the public have lost sight of the program's intent, most of the social work profession has refused to grapple seriously with the critics' discontent. The grumbling over the morality of ADC adults has been dismissed as irrelevant in edict after edict. These pronouncements have been about as successful as separating the ingredients of a bowl of fish chowder. Because the public believes this to be an issue, it has become an issue. The dilemma will not be altered by the professionals' insistence that the only factor is need.

The fact is the Aid to Dependent Children program in many instances is but a reflection of family breakdown across the breadth of America. In most homes the difficulties of the unmarried niece who found herself pregnant or the cousin whose husband ran off can be confined to whispered family gossip. This is because the participants have the financial ability to absorb and pay for the damage. ADC is the government net for those who do not. It is the catch basin for family failure shorn of family finance and, as a result, the bill is sent to the taxpayer.

These disturbing family shifts have been both multiple and basic. They are recorded in the mass of charts, graphs, and statistical columns of the Bureau of the Census, the Department of Health, Education, and Welfare, and the National Office of Vital Statistics. Together they paint a sociological portrait of Americans and together they give important clues to the failures that are tenants in the local welfare department.

The American family has not only changed its habits, but its location as well. It has left the homestead in droves. Farm population fell from 34.7 per cent of the total in 1910 to 7.7 per cent in 1962. Left behind, too, was the interdependence that was a part of hayin', milkin', and mornin' chores.

The exodus was followed by a gradual de-emphasis of religion. Dr. Helen Mayer Hacker, who examined these changes in the home for the Family Service Association of America, put it this way: "The religious function of the family is declining, especially in regard to the urban Protestant family. Grace at meals, group Bible reading, and prayers and devotions are less and less family activities. Church attendance and membership may remain relatively high, but religion is not the vital family concern that it once was."[3]

Attitudes about marriage also have changed. When Teddy Roosevelt was the occupant of the White House and the parlor still was an institution instead of a relic, those who held hands there were slower in asking the vital question. The median age for women marrying was 22, and for men 26.1. In 1960 the figures were 20.3 and 22.8, respectively. Sociologist Harold T. Christensen estimated that one of six American brides is pregnant at the time of her marriage.[4]

Illegitimacy, the word that an angry public has allied with ADC, has increased by almost 300 per cent in two decades. The rate per 1,000 unmarried females has jumped from 7.1 in 1940 to 21.0 in 1960. Federal reports show that in 1940 illegitimate births numbered 89,500; twenty years later they totaled 224,300, and the estimate for the sixties is another 40 per cent increase. Uncounted in these figures is a Planned Parenthood Federation of America estimate that there are now about 1 million abortions performed in this country every year.

The increase in pregnancies in the high school serves as a neighborhood barometer for these problems. Although the illegitimacy rate has doubled in the last twenty-five years among the fifteen- to nineteen-year-olds, this still is the lowest increase among the age groups. The rate among twenty- to twenty-nine-year-olds has more than tripled. In this group are a large number of the middle-class girls about whom we say euphemistically: They have made a "mistake."

"This is the socio-economic group about whom previous studies have provided the least information," Dr. Clark E. Vincent, family sociologist observed. "They do not threaten sex mores or impose a burden on taxpayers; and they provide childless couples with adoptable infants. These women are likely to travel incognito from their own state to another where they are attended by physicians in private practice, live independently during pregnancy, and have their medical expenses paid by couples to whom they release their children for adoption."[5]

But beyond the pre-marital problems of the family, its ability to hold together has been sharply reduced. In 1900 the divorce rate per 1,000 marriages was 3.4, immediately after World War II it hit 18.2 as a raft of servicemen marriages were dissolved. In the last few years it has leveled off between 9.1 and 9.4, almost triple the rate at the turn of the century. "A new marriage has about a one in four probability of ultimately ending in divorce," Dr. Paul H. Jacobson said.[6] To the almost 2 million divorces in the nation must be added almost an equal number of separations.

In all of these family difficulties the dollar sign looms large. The suburban parents who can find an abortionist and are willing to risk their daughter's life in his hands must pay anywhere from $300 to the thousands the illegal practitioner thinks the market will bear. A trip to an out-of-state private maternity home costs anywhere from $500 to $1,500. Even a bargain divorce requires several hundred dollars.

The phrase that "separation is the poor man's divorce," is not just a glib speculation. In Chicago, I asked a relief client, separated from an alcoholic husband for six years, if she ever thought about getting a divorce:

"Yes, I've thought about it. I even went. Had a half-hour interview with this man, and when I got through he tells me it's goin' to cost $200. That half-hour I talked to him he charged me $15. For that money I don't need no divorce. He don't bother me and I don't bother him."

Sometimes not even money can resolve these problems. This is particularly true for Negroes who are the ADC majority on most large city relief rolls. They are rarely involved in abortion, will not be admitted or cannot afford a private maternity home, and infrequently find parents to adopt their children. In Greenleigh's ADC study of Cook County, he found that in one year almost 99 per cent of the illegitimate children who were adopted were white. "Of all the children born out of wedlock in Cook County, the chance that a white child will be adopted in the first year of life is 166 times as great as for a Negro child," he said.[7] In New York City early in 1962 the home shortage for infants, even for temporary foster care, required an emergency campaign to get 162 perfectly well babies out of hospital cribs where they had been consigned because nobody wanted them. Four-fifths were Negro.

The sum of these tremors within the American family annually has put more strain on the ADC program. Not only does the ADC mother lack money to relieve the problems, but she has the least educational and, consequently, vocational equipment with which to solve them. The government's Bureau of Family Services in 1963 compared her characteristics with those of other American women. It was a study in contrast.[8]

When it came to schooling, the ADC mothers lagged behind like this:

More than a third failed to complete elementary school while fewer than an eighth of the other women did not complete it. Only 16 per cent finished high school, but 56 per cent of women in general did; and only 2 per cent had a year of college work while 16 per cent of other women reached that level. The median school completion mark for ADC mothers was 8.8 years and for other women it was 12.1 years.

When it came to jobs, the ADC mothers were clustered on the bottom of the vocational rungs like this:

The majority—54 per cent—were service and domestic workers while only 22 per cent of women in general were in this category. A total of 17 per cent were classified as unskilled laborers while less than 1 per cent of other women were. Only 10 per cent of the ADC women were in the white-collar group while the majority of other women—57 per cent—were in that category.

These are the underdeveloped Americans who head the largest number of relief families in the nation. It is doubtful that they were uppermost in the minds of legislators who wrote the Aid to Dependent Children program into the 1935 Social Security Act. The congressmen envisioned ADC as a kindly government provider for widows and orphans, a group for whom Americans long have reserved their best charity impulses. For the first few years this group did, in fact, dominate the rolls. But as time and additional legislation brought an ever greater number of persons under the umbrella of the social security insurance program, the widow no longer sought aid at the local welfare department. She still was in need, but now she could claim the monthly social security benefits for which her husband and his employer had made weekly contributions. In 1962 more than 3.5 million families received social security payments because of the death of the breadwinner.

The majority of ADC children today still are without a father, but his death is the least frequent reason they are on the charity rolls. The principal cause of their dependency is because the father has fled the home. He has deserted the mother of these children, is divorced or separated from her, or never was married to her. The most recent analysis of the ADC program by the federal government gives these major causes of dependency:[9]

TABLE 3

Major Causes of Dependency of ADC Recipients: 1961

Cause		*Per Cent*
Father dead		7.7
Father disabled		18.1
Father absent:		66.7
Divorced or separated	21.9	
Not married to mother	21.3	
Deserted	18.6	
Imprisoned	4.2	
Other reasons	.6	
Father unemployed		5.2
Other status		2.2

The absent father has become the ghost figure of the ADC program. He haunts the rolls from the smallest rural county to the largest city. Information about him is scant. "We have pages and pages that give a detailed history of the mother, her parents, and even her grandparents," the head of a large adoption agency told me, "but when it comes to the father, there may be a paragraph that says 'he's 24 years, 6 feet 2 inches tall and has brown hair.' "

However, one thing is clear. In many cases, ironically, it is ADC that helps drive him out of the house. Public welfare workers believe this happens frequently with men who are separated or have deserted. This is why:

The majority of states require that the father must be out of the home before the family can apply for ADC.* If the individual community provides no general relief funds or gives only token assistance to unemployed parents, the father has no choice. He must leave if his children are to eat.**

Occasionally a case record will document how this welfare program can be a home breaker. A Chicago municipal court report does this:

> The F's have been separated for the past year because of Mr. F's seasonal work and his inability to meet the needs of the family. This was the major cause of the separation.
>
> Mr. F has been employed for the past ten years by the Acme Co. Mr. F's employment was verified 7/12/62. Mr. F is currently earning $75 per week; however, his take-home pay is averaging $40 a week. The employer is withholding money for weekly payments to Mr. F's creditors.

* At the beginning of 1963 only fifteen states had taken advantage of a federal provision approved two years earlier, that permitted ADC funds to go to families with unemployed fathers in the home. About four-fifths of the total cases were concentrated in four states. One state, Washington, had the expanded ADC program but dropped it. The other states were: Arizona, Connecticut, Delaware, Hawaii, Illinois, Maryland, Massachusetts, New York, North Carolina, Oklahoma, Oregon, Pennsylvania, Rhode Island, Utah, and West Virginia.

** Some counties have no provisions for relief to any family that contains a potentially employable father. A 1962 study of services to children and families in Jackson County (Kansas City), Missouri, observed: "The failure to provide general relief for families of employable fathers no doubt actually encourages some fathers to desert their families to make them eligible for ADC."[10]

In this way wage assignments and garnishments are being forestalled. If garnishments were to be made, the employer stated, he would be forced to lay off Mr. F.

The creditors are:

General Finance Co., unpaid balance $225. Weekly payment $10.

Mercantile Discount Co., unpaid balance $91. Weekly payment not yet determined. Garnishment papers were served 7/10/62.

Chicago Housing Authority, unpaid balance $138. Weekly payment $5.

Gas station, unpaid balance $25. Weekly payment $5.

Mr. F is described by his employer as being "A good worker, reliable and a fine person" but "poor about managing money." Mr. F's work is seasonal.

Until late in her last pregnancy, Mrs. F (mother of four children) was able to work during her husband's periods of unemployment and by so doing could meet the family expenses. When they were without income and unable to manage, *Mr. F left home so his wife could apply for ADC.*

These financial problems are typical of the economic snare in which a large number of ADC fathers find themselves.

Negro fathers are particularly hard hit. For example, their chances of being listed in the Labor Department's unemployment statistics are twice as great as their white counterparts. When they are laid off the period of joblessness usually is longer than for white workers. Because of this they frequently become an economic drag on the family and are simply just another mouth to feed.

Furthermore, many ADC fathers enter the marriage contract with a limited set of job skills that dictate a limited income. These remain static while the size of the family does not. Responsibilities increase and the bills that come with them are temporarily stalled by turning to the finance company or the well-advertised "no money down, $2.00 a week" purchase plan. But the high-interest rate loans become due and the $2.00-time plans mount. A temporary job layoff, no matter how brief, tips the delicate financial balance of the family. A couch, a television set, or even the kitchen stove are repossessed. As they are carried out the door the father's vital self-respect as a provider goes with them. There is only one steady "income" that he sees and that begins when his wife fills out an application at the local welfare office and he moves "around the corner."

Efforts of the law to retrieve him have been sporadic, frequently dependent on the zeal of a particular welfare attorney. Even when the fathers are apprehended, the results often are negligible.

Fewer than one-fifth of absent ADC fathers contribute anything to the families they have left behind. Their limited skills and low wages are unchanged even though they are collared by the local sheriff. "So I have this man in front of me," a judge told me, "and I'm supposed to try him for non-support. Am I going to order him to pay $40 a week when he hasn't had a pay check for the last six months? If I put him in jail, it's going to cost the taxpayers more and I've made it a certainty that he isn't going to get a job."

The father who is pushed out the door because of financial troubles or who slams it himself because of other stresses and temptations becomes a floater. He frequently turns into a combination journeyman parent and itinerant lover whose stops are recorded in the local welfare department by the arrival of another child. He may be represented in several ADC cases, and as a result he takes on the role of the double culprit—deserting parent and unwed father. Paternity and non-support actions in city courts across the nation occasionally mark these way stations. In Chicago's Municipal Court, I observed separate cases one morning that involved an uncle and his nephew. Both were accused in paternity actions brought by the Cook County Department of Public Aid. The judge asked each of them: "Why don't you marry the girl?" Each of them answered: "Already married."

In the face of welfare criticism frequently an awkward attempt is made to explain away the papa problem by pretending he does not exist. The press releases and reports single out statistics that show how few employables there are on the rolls. They explain carefully that the ADC problem involves children too young to work and mothers who must stay home to mind them. This is carrying the babies-are-made-in-heaven theory a little too far.

The missing father is as much involved in the Aid to Dependent Children family today as he was in the bedroom. That no welfare dollars go to him does not weaken the fact that most often his failure has forced the government to be his substitute. His employment, his educational and cultural shortcomings are part of the basic problems of ADC. Far more research should be done about his difficulties in all of these areas. Social workers and their influential allies should urge this upon every community rather than label him simply among the missing.

But if the absent father has been nudged out of the debate, the illegitimate child he may have left behind, has not. Illegitimacy has become the noisiest argument in ADC. Accurate statistics are almost impossible to obtain. In large cities where most welfare recipients live and where the debate, of course, is the loudest, the figures are the highest. Greenleigh found in Chicago in May 1960 that one-half of the children on ADC were illegitimate. Ten years earlier the figure was one-third. He made a comparative study of other urban welfare districts and found the percentage of illegitimates on ADC to be:[11]

TABLE 4

Percentage of Illegitimate Children on ADC in Selected Urban Welfare Districts

District	*Per Cent*	
Baltimore	16.0 (1941)	37.5 (1958)
New York (county)	Not available	41.1 (1959)
Philadelphia (county)	40.0 (1951)	39.0 (1958)
St. Louis	29.6 (1946)	47.7 (1958)
Washington, D.C.	18.0 (1948)	38.0 (1958)

Greenleigh also warns about the accuracy of these percentages.*

* The definition of illegitimacy occasionally varies from state to state. He found Cleveland reporting 24.0 per cent according to Ohio law and 38.0 per cent according to Illinois law.

Further, the statistics offer another pitfall because they count individual children and do not give an accurate appraisal of what is happening within the ADC family. When he dissected the families, Greenleigh found that almost 70 per cent contained one or more illegitimate children. "In many cases," he reported, "the mother had been married, was deserted by her husband and had children by another man."[12]

In my interviews with scores of ADC mothers, many have given answers that provide better clues to the rising problem than the force of its statistics.

"You know," the ADC mother in the walk-up apartment told me, "they expect us to get off ADC by finding ourselves a job or if we can, another husband. That's really the only two ways we are goin' to make it, right? Well, for me to find another husband, I got to at least see another man, don't I? As soon as I do that, and this neighbor woman down the street sees me with him on a Saturday night, then she thinks—I'll tell you what she thinks—she thinks 'There goes that ADC whore.' "

A family counselor in an urban area, whose job was to talk with welfare parents, summed it up this way: "We expect too much. We expect this woman to sit home and eke out an existence on the minimum allowance we give her. We don't think that she gets lonely and then some guy will come along and tell her just a few things, maybe how nice she looks. Now he knows and we know that she don't look nice—she's got nothing to look nice with. But he tells her and she hears it and likes it, and it may be the first time somebody said something nice to her for a long time, so she gives him what he wants."

My interviews with clients echo this statement. No one is better qualified to explain the relationship between illegitimacy and public welfare than the woman who can claim title to both.

The woman in the Chicago housing project apartment was a divorcee and mother of four children. Three of them, according to the welfare department, were legitimate. The fourth, a girl, born two weeks before the interview took place, was not.

Q. How did you get involved in that situation?

A. I got involved in that situation due to the fact that I had a lot of confidence in this person and was takin' a chance with him.

Q. What do you mean by "a lot of confidence"?

A. When I say "a lot of confidence" I believed that if anything would happen to me—and it just wasn't in my opinion 'cause he told me—he would take care of things. This man was single and he was well able to take on a family, but he said he didn't want a ready-made family unless he knew that he could have a family of his own. Meanin' that he would like to know that the woman he was marryin' could give him a child. So I believed him. And so I did the things people do when they have confidence in people, I suppose. And then when he found out about the baby. . . .

Q. Did he live with you during this time?

A. No, he didn't. We only saw each other.

Q. How long did you see him?

A. Before I got the baby? About a year and six months.

Q. And then there was the baby. Did you tell him right away that you were pregnant?

A. Yes, I told him. The minute I knew I was pregnant I told him.

Q. And then what happened?

A. Then he sent me to the doctor and we found out for sure that I were and . . . he stopped coming around.

Q. That was it?

A. Yes. I was very upset about it, very upset about it.

Q. What do you mean?

A. 'Cause I was ashamed. And there was nothin' I could do about it. Because when he actually told me he wasn't going to marry me, which was the proper thing to do when you get a baby out of wedlock if you aren't married, if you're in a position to get married. And the minute he told me this wasn't going to happen, that was the minute I got upset.

Q. Did he give you any reasons?

A. No, he didn't give me no reason; he just didn't want to get married. He said he thought he wanted to marry me but he changed his mind.

Q. Were you lonely or . . .

A. This is the thing you will learn about me in the community if there was such a thing as asking around. I don't care for a lot of men. I like a lot of attention and I like to feel that I'm appreciated. So I feel you can't get this from a lot of men, you can only get it from one at a time. And this has been my way of livin' since I have been eighteen years old.

Q. What do you mean by attention, what kind of things . . . ?

A. Oh, now what I consider as attention is to have somebody to take me and kids to the movies, to the park, and give me the little things that a person that you would associate with would do if they appreciated you. And then only natural, with three kids to educate and to raise and you feel like if you only associate with one person at a time they might be interested in you enough, they might want to help you educate your children and help you raise your children. If you see this in a person the only natural thing to do is lookin' forward to marriage.

Q. How about the other kids? Has this had any effect on the other children?

A. No. They're feelin' fine now. They were upset. I guess it's all my fault 'cause I told 'em I was going to give the baby away. They was upset for a while, but now it doesn't bother them. But then I guess they're not old enough to understand.

Q. Did you really think that you wanted to give the baby away?

A. Yes, I did.

Q. What made you change your mind?

A. The head nurse over here at Station 19. She told me to think about it. Then I felt like it wasn't the baby's fault and number one, I was raised in an orphan home myself and I've never forgiven my father for it and there is a possible chance that this child might find out who I were and never forgive me for it. So I just said well, I'd bring it home and do the best I can. It wasn't her fault that she was brought into the world. Even though somebody else could give her richness I feel as though I could give her love and in some cases that's more important.

This child is another statistic on Chicago's illegitimacy records and in the files of its welfare department. Both are increasing. But neither is responsible for the other and the only thing it proves is that the dramatic national rise in illegitimacy is mirrored most easily where it is most noticeable—on the welfare rolls. However, it is time to call a halt to the pooh-poohing of illegitimacy as an issue. For too long some of ADC's defenders have been sifting out statistics to falsely minimize the problem. The favorite in the last few years was taken from a 1960 federal study ordered by the

Senate Appropriations Committee: "Illegitimacy and Its Impact on the Aid to Dependent Children Program."[13]

It said that about 13 per cent of all illegitimate children in the United States are on ADC. This has been repeated again and again. But it does no more to address the issue than the little boy who announced "my face ain't as dirty as sister's." Furthermore, the figure is deceiving. The public is not preoccupied over what percentage of the nation's illegitimate children are receiving ADC. Instead the public is disturbed with a wholly different measurement: namely, that so many ADC children are illegitimate. The latest federal survey showed that almost one-fourth of the ADC children were illegitimate.

Those who have sidestepped the issue should acknowledge that what has happened in the Aid to Dependent Children category, in short, is that the socially accepted, the widows, orphans, and youngsters of disabled breadwinners have been displaced in a large measure by the social outcasts, the runaway husbands, the bachelor parents and their offspring. In the sixties they represent ADC, and all the orphan feature stories are not about to bring back the good old days of blue bows and pink ribbons.

Since critics of the program have yet to receive an admission of this change from some social workers, their more flamboyant brethren have been encouraged to hurl irrational generalities at the entire program. The leading one is that ADC provides an incentive plan for a mother to have another child so her monthly check goes up. If this is true then ADC mothers have managed to contrive the worst example of the profit motive in the United States. In March 1963 the average monthly grant per person on ADC was $31.38, or just about a dollar a day. Among the scores of relief recipients I have interviewed, I have never met one who gave me even the slightest indication that she increased the size of her family to add to her relief check. Many of them who were struggling with large families were in that predicament because their child planning was patterned after their life planning—from day to day and week to week.

Faced with the rising ADC population and its increasing cost, a frequent demand is to take away the mother's children. In some instances this might be helpful, but if it were to be done on a large enough scale to affect ADC, the price for the alternative most likely would more than triple. In a report to its taxpayers, Monroe County (Rochester, New York) noted that it cost an average of $38.16 a month to keep a child in its own home.[14] Placing it in a foster home would cost $67.71 a month, while institutional care ranged from $141.90 to more than $300 a month.

This threat of taking children away from mothers is an important element in a punitive device called the suitable home law. Sixteen states have such laws and enforce them in varying degrees. In several southern states they have been used as anti-Negro laws. Eight states, for example, consider a home unsuitable if the mother has an illegitimate child after she receives a relief check. This was the legal basis Louisiana used in July 1960 to drop 22,500 children and their parents from the rolls. Three months later an Associated Press dispatch quoted a cosponsor of the law saying that children in his parish were found eating out of garbage cans.[15] "There is reason to suspect," Social Security Commissioner William L. Mitchell said in a classic bit of understatement, "that Louisiana Act 251 was concerned more with controlling illegitimacy and disciplining parents than it was with assuring that children receiving public aid should be raised in suitable homes and wholesome surroundings."[16] He held that a modified version of this legislation did not conflict with federal requirements and that aid would continue.

If controlling illegitimacy is the intent of some of these laws, then they may have been just about as effective as New England pulpit admonitions against bundling. Very few states have bothered to take a second look to see if their intent was achieved. In Mississippi, however, the Children's Code Commission interviewed families with 1,100 children three years after a suitable home law went into effect.[17] The majority of the 323 cases were closed because of an illegitimate birth or pregnancy. In 1957, when the families were re-examined, 187 births had occurred since the cases were closed. All but eleven were illegitimate. For those legislators who thought they were putting an end to illegitimacy, these statistics offer dreary proof indeed.

"When asked by interviewers how they had been getting along without ADC assistance, answers ran the gamut from hopelessness and defeat to wit and cheerful outlook," the report said. In most cases the income was described as "very low" and "irregular." An excerpt from a case record, written by a Mississippi interviewer, said:

> Although Betty is now married, she and her husband have been separated for about a year. He is, however, making a crop for her and her family. The children (9) who are not sick or too small, work in the field. She said that since she had been sick, she has been unable to plant a garden; therefore, she is forced to buy food for herself and her children on $20 a month which she gets from her husband's crop. She has no outside help except from her sister who sends the children clothes; some of the children wear clothes made from flour and fertilizer sacks. When the mother was in the hospital, some of her colored neighbors sent her an occasional fifty cents.
>
> Nevertheless, Betty was not so worried about the children's clothing; but when they cry for food, that does bother her. Tears rolled down her cheeks as she said, "The biggest time my children get a piece of bread and go on. Sometimes I take flour and make gravy for them."

When reviewing cases like this the social auditor has to decide whether his scale weighs people or monetary savings. Restrictive policies that deny aid to children keep both them and their errant parents off the welfare rolls. Texas, for example, which denied assistance to any child above fourteen until 1963, can produce an admirable record on the financial ledger.* But can it give an adequate answer when someone asks what is happening to these people? Too often legislators and those who beat the public drum for

* In April 1963 the Texas legislature permitted ADC payments to children up to the age of sixteen.

tax cuts have operated under the theory that when you remove the people from the welfare rolls you remove their problems as well. Instead, their difficulties may be camouflaged and frequently compounded on a country back road or on the upper floor of a city tenement. They stay conveniently out of sight until a man or woman comes back with a notebook that says "Some of the children wear clothes made from flour and fertilizer sacks."

Most ADC families in the United States receive less money than the amount the U.S. Department of Agriculture says is necessary to live on its low cost food plan. In Florida, for example, the average ADC child receives 52 cents a day for food, clothing, shelter, and medical care. Seven other welfare departments provide less.* Since 1951, Florida has had an $81 monthly maximum grant per family regardless of the number of children in it. It is the lowest in the nation. The state, like many others, provides far less for its needy children than for its needy adults. The following figures show the extent of that disparity:

TABLE 5

Public Welfare Grants Provided by State of Florida: Averages for August 1962

	Need Set by State	*Grant*	*Per Cent of Need Met*	*Medical Benefit*
Old-Age Assistance	$ 49.41	$46.74	94.6%	$14.31
Aid to Blind	$ 66.03	$57.26	86.7%	$ 6.41
Aid to Disabled	$ 63.49	$55.41	87.3%	$10.40
ADC per family	$106.81	$60.45	56.6%	$ 1.57
ADC per person	$ 28.59	$16.18	56.6%	$ 0.42

The ADC need is figured on average of 3.74 people; the other public assistance budgets include the needs of 1.2 people.

SOURCE: Florida Department of Public Welfare.

* These are: Arkansas, South Carolina, Alabama, Mississippi, Puerto Rico, Guam, and the Virgin Islands.

But if there is a financial disparity in ADC, there is a disparity between aim and achievement as well. The program in its third decade has failed to break the cycle of dependency and in a number of cases may have prolonged it. There is a hard core of ADC women today who may once have been married to a man, but now are married to ADC. It may not be a scheming, willful marriage, but often it is a marriage of convenience and sometimes of necessity. The monthly ADC grant for many of these women is the most regular "pay check" they have seen. Even though it might be less, it sometimes is superior to the income of a husband who may be laid off three or four times a year or who squanders his money in the neighborhood tavern.

In the Washington welfare study, one investigator reported that a Mr. N told the worker "his wife refused to take him back because she could get more from [the] Public Assistance Division."[18] The fact that federal statisticians announce that the average stay on the rolls of a family is 2.1 years does not shatter the argument. One-third are repeaters whose self-support time may be as brief as a week or a month.

The second and third generation relief families are increasing. There is a perpetuation of dependency from one generation to another in one out of every four Home Relief, ADC, and Aid to Disabled cases, the Greenleigh investigators found in their New York Study.[19] Among the group who, the interviewers felt, had an alternative to welfare, a low of 5 per cent in one county and a high of 23 per cent in another were satisfied with the status quo of relief.

The status quo also has attracted too many of the program's supporters. The comfortable and cherished assumptions of the past are repeatedly superimposed over the new problems of today even though the pattern often does not fit.

In some states we still hold to the policy that no ADC mother should work even though 8 million mothers in the United States are in the labor force. At the same time, nationally, we argue for more federal funds to set up day care centers.

In some states where ADC mothers are urged to work—and 15

per cent of the national total do—we expect a mother to take three or four different day work jobs in one week, travel to several different homes in the suburbs, and then have every penny deducted from her relief check.

We are so concerned with relief ineligibility that the most frequent question a rushed caseworker asks is: Are you working? And then we are dismayed when we find a sizeable group of recipients concluding that work is something to avoid if you want to stay on ADC.

We may acknowledge that changing sexual mores and behavior in America are affecting the ADC rolls, yet in most communities we refuse to discuss family planning.

We admit that the average ADC mother barely has an elementary school education while other mothers have graduated from high school, but we expect both to manage their housekeeping budgets equally well. A chorus of social work howls rises when someone suggests that a check should be sent directly to the landlord—in the same way physicians are paid for treating recipients—if a family cannot handle its money.

But above all, in the hurly-burly of controversy over the parents, we have neglected to ask penetrating questions about their children. We have been delinquent in taking a hard look in their direction. The swirl of oratory that has orbited around the worn bromide: Does ADC subsidize illegitimacy?, would be better directed to the basic questions: *What does ADC subsidize?* What do the annual billions buy?

Some of the answers are not at all reassuring. Even in the minority of states where ADC children receive the necessary minimums for adequate shelter, food, and clothing, the program really has not bought much more. The fact is that it has failed to purchase the most vital commodity for the ADC child—the chance to drop the shackles binding its parents. The poverty bonds already are leaving their marks on the young.

The measure of government charity cannot be simply a full stomach. It must be in what the sociologist calls "upward mobility," and what most of us describe as improving on yesterday. It is here that ADC is failing. There are the success stories, to be sure, of the prominent writer, the athlete, the business executive, whose names are inscribed in old relief records. But the exception, no matter how dramatic, provides no solace for the average. And across the nation the average ADC child is accumulating the same characteristics that shaped the dependency pattern of its parents. The American Public Welfare Association's recent comprehensive ADC study provides statistical backbone to push the argument out of the realm of speculation.[20] It showed clearly that in the key area of education, ADC youngsters are falling far behind:

School drop-outs among ADC children between the ages of fourteen to seventeen were more than twice as high as for all other children in this age group.

While 13 per cent of all Americans in this age group did not graduate from high school, nearly 70 per cent of the ADC youths failed to get a diploma.

While 19 per cent of all young people in the same age bracket went to college, fewer than 3 per cent of the ADC youths did.

Furthermore, in the last decade, while American youngsters made major forward strides in educational achievement, ADC children held on to their poor record. In 1950 the American Public Welfare Association did a similar study which permits comparison with the more recent survey:[21]

In the 1950 sample 71 per cent of the ADC youths between eighteen and twenty failed to finish high school, and in the present sample 72 per cent of the eighteen- to nineteen-year-olds failed to finish.

In the 1950 sample 3 per cent of those eighteen and older went to college, but at the end of the decade even fewer (2.6 per cent) of this group went on to higher education.

The behavior or lack of behavior of the ADC parents may capture the headlines. However, the educational performance of their children virtually guarantees a new generation of dependency—this is the real shame of the ADC families. It is the shame of every community that permits it to exist.

4

THE OBSOLETE YOUNG

I'll tell you, man, I go to Catholic Charities, to the Youth Center, down by the employment people—a couple of weeks ago I try to buy a job—I talk to social workers. . . . You go from place to place, you know, and you get tired. I guess you get bored. Guys say no work, no nothin', no work, and then you say, "To hell with it. Let the job come to me."

The seventeen-year-old boy speaking is one of nearly a million youths between the ages of sixteen through twenty-four in the United States who are out of school, out of work, and, too frequently, out of skills anybody wants. They are native Americans who are displaced persons. They are a new breed of economic hoboes, with peach fuzz instead of beard stubble, who inhabit street corners instead of tank-town railside jungles. But they share a basic commodity with their elder brethren of the Depression. It is an overabundance of time.

They can be seen among clusters of their companions on the sidewalks and in alleys of the big city slums, and they can be found in the rural crossroad stores and garages tinkering with a hot rod whose engine performance has been checked scores of times—because there is nothing else to do.

These idle youths may be public welfare's most serious problem. For they are its recruits who are in basic training for tomorrow's welfare rolls. Many of them will begin collecting relief checks with a regularity they have never experienced working for a pay check. They will marry on relief, and they will raise their children on the dole.

It is easier to find the idle young on a street corner than in accurate statistical columns. But one thing is clear from the U.S. Department of Labor statistics reports: Unemployment among youthful workers has been pushing upward at such a rate that it has more than doubled in the past ten years. The following chart shows the annual percentages:

TABLE 6

Percentage of Young People Unemployed: 1953–1962

Year	*Per Cent* 14–19 *Yrs.*	*Per Cent* 14–24 *Yrs.*
1953	6.5	5.2
1954	10.7	9.5
1955	9.6	7.8
1956	9.7	7.7
1957	10.8	8.8
1958	14.4	12.6
1959	13.2	10.6
1960	13.6	11.0
1961	15.2	12.6
1962	13.3	11.0

SOURCE: Prepared by Bureau of Labor Statistics, Department of Labor.

In May 1963 the Labor Department announced that the unemployment rate of teenagers reached an all-time record of nearly 18 per cent, three times higher than the national average. This meant that the out-of-work figures for youths matched those estimated for all workers during some of the Depression years. Secretary of Labor W. Willard Wirtz said this youth unemployment situation "could develop into one of the most explosive social problems in the nation's history."[1]

But the national figure of nearly 1 million unemployed youths does not tell the total story. To this must be added a second group also out of school, out of work, and, more significantly, out of energy to look for a job. They may number an additional 300,000, according to Eli E. Cohen, executive secretary of the National Committee on Employment of Youth.

"In some of our larger cities there are possibly as many unemployed youths not looking for work as there are officially recorded unemployed youths," Mr. Cohen told me. "When the government numerator comes around he asks the boy: 'Do you have a job?' He says 'No.' 'Have you looked for a job?' and he says 'No' again. This boy now is not counted as unemployed because the government considers him out of the labor force."

If these figures are alarming, they are but a prologue for the sixties. In this decade 26 million young Americans, the bumper crop of the post-World War II years, will enter the labor pool—40 per cent more than in the fifties. Yet of these work seekers, an estimated 7.5 million will be lacking what now has become a twin job requisite with the social security card—a high school diploma. More than 2 million will have failed to complete the eighth grade.*

There are some research previews of what will happen to this large group in the sixties. Late in 1962 the New York City Mayor's

* The drop-outs in the labor market today have an unemployment rate twice that of graduates. U.S. Department of Labor Statistics survey reports showed that in October 1959 one out of every four drop-outs (sixteen and seventeen) was out of work. They earn an average of $27 a week less than graduates and the gulf widens as they get older. In 1959 the median annual income among urban men was $1,389 lower for those who had not completed high school than for graduates. They are three times more likely than graduates to wind up in low-level jobs.[2]

Of the estimated 900,000 who quit high school in 1961, Dr. Glen Stice, a research associate of the Educational Testing Service, estimates about 50,000 would have made excellent college material.[3]

Task Force on Youth and Work released a study that showed at least 76,800 youths within the city were having job problems in one of three ways: 30,200 males and females between the ages of fourteen and twenty-four were unemployed, out of school, and looking for work. Another 13,900 out-of-school young men in the same age group had part-time jobs because many of them could not locate full-time work. But the largest group mentioned in the report comprised 32,700 young men between fourteen and twenty-four who were not in school, not in the labor force, and were presumed not looking for work. "The report proves beyond a doubt," Task Force Chairman Walter A. Miller said, "that New York City has a massive and serious problem of youth unemployment."[4]

But this enumeration of thousands of drifting youths is diluted in a city of 8 million inhabitants. Only when the count is localized in the specific neighborhoods where the majority of these unemployed live does the full significance of the problem become apparent. The Cleveland public schools in 1962 completed a survey of out-of-work youths in four neighborhoods that had these common characteristics: high rates of public assistance, crime and delinquency, school drop-outs, and unemployment. Three of the neighborhoods were predominantly Negro; the fourth was white. Some of the major findings were these:

Two out of three, or 63 per cent, of the out-of-school youths between the ages of sixteen and twenty-one were unemployed. In the three Negro neighborhoods the figures were 68 per cent, 77 per cent, and 80 per cent. In the white neighborhood it was 43 per cent.

In the four areas high school graduates appeared to have a 50-50 chance of finding a job—53 per cent were employed, 47 per cent were unemployed. In one Negro neighborhood 66 per cent of the high school graduates were unemployed.

Approximately three out of four of the school drop-outs were unemployed. Three out of five of all the unemployed said they had never had a full-time job.[5]

Until other major urban areas analyze these job problems on a neighborhood to neighborhood basis, it will be difficult to make accurate national generalizations. However, it is clear that citywide youth unemployment figures may be as misleading as an analysis of a patient's illness that reports only 6 per cent of the body consumed by cancer. Behind that figure may be the fact that most of the cancer is located in the stomach, and 80 per cent of that is affected. The urban disease of out-of-work youth is gnawing at specific sections of a city and may act upon the total body of the community in the same fashion that the cancerous stomach lays low the patient. Particularly susceptible are the minority neighborhoods, which in most cities mean the Negro ghettos.

Dr. James B. Conant, in his book *Slums and Suburbs,* observed:

> For without being an alarmist, I must say that when one considers the total situation that has been developing in the Negro city slums since World War II, one has reason to worry about the future. The building up of a mass of unemployed and frustrated Negro youth in congested areas of a city is a social phenomenon that may be compared to the piling up of inflammable material in an empty building in a city block. Potentialities for trouble—indeed possibilities of disaster—are surely there.[6]

The difficulties that these socially handicapped youths face are compounded by a radically changing economy in which the machine is displacing man in hundreds of thousands of jobs around the nation. They are part of a new labor pool that is struggling with automation—a second industrial revolution dominated by computers, stacks of notched data processing cards, and push-button assembly lines. They are at the dawning of a new labor casualty—the de-skilled American, who possesses talents for a task that has been stripped of its human component.

Much of the automation debate has revolved around the displaced older worker, who is the most visible casualty. Yet the new young worker may be hit as hard if not harder. Frequently the effects of automation are absorbed within a plant. Men are reassigned to other jobs. But these shifts have clogged up the normal hire-retire cycle. The lower echelon jobs may now be filled by the displaced man from above and not by the "new boy." The National Committee on Employment of Youth estimated that jobs for new workers were disappearing at the rate of 250,000 a year.

That this second industrial revolution has affected all areas of our economy is revealed by the statistics:

In agriculture, farm worker employment dropped from 9.5 million in 1940 to 5.2 million in 1962, pushing a massive contingent of unskilled men into the urban labor force. In manufacturing, the Bureau of Labor Statistics reports peak employment of almost 18 million workers was reached in 1943 and never has been equaled since. There were fewer workers in manufacturing in 1959 than in 1953. While white-collar employment increased between 1948 and 1961, blue-collar employment fell. Union leaders say that from 1956 to 1962 a total of 1.5 million production jobs in factories was lost.

A look at one large union highlights some of these problems. Particularly significant is the Building Service Employees' International Union with a total membership of almost 300,000. They are men and women with limited skills, who, if displaced, most likely will become part of the long-term unemployment core and eventually may apply for welfare. While total union membership gradually has been increasing, this has been accomplished by vigorous organizing far afield—from race track personnel to grave diggers.* David Sullivan, general president, a national leader in the automation debate, provided these examples to underscore his concern:

In Chicago his union's Local 66 Elevator Operators and Starters in 1956 had 4,328 members. Four years later the membership was down to 3,929 or a loss of almost 10 per cent.

* Even grave diggers are not immune to automation. It takes about ten hours for two men to dig an eight-foot grave. If a grave-digging machine is used, it takes about twenty to forty-five minutes to dig a ten-foot grave. The machine, which can dig seven to eight graves a day, is operated by one man and an assistant.

In New York, Local 32B, one of the three largest locals of any union in the country, lost approximately 25,000 jobs to automation. Union records of one building, the famed Chrysler Building, show what happened in seven years:

TABLE 7

Effect of Automation on Employment of Building Service Personnel in Chrysler Building: 1956 and 1963

	Number Employed	
	1956	*1963*
Elevator Operators	74	38
Security men	12	12
Porters	61	40
Total	147	90

"The elevators in the Chrysler Building East have been completely converted to automatic. Building West is in the process of conversion and it is management's intention to convert all but two freight cars," a notation on the record said.[7]

An advertisement in *Building Maintenance Magazine* illustrates how the new technology can affect the many porters and cleaning women in the union. It reads like this:

8¼ Man Hours in One!
The New Advance "Convertamatic" scrubs and vacuums 12,500 square feet of floor an hour—over eight times the area one man can clean with 19″ floor machine and vac![8]

Most readers can flip through their own vocational memory cards to find a personal experience that indicates the effect of a new machine-orientated economy. Some may remember the grocery clerk's job that disappeared when a new self-service supermarket arrived. Some may recall the delivery boy whose need has nearly vanished since women began driving to shopping centers. For me, the point was made when I spent a recent weekend on the farm where I grew up. For a few hours I rejoined the agricultural labor force of which I once had been a member.

There were five of us and we split up into two teams. Two baled six acres of hay and stored it in the barn with mechanical loaders, while three of us cut corn silage for one of three silos. In six hours we filled six doors of the silo.

Fifteen years ago, when I was part of a seven-man haying team, we loaded it loose and used horses to bring it into the barn. Three men worked inside with pitchforks to distribute each load, and it took days instead of hours to bring in six acres of hay. When the same crew was turned to silo-filling—which fifteen years ago meant hand-loading handcut bundles of cornstalks into wagons—we considered it a good day's work to fill one door of the silo.

Agricultural journals chronicle these advances in terse little paragraphs:

In the southern cotton areas hand labor virtually has disappeared. The 1960 crop was handled almost entirely by tractor power and more than 50 per cent of it was mechanically picked.

In the cherry country of Michigan, New York, and Pennsylvania mechanical tree shakers are coming increasingly into use. One machine does the work of eighty hand pickers, and costs are cut from $60 a ton to $20.

In industry the examples of a machine "harvest" are just as impressive:

Fourteen persons running fourteen machines today can make 90 per cent of all the light bulbs in the United States.

A furniture company now makes 1,000 quality upholstered chairs a day with 25 workers. Formerly the same production schedule required 300 workers.

Two men now produce 1,000 radios a day on an assembly line that used to require 200.[9]

With blue-collar labor shrinking, economists have placed great hope on the expansion of white-collar and service jobs. Donald N. Michael, in his 1962 report for the Center for the Study of Democratic Institutions *(Cybernation:* The Silent Conquest)* doubts this:

> In the first place, service activities will also tend to displace workers by becoming self-service, by becoming cybernated, and by being eliminated. Consider the following data: The U.S. Census Bureau was able to use 50 statisticians in 1960 to do the tabulations that required 4,100 in 1950. Even where people are not being fired, service industries can now carry on a vastly greater amount of business without hiring additional personnel; for example, a 50% increase in the Bell System's volume of calls in the last ten years with only a 10% increase in personnel.[10]

Amid this mounting information that indicates we may be faced with a significant number of superfluous people, the twin demands of "find more jobs" and "retrain workers" have become more audible. Union leaders, politicians, and industrial spokesmen have repeated them with such frequency that the identity of their concern has been presumed.

But do we really know who these jobless are?

I don't believe we do. We are planning for people—particularly our out-of-work youth—whom we know largely from the numerical reports of the U.S. Department of Labor's Bureau of Statistics and from the graph that records the drop-outs. Too frequently we make judgments about them based upon our youthful experiences rather than theirs. We assume these are the same even though they may never have experienced a way of life that remotely parallels ours. We assume too, that somehow, somewhere, they have recognized a value in work. We assume, in short, that they want a job.

We forget that many, like the boy in the beginning of this chapter, have said ". . . to hell with it. Let the job come to me." Sometimes we are unaware that others may never have gotten that far; that they have never looked. When an interviewer asked one boy

* Mr. Michael's word "cybernation" refers to both automation and computers. He fashioned it from "cybernetics," a term invented by Norbert Wiener to mean the processes of communication and control in man and machines.

I know, "How do you feel when you are unemployed?" he replied with a shrug of the shoulders and a word—"Nothin'." A few segments of a tape-recorded interview with him may show why he felt "nothin'."[11]

Q. Tell me about your mother. How do you get along with her? Was there anything about her that bothered you?
A. Uhuh.
Q. What?
A. She used to go out all the time with other men, and whenever I was goin' to school she would have one of her boy friends in the house, and every time she has a boy friend in the house, she don't want me around. I would go in early back from school and she would tell me to go on back outside and everythin'.
Q. This happened often?
A. Uhuh.
Q. How well does your mother know you?
A. I don't think she knows me too well because when I was six years old I was taken away from my mother by some people and put in this place. Well, I never saw my mother, I think, it was four years. I saw her when I was ten. She came and took me out of this place. Then I started runnin' around the street and gettin' in trouble. Then I got put in another place for a year. Then I came back out, yeah, I came back out for two weeks, and then I got sent to another place and I came out of that place when I was fifteen. Then I got sent to another place when I was sent upstate.
Q. Tell me about your father. What kind of a person is he?
A. He's nice. He only has one thing wrong with him. He drinks a lot.
Q. How well does he know you?
A. He knows me a lot. When I was in that place he used to come up every Satiday and see me.
Q. Did he understand how you felt about things?
A. Uhuh.
Q. Could you ever talk over problems with him?
A. Uhuh.
Q. And he understood?
A. Uhuh.
Q. What does your mother expect you to become?
A. She don't 'spect me to come anythin', I guess. She keeps tellin'

me I'm not goin' to amount to nothin' and I'm goin' to be just like my father.

Q. What is courage? Do you think you have courage?

A. Yeah.

Q. What have you done to show that you have courage?

A. Fought a whole lot of guys.

Q. Tell me about your neighborhood. What kind of neighborhood do you live in?

A. Junkies. Prostitutes. All that sort of thing.

Q. Do junkies ever bother you?

A. No, they don't bother me.

Q. What about the prostitutes?

A. No, I don't mess around with them. I don't need to buy no sex.

Q. What does the word "fair" mean to you?

A. Supposin' I had a fight with this guy and all of a sudden he fell on the floor. Instead of me stompin' him or somethin' I'd help him up, somethin' like that.

Q. Would you like to be considered fair?

A. Yeah, you know, if I were fightin' with a guy, the only time I wouldn't fight fair, if he don't fight fair. Thas if just he and me was fightin'. But if like my boys, if we was comin' down in a gang fight or somethin', I wouldn't fight fair then. . . .

Can we expect this boy suddenly to discard his past experiences and the jumbled values they gave him, and become a job-seeker? Admittedly, this member of what Harrison Salisbury called "The Shook-up Generation" is among the minority of unemployed youths.[12] However, he is not unique, and the interviewer does not have to go through too many candidates to find others whose biographies show a zigzag course from the street corner to "this place, and that place. . . ."

There are other unanswered questions too. These concern the many youngsters who at least are motivated to go to an employment agency or to follow through on a help wanted ad. Do we really know their capabilities?

Again, I don't believe we do. We presume they know what a job requires, and we presume they are capable of filling it. It is here that our national zest for telling each other that all of us are equal comes into sharp conflict with reality. For our difficulty with the unskilled and semiskilled worker is not one of retraining. It is one of training—but not training on computer operation or assembly line maintenance; rather, how to read, and how to write, and how to make change for a dollar. It is training to fill out an application blank for an employer. It is training how to dress when asking a man for a job. For the woman in the household, often it is training to use a baby formula or to read the instructions on the back of a soup can.

I remember one afternoon making a home call, as a caseworker in Buffalo, to the house of a woman who had just come in from grocery shopping. I talked to her while she unpacked a variety of goods. I was surprised, because with but two exceptions she had bought only one of each item. I asked her why she bought "singles," and gradually during our conversation I realized that she was unable to figure that three cans costing 49 cents made a 2-cent saving when you bought them that way instead of at 17 cents apiece.

The 1960 Census told Americans that 2.4 per cent adults were illiterate, one of the smallest percentages of any nation in the world. There appears to be a serious gap, however, between this ostensibly low statistic and performance.

Personnel managers in major industries are learning that the school grade a man said he completed does not mean that he can do work at that level. More and more companies are giving prospective employees basic reading and writing tests, many of which do not go beyond the elementary or early high school level. The scores often startle personnel experts. In Massachusetts the personnel director of a large corporation told me:

> We have been testing for about ten years. We give simple spelling and arithmetic tests to all the high school graduates who come in here, and frankly we are surprised at the number who can't pass. I'd like to give you the exact figure, but some time ago one of our men mentioned the high rate of failures and it raised such hob in the community that we decided it would be better if we kept them confidential.

Industries which have attempted to assist in retraining employees whose jobs have been eliminated by automation or consolidation have found the efforts disappointing because the educational foundation presumed to be there was not. A key case is the experience of Armour & Company and the packing house and meat cutters unions.

In the 1959 labor contract between the company and the unions was a section which set up a joint automation committee whose task included organizing a "program of training qualified employees in the knowledge and skill required to perform new and changed jobs. . . ." In July 1960, when the company shut down its Oklahoma City plant, invitations were sent to 431 production workers to take aptitude tests and counseling interviews for future training. The program, conducted with the help of the Oklahoma State Employment Service, got a response from 170 workers. Tests showed that only 60 might be helped by some vocational training. "The balance," the Automation Committee's report said, "65 per cent of the total—were simply told that the best chance of employment would be in casual manual labor."[13]

The most significant report of how this problem affects public welfare was produced by Chicago's Cook County Department of Public Aid.[14] The findings permit more than idle speculation that many of the unemployed youths of today will be members of the relief population of tomorrow. The study, prepared under Dr. Deton J. Brooks, Jr., the department's director of research and statistics, included 680 able-bodied persons from families containing almost 2,000 children. All of them lived in a south Chicago area known as the Woodlawn community. It is an almost all-Negro neighborhood of 60,000 persons, of whom almost 25 per cent are on relief. The area has poor housing, a high crime rate, and low average income.

The welfare department conducted detailed interviews with the recipients in the study and gave each the new Stanford reading test for grades 2 to 9. From the interviews the researchers learned what grade each had completed in school; from the tests they found out what level work they actually could do. The difference between the two was acute.

While the interviews showed that 6.6 per cent were functionally illiterate because they had completed less than five years of school, the tests showed that more than half (50.7 per cent) were functionally illiterate because they could not read well enough to do fifth grade work. Women did better than men as this breakdown indicates:[15]

TABLE 8

Cook County, Illinois, Department of Public Aid Study to Determine Literacy Level of Able-Bodied Public Assistance Recipients, by Sex: 1962

	Average Grade		*Per Cent Functionally Illiterate on Basis of*	
	School Level	*Test Level*	*School Level*	*Test Level*
Male	8.1	5.1	13.3	59.8
Female	8.8	6.0	5.4	49.0

The gap between education and ability to perform is underscored further by the fact that four out of five who completed the fifth, sixth, and seventh grades were functional illiterates; three out of eight who finished grammar school or higher—"a point above which," the report said, "it would be expected that at least basic literacy education had been completed"—also tested out as reading failures.[16]

The study showed that much depended upon where in the nation the recipient received his education. There were marked differences between those who received their education in the urban North and those in the rural South. The two extremes were Illinois and Mississippi:[17]

TABLE 9

Cook County, Illinois, Department of Public Aid Study to Determine Literacy Level of Able-Bodied Public Assistance Recipients, in Urban (Ill.) and Rural (Miss.) Areas: 1962

	Average Grade		*Per Cent Functionally Illiterate on Basis of*	
	School Level	*Test Level*	*School Level*	*Test Level*
Illinois	9.4	6.8	1.2	33.4
Mississippi	7.6	4.4	14.2	76.9

The figures show that three out of four Negroes who come from Mississippi schools lack the reading skills required by the employment market. At the same time, the statistics indicate the failure of the Illinois and particularly the Chicago schools to do the job. While almost 99 per cent of the Illinois-educated recipients completed the fifth grade or better, fully one-third could not do the work.

What are the implications of these findings? They show clearly that half of the relief population surveyed is unfit for almost any kind of available work because of serious educational infirmities. All the admonitions of legislators and taxpayer groups to "get the loafers off relief" are to no avail when confronted with this evidence. But beyond the ability to obtain a job, there may be even more serious implications. For how can society's values be taught within a family unit if the adults have not experienced those values and cannot even read about them?

This is particularly relevant, it seems to me, since more than four out of five of the adults in the survey were women, the vast majority of whom represent the only grown-up in the family. The Cook County report makes these observations about them:

. . . This study reveals that upwards of 49% of these dependent women, who are either mothers or potential mothers, have not attained the basic literacy levels necessary to communicate freely with society, much less interpret that society to their young. Thus, seeds of a new generation of limited, handicapped social misfits are already germinating. It seems almost inevitable that a new crop of adult dependents will grow from the present seedlings of dependent children unless these children are nurtured in a different kind of social and cultural soil than they are today. . . .

Another factor which accentuates the seriousness of this problem is the relative youth of these able-bodied adult dependents. This study, like all the others conducted by the Cook County Department of Public Aid dealing with the social characteristics of able-bodied adult dependents, confirms the fact that they average approximately 33.5 years of age, with 50% of them being under 32.3 years of age. Thus, we have the appalling aspect of a whole host of persons who will themselves be long-time dependents unless something is done that will improve their employability status in our present-day labor market. These adults are not only dependents at a time they should be in the full flower of economic productivity, but many are illiterate at a time they can be expected to produce more and more children.[18]

The findings in Chicago's Woodlawn community—called by the researchers "its most serious welfare problem"—are not unique to the second largest city in the United States. They could be duplicated in the urban areas of Los Angeles, Detroit, Pittsburgh, Cleveland, New York, or Philadelphia. The facts are that a substantial number of America's able-bodied relief population is educationally unfit to find a job amid increasing demands for skills and, further, is ill-prepared to raise children who must make major advances over their parents if they are to avert dependence on a monthly welfare check.

The evidence is substantial from many parts of the nation that thousands of youths now share the characteristics of the Woodlawn adults. And these statistical likenesses are not confined to the level of educational achievement but include the social implications that the Woodlawn study warns about.

In New York City one of the most comprehensive efforts in the nation to find jobs for unemployed youth was started in 1960 by establishing a separate Youth Employment Service. The statistics at first glance show that employment counselors obtained thousands of jobs for these youngsters. A closer examination reveals this:

In two and one-half years of operation, 33,000 youths were interviewed. Thirteen thousand jobs were filled, but many of them were considered only as temporary. Since there is no follow-up once a youngster is placed, the length of time he stays on the job is a matter of conjecture. The best estimate is that only 10 per cent of these placements are "reasonably permanent." This means only one out of twenty-five young men and women who came to the Youth Employment Service because they were out of work received a reasonably permanent job.

"Unfortunately, jobs in private industry are not the solution to the unemployed youth problem," said Mrs. Marguerite H. Coleman, Supervisor of Special Placement Service, New York State Employment Service. "This program worries us because it's very expensive, terribly expensive. If we could just help those for whom there is a job in private employment, we could help more. But our people spend more time with kids who shouldn't be in here than with those who should. We also worry about the kids who say: 'This is just one more place you went where they didn't get you a job.' "[19]

I spent some time with these New York Youth Employment Service interviewers. In one particular afternoon I recall seeing only three of sixteen boys dressed in a shirt and tie. Several came to the interview in dirty or ripped clothing. Others had to be sent job-hunting dressed in unironed shirts. One girl wore sneakers without socks or stockings while the temperature outside was 18 degrees.

The presumption of social equality is badly disjointed here again. It is clear to me from talking with these youngsters, and from those who were in my caseload when I was a welfare worker, that many came from homes where an adult might not have known how to iron a shirt or known that a necktie and a shoe shine were part of the equipment in the kitbag of job hunting. And these were not isolated instances.

"We have to tell them very often to shave, to change their clothes, to bathe," an interviewer told me. "We have to tell the girls about make-up, about putting on lipstick, and all kinds of personal hygiene. In a half-hour interview and pep talk what we really have to do is try and make up for sixteen years or more of indifference of things that a mother, a teacher, and a father should have done but didn't. By the time they come here it's too late."

I have talked to interviewers who have sent boys to look for a job and found that if the address was at the corner of 42nd Street and Lexington Avenue, they would make their way to the numerical street which they could find and then walk along looking up at the corner street signs until they located the cross street whose letters matched those on the piece of paper.

"The other day one of my boys came back three days after I sent him out for a job and said he was still out of work," one of the interviewers told me. "I asked him what happened and he said he couldn't fill out the application at the plant. I couldn't understand that because he had filled out the application here for me and I asked him about it, and he said, 'Well, you see, it was Thursday and my friend couldn't come along.' His friend, it turned out, had come with him to the Employment Service and went with him whenever he looked for a job so that he could fill out the application forms. That Thursday his friend had to be in school to take a test."

The employment counselors need not be told that these youths come from another portion of society whose image and guideposts are foreign to the traditional portrait of middle-class behavior. After a while candid answers ranging from crime to sex become matter of fact, both to the interviewer and interviewee. One afternoon I was talking to a sixteen-year-old drop-out about the possibility of making money. I asked: "What do you think the best way of getting money is?" He answered: "What do you mean, by working for it or stealing it?"

No visible line divided the two except that "stealing it" may have involved a risk with the law; no hint came during my talk with the boy that this risk had anything to do with a moral code. The risk was comparable to crossing the street against a red light. This was no isolated experience. Another employment counselor summed up a recent interview like this:

> This kid was dapper, he was well dressed, he came in at Christmastime, and I asked him what he had done before and he said he had worked as a runner in the numbers racket, and he gets $75 a week plus bonuses. And then I asked him what he was doing here looking for a job now, and he said around Christmastime he knows the police crack down and they just picked up somebody to book him, and he didn't want to be booked so he would look for work to pick up some money for the Christmas season. But he was going to go back in as a runner.
>
> Now, it's pretty hard to change their attitudes. He is accepted in his community because they don't look down on runners. Now if he were going to change he would have to finish his schooling—he was a drop-out—and start in the labor market at the bottom, but now if he continues as a runner, eventually if he has it on the ball he will become a banker. I mean how can you sell a boy like that? You can tell him about the moral aspects and you can tell him about the chance of being arrested.

One counselor I know gives youngsters a list of twenty questions and answers to memorize before he sends them out for messenger jobs, and most afternoons I could hear him drumming at the same questions again and again:

"Where is Wall Street? . . . Where is Times Square? . . . Where is City Hall? . . . What is the shuttle? . . . What is the Avenue of the Americas? . . .

These are some of the questions asked of the boys by employers, and the employment counselor learned that unless he coached his charges they came back empty handed.

I asked the operator of a messenger service about some of his problems, and the reply came in a torrent:

> You ask about these kids—well I'll tell you. They don't want to work. They don't know how to work. Some of them don't know

enough to wipe their noses. They don't find the places we send them to. Simple places, you know, everything written out, printed, and they don't find it. And you may send a kid out on a call and you don't see that kid again, ever. Somewhere along the way he decides he should quit, and right then and there he does. They last a day, three days sometimes, maybe a week. . . .

These experiences, again, are not isolated. Experimental programs by the New York State Division for Youth, indicate that these youngsters have to be told not only how to do a simple task but, more importantly, the value of doing it, and why they should keep doing it. Training for work counseling sessions includes such subjects as how to file, how to wrap, making and answering calls on the telephone, learning to travel in New York, and grooming and personal appearance. Under "Job Etiquette" are lessons in punctuality, attendance, responsibility for work assignment, calling in sick, the rights of others, and good manners.

During a remedial arithmetic session which I attended, seven boys and a girl sat around the table watching the instructor identify different currencies as a first step in an exercise to teach them how you make change for a dollar and more. Their curiosity for arithmetic was aroused during a previous lesson because they were going bowling and consequently had to learn some math in order to keep score. All of the youngsters were either sixteen or seventeen years of age. A number of them failed to answer a question that asked: There are —— quarters, —— dimes, —— nickels, and —— pennies in $1.87?

Many have come to recognize their own shortcomings far more clearly than has the society from which they are being excluded. They themselves point up the differences between "me and some other kids." Among the older ones, the educational lack is most frequently expressed.

"Really, once you are out of school you only realize how hard it is to get a job without a high school diploma," the seventeen-year-old girl said. "I tell my friends 'Don't you quit school' because I know what it's like. Before, I was the first one to say 'Yeah, I'm going to quit school,' but after you quit you really know what it's like to be out without a diploma. Sitting home and doing nothing all day is probably the worst thing. You could go out and walk and window shop but I can't go round and window shop all the time. I have to be doing something steadily all day or otherwise I get very bored."

This self-analyzed inadequacy gradually turns into hardened barriers which, to the youngsters involved, are insurmountable. Listening to tape-recorded interviews with these young people, it is difficult to keep in mind that the voices talking are barely over their middle teens. In many cases I have had the feeling I was listening to adults who, decades earlier, had made a host of wrong decisions. Take an interview with a sixteen-year-old boy who had been sent to a state training school for truancy and jail for car theft. It sounds like this:

Q. And when you came back [from jail] did you go back to school?

A. I went back into school but started to do the same thing again so I finally decided to get a job. If I was going to play hookey I might as well go to work and get a job.

Q. Do you think you have as good a chance to get a job as anybody else?

A. As good a chance as anybody else who has played as much hookey as I do.

Q. What do you think a boss looks for when he hires somebody?

A. He looks for somebody he thinks can handle the job. Like I can't get a job in an office. So there's no use of me tryin'. I don't even know how to type well. I know how to type a little, but not well enough. 'Cause there's always a chance the boss will ask you some hard words that you got to look through the dictionary to find out what he's talking about. You know, they can't give you a job where you have to be lookin' in the dictionary every day to find out what the boss is trying to tell you.

Q. Of the people you know, who do you think has the best job?

A. The people that I heard about are the ones that sit down behind a desk and that's a lot of them, but they all went to college.

Q. What kind of job would you like now?

A. Auto mechanic, 'cause that's the only thing I know.

Q. I'm going to read you a list of jobs and as I'm reading them, think of the one you would most like to be—teacher, policeman, lawyer, garbage collector. . . .

A. A lawyer, well, you know, the only chance you got of being a lawyer is learning everything while you were in school. I didn't learn that much so there's no chance of me bein' a lawyer.

Q. How about a teacher, have you ever thought about being a teacher?

A. No.

Q. Why not?

A. I can't even teach myself how to get a job, how can I teach anybody else?

Q. How do you feel when you don't have a job—what's the worst thing?

A. Well, I feel like, you know, when people are not working and they don't go to school there isn't anything they can do for themselves. And really, I'm tired of getting money off my mother. Every time I need something I go up to my mother and I ask her for it. You know, I don't like that. Only when I'm real desperate and need something, like take some girl to the movies I go up to my house but other times I like to do things for myself.

Q. What does getting ahead mean to you—making it big?

A. It doesn't really mean much to me. I don't want to be ahead of anybody, you know, I just want to be level with them, you know? I mean, the way I stand now, I can't jump ahead of anybody, like somebody even younger than me that might be workin' now, maybe they makin' $5.00 a week by just working a couple o' hours a week, he still ahead of me. Even if he doesn't go to school he's still ahead of me. I'm doing nothin'.[20]

This is a partial biography recorded on a celluloid tape. It may well become capsuled into the brief summary phrases that make up a welfare case record. Job-hunting efforts of this boy will be frequent and sporadic, and as he gets older and acquires a family, more difficult. Exactly how difficult they may become can be seen by glancing at the job record of a welfare recipient in the generation ahead of this boy. The record comes from the files of the Cook County Department of Public Aid's Industrial Training Center, which prepares relief recipients for work and runs its own employment program. It begins March 3, 1961, after the recipient was assigned to the training center.*

3/3/61: States that he wants a job very badly in order to support his two young children.
4/10/61: Rfd. to Johnson's Restaurant as cook's helper.
4/17/61: Rfd. as porter-dishwasher to Charlie's Snack Shop.
5/5/61: Rfd. as porter to Swift Candy Co.
6/2/61: Appointment for 6/5/61.
6/2/61: Rfd. to National Time Co. as porter.
6/5/61: Rfd. as porter to Standard Hotel.
6/7/61: No suitable opening.
6/9/61: Rfd. to Joe's Drive Inn as porter.
6/13/61: Client hired on above referral, but stated that he had difficulty obtaining transportation from that address after 2:00 A.M. He was picked up by police and questioned regarding being in the neighborhood and was threatened by a motorist. Client did not return to job. He is to report 6/14/61 for a day's pay.
6/20/61: Rfd. to ISES [Illinois State Employment Service].
6/23/61: Rfd. as porter to Rosa Restaurant.
6/27/61: Rfd. as dishwasher-porter to Lefferts Restaurant.
6/30/61: Client is in today saying that he could not find the place where he was referred.
7/5/61: No suitable opening.
7/6/61: No referral.
7/12/61: Complained of toothache.
7/20/61: Complained of post-dental complications.
8/3/61: Sent to ISES.
8/10/61: No employment available.
8/17/61: No suitable opening.
9/5/61: Transfer to another load. Record held in ITC over 60 days after graduation.
9/25/61: Referred for current evaluation of employability. Still registers physical pain on left side.
9/28/61: Is employable and restricted to medium-light-type work.
10/13/61: No suitable opening. Referred to Work Relief.
11/2/61: Telephoned—left message with landlady. Referred as dishwasher, Lake Isle Restaurant.

* The real names of companies in the record have been changed.

11/3/61: Hired as dishwasher—Lake Isle Restaurant @ $40 per week—72 hr. work week—6 day week (includes meals and uniforms).
11/15/61: Worked 1 day on the above job—earned $4.50. To continue on Work Relief Project.
12/5/61: Intensive dish washing and pot washing job solicitation made, but to no avail. Return Appt. 12/8/61.
12/7/61: Could not be reached by telephone. Telegram sent—referred as bus boy to Sam's Restaurant.
12/7/61: Sent wire to Sam's.
12/8/61: Was not hired at Sam's today, however, was told to return next week for possible openings.
1/8/62: Employed (City Restaurant) to telephone 1/9/62—3:00 P.M. re: possible opening.
1/12/62: Referred as dishwasher and kitchen helper to Delfin Restaurant.
2/9/62: No suitable opening.
3/30/62: Telegram sent. Referred as machine dishwasher to Tip Top Restaurant.
4/3/62: Telegram sent. Referred as dishwasher to Carla Rest. Home.
4/4/62: Hired to start 4/5/62 @ $35.00 per week.

Employment records like this will be written with increased frequency in the sixties. They may be briefer, because there just will not be as many places to send people.

And they will include more and more young people consigned to the welfare rolls, because on the day when they looked for their first job, they were obsolete.

And they were obsolete, in part, because we are assuming that their desires from life are the same as ours, even though their parents may have never experienced them, could not talk about them, and therefore did not teach them to their children.

And they are obsolete, in part, because they have been plunged into a school system largely designed for middle-class Americans, where an academic high school diploma is a matter of course and in many neighborhoods the question of college only a matter of choice.

We have failed to admit that not all of our young people can graduate from high schools as they exist today, while at the same time we have mandated that they must, if they are to be participants in our technological society.

Because of this, we are creating in the sixties a major economic anachronism: We shall have difficulty in filling a significant number of jobs in one level of our economy, while we shall have large-scale unemployment in another. We shall have thousands of openings for the technicians who will operate our computer- and machine-oriented economy, and below them we shall have hundreds of thousands of young men and women floundering for some jobs for which they are unqualified, and for others that no longer exist.

5

65 PLUS

Nowhere is America's zest for euphemisms more apparent than in the descriptive language we have allotted to that part of our population we call the aged. Over sixty-five has been transformed by the sloganeers into mellow titles like "Oldsters," into political parlance like "Senior Citizens," into time segments like "Golden Years," and occasionally into ten-foot highway billboard lettering like "Sunset Court," a trailer camp for gray-haired migrants seeking the Florida sun.

The phrasemakers clash with the President's Council on Aging, which, in the spring of 1963, told John F. Kennedy that "the problems of the older American . . . have come dangerously close to making him a second-class citizen."[1]

Nearly 18 million Americans are now over sixty-five and their number is increasing by 1,000 every day. Estimates are that there will be 20 million by 1970 and more than 32 million by the year 2000. In contrast, in 1900 there were only a little more than 3 million over sixty-five. The life expectancy at birth then was forty-nine years; now it is seventy. While United States population in this century increased by 250 per cent, the aged population increased by 600 per cent. The newspaper feature story that paid reverent tribute to the centenarian is on its way toward extinction. There just will be too many to make it news. In the last decade the number of Americans aged one hundred years and older more than doubled to a record 10,369.

This gray-haired population explosion and the problems it contains today are among the forefront of domestic issues. They have been pushed there by a combination of the voting-booth power of the elderly and a self-conscious America remembering the Biblical injunction to "Honor thy father and thy mother."

Once an American crosses that numerical marker of sixty-five he joins the most surveyed, counted, probed, researched, and analyzed group in the nation. One federal agency alone, the U.S. Public Health Service, which in 1953 spent a paltry $100,000 trying to find out what happens to him as he grows older, ten years later had $15 million reserved for the same purpose. In January 1961 a special White House Conference was devoted to him and two years later he was the subject of a special Presidential message. In the White House he is represented by the President's Council on Aging, in the Department of Health, Education, and Welfare by a new Office of Aging, and in the U.S. Senate by a Special Committee on Aging.

A recent monthly government publication, *Aging,* included a two-page table of thirteen different departments, agencies, and special programs which provide federal grants for projects for him.[2] Among them were such cabinet divisions as the Department of Agriculture (which provides surplus commodities and food stamps) and the Department of Commerce (which provides, under its Area Redevelopment Administration, loans for constructing proprietary nursing homes).

In 1963 a total of forty-seven governors had special committees on the aging which were duplicated in miniature in hundreds of counties and cities in the nation. In these communities there are now more than 700 centers for education, recreation, and other activity for the elderly. These are augmented by an estimated 3,000 clubs for the aged sponsored by welfare, recreation, religious and labor groups.

However, there is a large "but"—particularly as it is expressed by the President's Council:

For all the interest and activity which has surrounded the Older American in the past 15 years, this one conclusion stands out: He has gained longer life—as a result of scientific, economic, and social advances in this century—but is left without the financial means to solve satisfactorily many economic, social and medical problems. This conclusion is one that we, as a nation, have not fully faced.[3]

This conclusion is all too vivid to the elderly. "I guess we've got the worries," a seventy-one-year-old man told me recently. "We've got the worries about running out of cash, about going to somebody and asking for something, about going on welfare. We've got the worries about the doctor bill, the medicine from the drug store, getting sick and the hospital and all that. And then we've got the worries about time, about all that time to do the worrying."

There are no neat dividing lines between the aged on relief and those who have so far successfully sidestepped the need for public charity. The problems of the two groups are more noticeable for their similarities than for their differences. As a matter of fact, the disease called poverty has its strongest hold among all the aged.

The median money income for older persons is less than half of what it is for those under sixty-five. Fifty per cent of the older couples in the United States have an income of less than $2,530 a year, and half of the single elderly less than $1,055 a year. Two of every three receive at least part of their support from Old-Age, Survivors, and Disability Insurance—the lengthy government label for social security.

Apart from earned government payments, the older American more than any other depends on public charity. While one of twenty-five children in the United States is supported by welfare's Aid to Dependent Children program, one of eight aged must rely on the relief check called Old-Age Assistance. A statistical portrait of OAA recipients shows:[4]

A median age of seventy-six
Two of three are women
Three of five have additional income
Two of three maintain their own households

Fewer than one of four with grown children
receive any money from them

These 2.25 million Americans are caught in the swirl of the relief controversy. They are branded by association and they know it. "Do they want me to go out and work?" a seventy-seven-year-old man asked me in Newburgh. Even the loudest welfare critic sometimes becomes self-conscious about including them in the verbal crossfire. And to relieve the conscience, he occasionally will bless them with the label "the deserving poor."

Among these older relief recipients is the bulk of the nation's middle-class poor. In the language of the athlete, their trouble is that they peaked too early. Many of their lives are threaded with modest success stories that were snared on the costly barbed wire of longevity and illness. They are the worn denials of the business bromide that "time is money," for they possess a surplus of the former and a shortage of the latter. The awkward ratio has contracted their lives into ritualistic patterns that pay homage to detail in order to drive out the ticking of the clock.

These faded middle-class biographies stock the Old-Age Assistance files of welfare departments throughout the nation. Take, for example, the story of a man who had been a magazine illustrator. A framed montage of covers he had drawn for *Liberty* magazine and the *Saturday Evening Post* hangs on the wall of his room. Four paragraphs in his case record show both the man and his routine. This is what his caseworker says:

He is a short, slim, well-groomed man whose appearance is very youthful. He is 71 but looks no more than 55. He has no legally responsible relatives living. He is not eligible for Social Security due to the fact that he was never covered when he was working. When I asked him whether he has checked employment possibilities lately, he said that it is impossible for him to find a job because he is part of "the economic leper colony" of older people. He said he is "tired of beating his brains out."

He claims to manage adequately on his public assistance budget and eats in economical restaurants, such as Grant's and Woolworth's, where he feels the meals are quite cheap. Client seems satisfied with living arrangements particularly because the house is a quiet one. However, the room he occupies is small and dreary looking. The walls are peeling but he does not want to have it painted because it is a nuisance and also he does not know what he would do with his parakeet called "Rumpus." He made a big fuss over the bird while I was there, rubbing noses with him and had him walk on a stick and then he twirled the stick around and the bird stayed on it. He seems very much attached to Rumpus.

I asked the client about his hi-fi which he had built himself and he played a record of Russ Morgan's for me. He seemed to get a great deal of pleasure out of listening to his records.

I asked the client whether he sees any friends and he answered, "No, when I lost my money and jobs, I dropped them before they dropped me." He listens to the radio, plays his records, goes to the library occasionally. He has a subscription to the *Saturday Review.*

If many of the aged on relief store with them the remnants of their middle-class past, they also have held on to the middle-class abhorrence of depending on welfare. "I saved all my life so I wouldn't cheat the old lady I'd one day be," a woman told a social worker from the Community Service Society of New York. "But the old lady is cheated anyhow."[5]

The relief check for the aged provides sustenance, but every time it is endorsed, the signature adds to the testimony of dependency. It is this constant forced acknowledgment of defeat that troubles the aged more than the penny budgeting that many welfare grants require of them. Some have refused to come to the relief office. They only will discuss personal difficulties over the telephone or when a caseworker makes an infrequent home call.

I remember when I was a welfare department worker one afternoon visiting an elderly client. Our conversation suddenly was interrupted by a knock on the door, which startled her. She did not want to answer until it was quite obvious that the person on the other side had heard our voices. The visitor was a friend, and before I had a chance to say anything, she introduced me as the nephew of a neighbor.

Sometimes the reluctance to admit dependency leads to a kind of charade with the caseworker, where both pretend that a situation is temporary that both know is permanent.

I recall the day I had to ask a man in his eighties to sign over title to his home to the Welfare Department, so that when he died the county could recoup some of the money it had invested in him. We talked about a number of minor problems before I asked for his signature on the document. He told me about the history of the house, how he had built and added small things through the years, how lightning had struck the back of it once, and how he had last painted it himself fifteen years earlier. Then he grabbed the paper, squinted at the legal language, which I had explained to him, and signed it, saying: "When I get some money I'll get it back. Don't forget I'll pay you back when things get better."

The necessity for charades like these is being reduced as the number of aged who must depend on relief is reduced. Today those over sixty-five no longer represent the biggest group on welfare. This dubious numerical honor now goes to dependent children, which took the lead at the start of the decade. In December 1960 there were 2,377,400 children receiving assistance and 2,332,000 men and women receiving Old-Age Assistance. In the last decade the Aid to Dependent Children program increased by 43 per cent while Old-Age Assistance dropped by 16 per cent. However, the largest monthly welfare expenditures still go to the aged. In March 1963 the nation spent $169,788,000 for OAA and $125,232,000 for ADC.

The drop in the number of aged who depend on relief cannot be attributed to a sudden improvement in their earning power, but rather has resulted from an expansion of the social security system.*

* A series of amendments to the 1935 Social Security Act is responsible for the large increases in the program. Since 1950 these changes included:

1950 Amendments: Benefits increased 77 per cent; coverage extended to 10.5 million workers.
1952 Amendments: Benefits increased 12.5 per cent.
1954 Amendments: Benefits increased; more workers covered; disabled workers' benefit rights protected.

In 1950 public assistance (OAA) accounted for about half of the money paid to the aged under government programs, while in 1961 it represented only about one-eighth.

More often than not the relief check supplements their income. For example, one out of every three received a welfare check because the social security check was too small to provide the daily necessities of life. The following chart shows the shift from OAA to social security:

TABLE 10

Number of Old-Age Assistance Recipients Compared with Number of Social Security Recipients: 1940–1962

	Number Receiving	
June of Year	*Old-Age Assistance*	*Social Security*
1940	1,966,000	66,000
1945	2,036,000	649,000
1950	2,787,000	2,095,000
1955	2,544,000	5,888,000
1960	2,355,000	10,454,000
1962	2,233,000	11,976,000

SOURCE: Prepared for the author by the Bureau of Family Services, Division of Program Statistics and Analysis, Department of Health, Education, and Welfare.

1956 Amendments: Benefits to disabled workers age fifty to sixty-five; made benefits available to women at sixty-two; more workers covered.

1958 Amendments: Payments to dependents of disability beneficiaries; benefits increased 7 per cent.

1960 Amendments: Benefits to disabled workers of any age; less work required.

1961 Amendments: Made benefits available to men at age sixty-two; larger percentage to aged survivors; minimum benefit levels increased.

Old-Age Assistance, like other relief grants, varies widely across the nation. In March 1963 the average monthly payment to a recipient was $76.67, with a high of $107.70 in California and a low of $35.24 in Mississippi.* These payments included a national average of $16.01 per recipient for medical care.

One thing is clear in this financial ledger of welfare: The aged on relief are the affluent among America's poor. The majority of states provide at least twice as much cash for an elderly citizen as they do for a child on relief. In some states the difference is three-, four-, and even fivefold. In Alabama, in March 1963, children receiving ADC averaged 39 cents a day compared with $2.01 a day for those on Old-Age Assistance. The disparity is even wider because more than half of the ADC families in the nation (55 per cent) have no other income except the welfare check, while fewer

TABLE 11

OAA and ADC Cash Payments in Ten States: March 1963

	OAA Cash Payments Per Recipient	*ADC Cash Payments Per Recipient*
All States	$60.67	$29.11
Alabama	60.40	11.67
Arkansas	51.76	15.97
California	94.84	42.40
Kentucky	52.32	22.84
Louisiana	69.08	22.79
New York	67.39	37.44
Ohio	66.58	29.57
Pennsylvania	62.22	27.28
South Carolina	40.95	15.42
Texas	58.07	18.96

* The territory of Guam paid $32.39 and the Commonwealth of Puerto Rico paid $9.21 to its recipients.

than half of the elderly (40 per cent) are without other resources. Here is a comparison of cash payments in ten states:*

But if state payments vary widely, so do their respective requirements of Old-Age Assistance. Liberal regulations have produced huge relief populations in some states, reflecting a pension rather than a relief philosophy. An example of both comes from the two most populous states in the nation. New York, with more aged than California, in June 1961 had less than 4 per cent (or 61,297 recipients) of its elderly on relief. California had almost 18 per cent (or 253,937 recipients) of its elderly on the welfare rolls.

In the West Coast state the old-age recipient can own his home no matter what its value, can own other real estate up to $5,000 in assessed valuation, providing it gives him income, and can have up to $1,200 in cash, stocks, or other property. In New York State, in contrast, an old-age recipient must have less than $250 worth of any property, and if he owns his home the welfare department can and does ask him to sign over title as well. Despite these stringent rules the average grant for the aged in New York still is about $30 higher a month than for needy children.

Legislators always have looked more kindly on the relief problems of the aged. Unlike children, they vote. Furthermore, in states that have tightened the noose on ADC because of the mushrooming Negro population, no such motive can be attributed when it comes

* Cash payment comparisons are made in order to eliminate the high cost of medical care for the aged, which further inflates their average grants. While medical-care payments average $16.01 for the aged, they average only $2.27 for ADC.

In California, for example, the State Department of Social Welfare is authorized to spend an average of $15 per month per recipient for outpatient medical services, but is under statutory limitation to spend only $3.00 per month per child and $6.00 per month per parent on ADC. "These latter amounts," Carel E. H. Mulder, chief of the department's Medical Care Division, told me, "are insufficient to purchase meaningful, comprehensive, and continuous care, necessitating the establishment of controversial priorities which has led to a history of successive program retrenchments and expansions."

to the Old-Age Assistance category. Nationally, four out of five of the OAA recipients are white.

Among the priority list of "worries" enumerated by the aging, none is more visible and controversial than health care. The question of who is to pay for medical and hospital bills has become a national debate. It has been spurred by the fact that illness has priced itself out of the free market place of the elderly. They simply cannot afford to pay for their infirmities. While the Department of Labor's Consumer Price Index has risen 26 per cent since 1950, medical costs have gone up more than twice that much. A 47 per cent increase in doctors' fees is dwarfed by a 125 per cent jump in hospital costs.

Furthermore, the aged spend an average of twice as much money for medical care in a year as younger Americans, but have less than half as much income to pay the bills. In his special message to Congress in February 1963, President Kennedy provided a statistical breakdown of some of these problems:

Our senior citizens are sick more frequently and for more prolonged periods than the rest of the population. Of every 100 persons age 65 or over, 80 suffer some kind of chronic ailment, 28 have heart disease or high blood pressure, 27 have arthritis or rheumatism, 10 have impaired vision, and 17 have hearing impairments. Sixteen are hospitalized one or more times annually. They require three times as many days of hospital care every year as persons under the age of 65.

Yet only half of those age 65 and over have any kind of health insurance; only one-third of those with incomes under $2,000 a year have such insurance; only one-third of those age 75 and over have such insurance; and it has been estimated that 10 to 15 per cent of the health costs of older people are reimbursed by insurance.[7]

The Brookings Institute, in a 1962 study of private health plans, said: "The fragmentary evidence available suggests that health insurance does not meet more than one-sixth of total medical costs of the insured or one-fourteenth of the total for all the aged."[8]

In an effort to stave off a government medical insurance plan under social security, the nation's insurance companies have blue-penciled a number of previous restrictions that discouraged and eliminated applicants. A recent full-page advertisement in the Sunday *New York Times* by one such company promised: "Everybody accepted. No health problems. No physical exam to qualify."[9] Combined hospital, surgical, and medical coverage (which still left the insured paying a substantial part of the bills) would cost $252 a year. At this rate half of the elderly couples in the nation would have to spend at least one-fifth of their total income for health insurance premiums alone.

It is this dreary arithmetic that has dulled the appealing prose of the insurance advertising writers. The facts are that too often the doctor's office and the hospital admissions desk are previews to poverty. The route to the local welfare department frequently is through their waiting rooms. In the first half of 1961 just about every third person approved for Old-Age Assistance needed it directly or indirectly as a result of health difficulties, said a report to the U.S. Senate's Special Committee on Aging.[10]

Nowhere is this drift toward welfare more apparent than in America's nursing homes, where patient stays are long and sometimes permanent.* One such home is the Washington Nursing

* Nursing-home care represents one of the most costly and problem-filled areas of welfare medical care. In 1962, for example, about one-third of the total $350.7 million in medical-care payments for Old-Age Assistance recipients was for nursing-home care. There are approximately 11,600 nursing or convalescent homes in the nation, which range from modern facilities that provide skilled nursing care to those that are but storage bins for the aged. Both contain many patients who have no medical reason for being there.

For example, a study conducted by Thayer Hospital of Waterville, Maine, found that more than half of the patients in six area nursing homes did not need nursing care. Physicians made weekly rounds for a period of six months. Dr. Harold N. Willard, director of the hospital's Chronic Care and Rehabilitation program, reported:

Center in Washington, Illinois. This forty-nine-bed facility is considered a model small nursing home. In April 1963 the home had forty-eight patients, half of whom were relief recipients. Significantly, nine patients who are now on the rolls of the Illinois Public Aid Commission entered the home as private paying patients.

Their case record potentially could be duplicated in most American families. One of the patients, for example, is an eighty-eight-year-old retired construction superintendent who suffered a back injury. Two months after he entered the nursing home, he went on relief. A summary of the case record provided me by the nursing home owner, said: "He was in the hospital for several years previous to nursing home admittance. When funds ran low, he started seeking a nursing home. His present rate is $200.35 a month. He has three children. One daughter contributes $35 each month and the Illinois Public Aid Commission the balance. The daughter helped pay his and wife's expenses for twenty years (until her death). She and husband are now retired themselves and can't afford entire expense."

Another instance of the transition from independence to public charity involved a couple who celebrated their sixtieth wedding anniversary in the nursing home. They had in excess of $10,000 saved. The case report tells the story:

Both admitted to nursing home in May 1954. Man 80 years of age, a lathe operator by trade. Admitted from Methodist Hospital after several weeks of hospitalization. He was a bed patient with an indwelling catheter but now has been able to participate in activities of daily living.

"In our evaluation of patients in nursing homes, we noted for each individual patient whether he needed care that necessitated complicated medical procedures or skilled nursing procedures. It was found that 51 per cent of the patients seen in nursing homes did not need either of these. About half of this group had no need for skilled nursing care at the time of admission, and the other half were appropriately admitted, but had improved to the point where they no longer needed nursing home care."[11]

Woman age 81 on admission, arteriosclerotic (required supervisory service rather than nursing care). But was admitted to the nursing home with her husband because of no family or near relatives to care for her.

Husband had a social security check of $82 plus a pension of $88 a month. Wife received social security check of $38.20 a month. They had their own funds to pay for nursing home care of $175 per month for each. They were able to pay their own way until July 1, 1957.

It is this trend—from self-sufficiency to charity—that in 1960 prompted Congress to pass the first federal legislation devoted exclusively to meeting some of the health needs of the aged. Public Law 86–778, popularly known as the Kerr-Mills Act, was counted as the vehicle that would bulldoze away the medical worries of the aged. It said that the federal government would pay from 50 to 80 per cent, depending on the wealth of the states, of the cost of medical care for those over sixty-five who had insufficient funds. The states were responsible for the remaining costs and were given the right to define what "insufficient funds" meant. The local welfare departments administer this legislation.

Kerr-Mills, despite the salutary prose that greeted its birth, became the fifth federal welfare program. In order to qualify in most states, the elderly have to be a hairbreadth away from poverty. They must go to the local welfare office and take a means test. This differs from the investigation that others seeking relief go through, not in kind but only in degree. It is this inescapable relief concept that has made Kerr-Mills less than successful.

An analysis of the first eighteen months experience with Kerr-Mills made in a report to the Senate Special Committee on Aging prompted its chairman, Senator Pat McNamara, to say that it "shows quite conclusively that measured against anticipated results, Kerr-Mills has fallen considerably short of the goals set by its more optimistic proponents."[12]

By June 1963, twenty-nine states were operating programs under Kerr-Mills, each with its own definition of need. The report to the

Senate Committee observed that at least fifteen states had tougher eligibility requirements for the new Medical Aid to the Aged than those states have under the Old-Age Assistance relief category.

In some of the twenty-nine states an infinitesimal percentage of the aged have been helped. In February 1963, for example, three states—New York, California, and Massachusetts—counted for almost three-fourths of the total expenditures for MAA in the country. If Michigan and Pennsylvania are added to the list, the five states spent 85 per cent of the total. New York State, with one-tenth of the aged population in the nation, claimed one-third of the $22.7 million used in February.

All but a small minority of those helped through Medical Assistance for the Aged in New York would have received care even if there were no Kerr-Mills legislation. What MAA really means in New York is that the state is simply getting more federal money to provide medical services it has been giving all along. Most of these aged would have received medical care under OAA, while many others would have qualified for the state's own medical-care program for the indigent. In the fall of 1962 the State Board of Social Welfare told a legislative committee that an analysis of MAA cases showed: "Of those now receiving care, approximately 15% are persons receiving care they would not otherwise have received if there were no Medical Assistance to the Aged program."[13]

In contrast, the American Medical Association, which approaches government-supported medicine with the objectivity of a Hans Christian Andersen dressed in a surgical gown, blithely reported this headline in its newspaper: "Kerr-Mills covers 93% of the aged."[14]

When the imaginative mathematics of the AMA and the attractive advertisements of the private insurance companies have been blunted by the simple exercise of matching promise with performance, one fact remains: This nation has yet to provide a workable medical program for its older citizens.

If the physical deterioration of the elderly represents their major problem, it is closely matched by a more intangible difficulty. It is best expressed by the man at the beginning of this chapter, who said: "We've got worries about time, about all that time to do the worrying." For the aged, there are three subjective definitions of this copious commodity. It can be called idleness, or loneliness, or retirement.

For many Americans, the phrase "over sixty-five" has yet to mean the orderly switch from the vocational world to private pursuits. For too many it has served as the numerical marker of a dead-end street. Pressed by company retirement regulations and encouraged by social security benefits, the elderly have been mustered out of America's labor force. Only one-fifth of those over sixty-five in 1963 were still working. Forty years earlier, one-third were counted in the labor force.

For the effects of this enforced mass leisure, one can go beyond the obvious rocking chairs lined up on the porches of homes for the aged and the well-worn checkerboards inside. For example, geriatric experts have found that it is a surplus of time that brings some of the aged to hospital clinics rather than an illness. In New York, day centers for the elderly have reduced the outpatient clinic visits among their members. Before these centers were opened, members went to the clinics simply because it was some place to go.

Walter M. Beattie, Jr., former planning director of services to the aging on the St. Louis Health and Welfare Council, had similar experiences.

I have had brought to my attention by several agencies the apparent utilization of outpatient clinics by older persons for social-personal needs. In one instance I consulted with the Social Service Department of one of our larger hospitals. Its concern was the number of elderly who were continuing their relationship with the clinics on a regular visiting basis over a period of years. The physicians complained that there was no real need for these persons to come to the clinics as frequently as they did, other than the fact that often they were there to talk to the physician and staff about personal problems.

The hospital was concerned because these older persons often came early in the day and stayed for a number of hours, making it difficult to serve persons with more urgent health needs.[15]

Caseworkers in public welfare departments throughout the nation have found that home calls on old-age recipients frequently are the most difficult to keep brief. Often the discussions range over a variety of subjects that have little or no relation to the concerns of public welfare. The elderly on relief, in short, simply want to talk. I remember one recipient who would put the coffee pot on the stove as soon as the caseworker entered. This would insure that she would have company at least until the ingredients were brewed and consumed.

However, such chatty visits are more often the exception rather than the rule. "We are still stuck with the original plan for older people on public assistance," Miss Ollie Randall, the dean among workers for the aged, said, "namely, that you send them a check once a month and then take a look once a year to see if they're still alive and eligible."[16]

Sometimes more than a year goes by between such home calls. For example, when I was a caseworker, the list in my office showed that some of the aged had not been visited in two and three years. Many workers, harried by problem families, usually leave the aged to the last if they carry cases from all relief categories. In a number of states, the Old-Age Assistance caseloads are so high that it would take more than three months for the worker to see all of his clients, providing he did nothing else. In 1962 caseworkers in half the states of the United States carried more than 200 Old-Age Assistance cases each. Texas led the list with 423 cases per worker, while six other states were well into the 300's per worker.*

It is difficult for most active Americans to comprehend what the incessant ticking of the clock means to their elders. It is hard to

* These states were: Alabama, 354; Arkansas, 341; Louisiana, 387; Mississippi, 360; Oklahoma, 316; West Virginia, 369.

explain to a businessman who may breakfast in New York, lunch in Chicago, and be back in his suburban home before the day is out. It is hard to portray for most of us who have our days sliced into busy time segments of seven hours of work, of fifteen-minute coffee breaks, of forty-five-minute lunch hours, of forty minutes commuting time, of after-dinner church and club meetings.

The hours of the elderly are not capsuled in a sentence or even in a paragraph. The dilemma may filter through a conversation about the day-to-day activity with an old man or an old woman. Recently, while interviewing Old-Age Assistance recipients, I discussed with one of them her activities of the previous day. This was our conversation:

Q. What did you do yesterday?

A. Well I get up—these fellows shriek me awake at six or seven and I uncover them.

Q. You uncover the parakeet?

A. Yes, the parakeet and the canary. And then I go back to bed and try to rest. I can't sleep any more. But I try to rest and keep the load off my heart as they told me. And then I have a breakfast—either cereal or I have two slices of toast and sometimes three slices of toast with margarine and marmalade, and two cups of coffee. I put one cup aside for lunch.

Q. Every morning the same thing?

A. About. Well, then I wash my few dishes. Then I look at my plants and I discovered that I had planted grapefruit pits in there and they were coming out and I had to transplant them. Then I cleaned the floor. . . .

Q. Did you talk to anybody?

A. No.

Q. Then what happened?

A. Then in the afternoon I went to the post office to inquire how much it would cost to send a package. And then I went and got heavy paper and the cord. And then I had a talk for half an hour with a woman about parakeets. She was an English woman.

Q. Which woman was that?

A. In Woolworth.

Q. Is she a friend of yours?

A. No. We were looking at the parakeets. And we started

talking about the birds. And I asked her if I had to have them flying out, and she said "Well, I have mine flying out. It's not nice to keep them in a small cage." And I said "Well, my ceilings are so high and I can't catch them." These are the talks we had.

Q. This was in the afternoon?

A. This was in the afternoon. In the morning I made my bed, cleaned the bathroom, cleaned the floors, and the sink and sometimes I find I tear a dress or something happens, and then I sit down half an hour and I talk to the birds and relax. Anything not to think, not to wander into the past.

Q. What do you talk to the birds about?

A. What do you think I should talk? I say "Hello, Hanschen," and this is Toni. Hanschen is German. It comes from Johannes. Every German bird is Hanschen. He sings very nice.

Then I went around and looked through the stores. I look at things. The newest things that come out and the way the prices go up. I noticed in the A&P the sugar has gone up to 35 cents instead of 32 cents. And the ginger ale, I allow myself generally a bottle of ginger ale, used to be 29 last week and now they want 33 so they can keep it. And then I went back home again yesterday after talking to the woman. And I looked at shoes. I always look at shoes.

I did some ironing. I have to do some more ironing today. And I sit there and look at the birds and turn on the radio. That went *kaput* today.

Then I had my supper. I just have two cups of tea with lemon juice. Oh, I also got a loaf of bread yesterday, black pumpernickel, you know. And I had pumpernickel and two slices of liverwurst and some cream cheese and Jello, and then two cups of tea.

Q. What did you do after supper?

A. I filled out my diary and my mail book. . . .

Q. What mail book?

A. Oh, I notice generally the mail I get and send.

Q. You keep track of it in a book?

A. Everything.

Q. The mail you receive . . .

A. And the mail I send.

Q. How do you keep track of it?

A. Look, all the mail I got already in a few months. You have to have something to do all the time, or you . . . One side is "received" and the other side is "sent." "Airmail letter from Kitty," that is my sister, or "Birthday card to so and so." You know.

Q. And that's what you did after supper?

A. Yes. It takes only a little while. And then I rest a while again, with the window open to get some wind and look at the trees, and I'm glad that I can look at them.

Q. How long did you look at the trees?

A. Oh, I can't tell you. Then I look at the television program because I buy no more papers since the paper strike. Then at 6:45 I have the television on, what's his name . . . Robert Trout. I listen to him and then comes Carol Reed with the weather and then that other chap whom I like very much, with the news from all over the world, and then it depends what is on. At 10:00 generally I retire to bed with a whole lot of books.

Q. Did anybody come to the door?

A. No.

Conversations like this could be part of the dialogue between a caseworker and an elderly relief recipient anywhere in the nation. They are not restricted to any region, to any particular state, or, for that matter, specifically to the aged on relief.

As their numbers continue to grow and their demands become increasingly audible, many of the problems of the elderly will be relieved. Fewer will have to turn to the local welfare department for help because of an expanding social security system. Medical worries will be reduced when Congress tires of the word battle and approves a medical insurance program. But there is no legislation for the intangibles that creep out of conversations about parakeets and keeping "a mail book." For the elderly, the simple word "time" may be the most complex dilemma of all.

6

THE TURNSTILE GUARDIANS

There are almost 35,000 public welfare caseworkers in the United States. They are the country's liaison with the wasted Americans. They are the national eardrum for poverty—the listening post of failure. Today, too few serve too many with too little skill. What they are as a group holds the patchwork of public welfare together. What they are not is the key to its biggest weakness. They are its foremost dilemma.

The often misleading public conception of the relief recipient is matched by the false portrait of the individual who serves him. The talk is of "social workers," yet social workers are missing from the personnel lists of many welfare departments. The graduate of a school of social work is more often outside than inside the largest welfare business in the nation. America's poor are served by an army of workers that is untrained.

There is one caseworker with full professional training for every 23,000 relief recipients.

One out of every three caseworkers in public welfare did not complete an undergraduate education.

Only one out of ten has taken any graduate courses in social work.

And only one out of a hundred has completed two-year professional social work training.

When I started as a caseworker in Buffalo, three of the eleven who started with me had taken a basic sociology course. None had majored in a subject that would provide a foundation for a helping profession. Included in our group was a girl who had majored in secretarial science, a law school graduate waiting to retake the New York State Bar examination, a real estate salesman whose business faltered in the winter months, and an aircraft company shipping clerk whose job had floundered in a wave of defense contract cancellations. Each had to have a college degree.* Some states had to forego this requirement in order to keep the ranks filled.

These guardians of the poor have come to the task by accident. Some have developed a desire to help people and have tried to practice it amid a whirlwind of discouraging forces. Others have brought to the job a string of failures in their own lives, failures they sometimes cannot suppress as they are called on to deal with the failures of others. And some come simply because there is just no place else to go.

In 1962 the commissioner of a large midwestern city explained his staff troubles to me like this:

> If I look back over the last fifty people I've hired, the biggest bulk of them would have been men at the forty-years-of-age level who have not been successful—let's say working in finance collection activities, working in small businesses that have been washed

* While all caseworkers in New York State must have an undergraduate degree, the commissioners of local welfare departments are not required to have the qualifications of their caseworkers. Of the sixty-five, forty-six are elected by the voters. Only one obtains his job through civil service while the other eighteen are appointed by mayors, county executives or boards of supervisors.

In 1960, in nine western New York welfare districts, only one commissioner had a college degree. The elective route to the commissioner's office requires that the aspirant first be an able politician. Other high administrative welfare posts then come under the political patronage umbrella. In one county a maintenance man in the welfare office was appointed deputy commissioner of welfare when his party was victorious at the polls.

out of the economic system, salesmen, librarians. The rather attractive beginning salary picks them up . . . a few lawyers, maybe . . . more of that kind than the girl or boy fresh out of college. The fresh out of college group, in the main, have been the girls who, I think, have been very high in their class, academic-wise, and have this desire to help people.

Q. But you have few people who initially are motivated into a helping profession?

A. Damn few . . . with the exception of the little girl who got it somewhere in church, or in the YWCA, or even the counseling process of her school and then moved into social work.

Many of the others enter the department "as guardians of the public purse." They are adversaries of the people on relief. I'm sure you must have found in your Buffalo experience that some of these boys with you said, "That son-of-a-bitch isn't going to get any more from me." Now that's a very crucial problem in public welfare. That's very, very tough. He reads in the newspaper that this is a dirty damn business we're in here . . . with chiselers and illegitimate children. It's just more respectable to agree with them.

Q. What do you do to change this attitude?

A. Well, not enough.

Q. Do you have a training period they go through?

A. A month. An induction period of a month. None of it has been as successful as I'd like it to be. It takes a devil of an impact . . .

The example that I'd like to use . . . well, here's a fellow from —— Motors Inc., a well-known company. . . . This chap who graduated from college in about 1940, so he has his B.A. degree. He worked for twenty years for —— Motors Inc. as a mechanic. He got laid off and he walked through civil service and emerged a social worker. And I have him on my staff.

We feed into these relationships with people such a variety of kinds of personnel. The reason I got him is when the '58–'59 recession hit we hired twenty-one people in a hurry. Here are people starving and you have to get troops into the trenches. Now his social philosophy I don't think is too bad, but he got it only by accident. He certainly is not a member of the helping profession. He's a mechanic.

Every year the need to draft additional "troops into the trenches" increases. In a recession year the welfare personnel files follow the unemployment graphs in their upward movements.

But even without economic disturbances, the staffs of public welfare departments will expand sharply in the next few years with the new emphasis on rehabilitation. The Bureau of Family Services estimated that the 1961 total of caseworkers will more than double and the number of supervisors triple by the end of the decade.[1] The Bureau's goal is to change the professionally trained caseworker ratio from the present one out of one hundred, to twenty-two out of one hundred by the end of the decade. This means 14,200 fully trained caseworkers by 1970. At the beginning of the decade the actual count in all welfare departments in the nation was 299.

No one has quite located the magic wand that will produce this new army of trained public welfare workers. And if the present rate of social work education continues, it will take a Houdini-like performance to supply the manpower. In June 1962 the total number of men and women who received graduate degrees from the nation's schools of social work was 2,318. If all of them had gone into public welfare—and only a small percentage did—their number would have been inadequate to replace the caseworkers who quit welfare departments in New York and Illinois alone. The annual increases in school of social work graduates (156 from 1961 to 1962) would not meet the requirements of one of the larger urban welfare departments in the country.* This leaves the task of filling public welfare jobs with trained social workers today like

* Even this increase created problems for schools of social work. While total enrollment in the sixty-three accredited schools rose almost 11 per cent in the 1961–1962 academic year, the increase of faculty was a little more than 6 per cent. The professional journal, *Social Work Education,* reported:

"Some of the newly established schools of social work have found it particularly difficult to recruit faculty and have had to depend on temporary and part-time appointments. Increasingly schools have had to employ practitioners without teaching experience, which makes even more necessary the need to provide an organized plan for the induction of new faculty into their teaching responsibilities."[2]

trying to wash your car with a water pistol.

Consequently, many of the newcomers in public welfare—be it the midwest mechanic or the real estate salesman from Buffalo—have only a fuzzy picture of what the job is about. They may have read a pamphlet on a bulletin board or a plea by a commissioner in a newspaper. There is a sudden discomfort in learning what is behind the walls of houses only a few miles from where you live. It takes—as one of my coworkers told me—"a little getting used to" before this new world finds its niche amid the middle-class repository of your mind.

The calamity of public welfare is that too few caseworkers stay long enough to get used to it. For they are the turnstile guardians of poverty. In some parts of the nation they are like tourists in a strange land of sagging doorways, padlocked mailboxes, and grimy walls decorated with four-letter words. They come, they look, and they go home.

"In public assistance," a caseworker from Connecticut said, "sometimes we don't even get to know the guy's name, in the same office. He walks through the door and turns right around and walks out again. Some of them are employed for as short a time as two days."

That caseworker was describing the exception, but the federal government has reported that almost two of every five caseworkers in Connecticut quit their jobs in 1961.

"The fact is," the Connecticut worker continued, "that you cannot run a program when everything we know in casework is based upon a continuing relationship, a one-to-one relationship in helping people resolve themselves and their problems to a degree that they can handle their problems differently, hopefully, better than they did before.

"But the hardest casework is the continuing relationship based upon study, diagnosis, and treatment, and you can't have this when you have a whole multitude of people parading through your agency—taking from your agency and giving very little in return."

In my caseload there were many welfare recipients who had to look on their identification cards for the name of the previous worker. The larger case records were biographies of dependency but written like an anthology. Literally dozens of persons contributed a page, two, or three. One recipient, on relief for fourteen years, faced seventeen different caseworkers.* A few she remembered because they coincided with the birth of a child or a problem. The others were just blurred faces whose names were recalled only on the "separation sheets" of the personnel department. Of the eleven caseworkers who started with me, five had quit after the first three months had gone by.

A 1960 survey in my welfare department produced these turnover statistics for caseworkers in public assistance:[3]

TABLE 12

Caseworker Resignations, Erie County, New York, Department of Social Welfare: 1960

Year	*Staff Positions*	*Resignations*	*Per Cent of Resignations*
1957	118	77	61
1958	91	55	60.4
1959	121	69	57
1960	141	79	56

The national resignation rate of caseworkers was 26 per cent in 1962. Among those plagued most were three states that have some of the largest welfare populations in the nation. These are California, 31 per cent; New York, 41 per cent; and Illinois, 31 per cent. Leading the list was Maryland with a 46 per cent turnover. A

* In Chicago, a welfare department supervisor complaining to me about the steady exodus of her workers, said:

"I could think of one particular caseload that was difficult to keep covered. Now this one was located in the slums and I think in one year there was something like seven workers came and gone and for a time it was uncovered for about nine months. Well, you never knew what was happening at all."

Baltimore public welfare department report for 1960 made these curt comments in a section titled:

THE FEW WHO REMAIN WATCH THE MAJORITY LEAVE

The minimum number of caseworkers needed last year to help the agency's more than 17,000 families was 406. The Department was allowed 343, but it could not hire even that number. At no time did the Department have more than 318 on the job. To maintain that level 213 were hired during the year to offset the continuous resignations. The staff turnover this year was 56 per cent. (The next year it rose to nearly 70 per cent.) A staff vacancy rate of 6 per cent at the Department at a most conservative estimate means that 6,000 clients receive but token service.[4]

This arithmetic is testimony of down-the-drain investing. Commissioners agree that it takes anywhere from six months to a year before a dollar spent on a caseworker is returned in performance.

A California Welfare Legislative Committee said the cost to counties for training each new social worker has been estimated from $500 to $1,800. "This," the committee report said, "is a considerable amount to invest in a person who does not remain with the county welfare department more than a year or two."[5]

What is the cause of this annual mass exodus?

Study groups, investigating committees, and legislative bodies have asked the question over and over again. There is no single answer. It may be a conglomeration of factors, among which these always seem to stand out: Pay, high caseloads, and paper work; their sum is general job dissatisfaction. For the girl with the YWCA exposure it is often told in a single sentence: "I came here to help people and I can't." For many others their haphazard arrival was forewarning of a similar departure. What discourages them is revealed from my own experiences in the first days as a welfare worker:

The eleven of us were moved into a small training room where desks were crowded next to each other. The personnel department had recorded from each of us the vital statistics. It was like freshman registration at college without the hurly-burly of milling people and IBM cards. Before the first few hours had passed that curious camaraderie of the unknown bound the new initiates together. The uncertainty of orientation was soothed by the fact that we were being paid to listen.

The lectures began, paced to keep the slowest within the periphery of progress. Within one week, man's historic inability to resolve poverty had to be capsuled for lay consumption. But it was dwarfed by the necessity to learn the intricate mechanics he had invented to try and relieve it.

A portfolio of forms began to grow. Rule books were added and our stenographers' notebooks began to swallow a helter-skelter of definitions and formulas. "To do the job," my neighbor observed, "you don't need sociology, just an adding machine." The budget cards of the practice cases had lost the taste of reality through repetition. But the lesson was learned. After a week we knew a little of the vague shape of public welfare, the various categories, a smattering of their requirements, and how to get a check to a family whose cupboard was empty. A few shreds of social philosophy may have stuck as a bonus. We were the five-day wonders of public welfare, ready to move from the classroom to a desk as a trainee in the office.*

Slowly the cases began to build up—two, six, nine, eleven. . . . The budget cards and the forms were familiar from the classroom. But the names on them were no longer fiction. They were people in trouble. As the first few weeks went by I got to know them.

"Enjoy it now while you can," a worker at the next desk told me. "This is the only time you can really do casework when you have a training load." The classroom instructor said the caseload would be built up gradually over the next three months. But the resignations kept coming and two months after I walked through

* Other departments may have a two-week classroom period. Some as much as four to six weeks. In the largest department in the nation—New York City—a monthly average of about ninety beginners receive four weeks of on the job training interspersed with occasional classroom lectures.

the door I had a full caseload. A few weeks later I counted 160 cases. Suddenly I was the government-assigned head of more families than live on some suburban blocks.

"You are not going to be able to work as carefully and conscientiously now as you did before," my supervisor told me. "You can't check things as much as you want to. If you do, you can't take it. The main thing is to get the aid out. You can always check things later if you have suspicions. . . ."

I now was part of the system—a system where help was measured only by what it bought at the grocery store and gave to the landlord. I had become a dispenser of checks and very little else.

"I just want to give you a little advice," a worker in my unit said. "I used to be just like you are. But I learned . . . you can't beat the system. If you try it, you'll crack up. You see things that are all wrong, but if you get exicted about them, you'll wear yourself out. This agency just wants you to get out the aid . . . anything else and you'll be sticking your neck out—and it'll be out there all alone. . . ."

The six workers in the unit were averaging 155 cases each. High man was my neighbor with 181, although down the hall a worker was inundated with 208. The department's monthly average was 139. Yet in 1962 a federal report showed that New York State had the lowest caseloads per worker in the nation.[6] The figure it gave was a monthly average of 67.

That same report listed six states with an average caseload per worker above 200. These are: Texas, 333; Alabama, 315; Mississippi, 261; Arkansas, 261; Oklahoma, 241; Louisiana, 219.

With assignments like these, casework becomes a fiction and public welfare becomes a function of the check-writing and adding machine. Alabama has its welfare program under the Department of Pensions and Security. The caseload figure indicates it is aptly named.

But northern states with their large urban welfare districts, also showed caseloads above the manageable size: Illinois, average 116 per worker; Ohio, 130; and Pennsylvania, 108.*

For these work loads the caseworker is invariably paid less than what has come to be an accepted public image of the "underpaid school teacher." My weekly take-home pay in 1960 was $59.62. The starting pay around the nation ranged that year from $2,940 in Jackson County, Mississippi, to a high of $5,820 in Milwaukee.

The salaries, with few exceptions, are set by local boards of supervisors, commissioners, or councilmen, whose absolute control of welfare spending often is restricted to deciding the size of a worker's paycheck. In some communities the allowance is so niggardly that a caseworker with a sizeable family is perilously close to the income he would receive if he were to join his recipients on the rolls.**

In New Jersey a legislative welfare investigation in 1963 detoured from its criticism of ADC to tell fellow legislators and the people they represent:

> The most regrettable experience with which this committee was confronted was a petition signed by every caseworker in one of our major counties outlining a whole list of complaints from low salaries to other inadequacies of major import. Investigation of these complaints corroborated their truth. An example of such conditions is illustrated by salaries and caseloads of workers employed in Atlantic County.[8]

The pay schedule showed the highest annual salary was $4,080 for one worker who, on April 1, 1962, had been on the job for twenty-eight years and nine months. Another worker with twenty-one years of service was paid $3,540. Of eight temporary caseworkers, all of whom had two or more years of service, only one

* The new federal provisions for rehabilitation require that caseloads for workers providing social work services will have to be reduced to a maximum of sixty by July 1, 1967. This will include almost all ADC cases.

** The 1960 Baltimore report said: "A caseworker last year started with a take home pay of $54.25 per week. The average take home pay of Baltimore secretaries last year was $62.90."[7]

received more than $3,120 a year. That "temporary" worker had been on the job for eleven years and four months and was earning $3,420.

For this sum, the span of knowledge should include a smattering of politics, law, other governmental agencies, sociology, psychology, religion, police work, the courts, accounting, and—above all—bookkeeping.

The last has been officially installed as the *bête noire* of public welfare. It has been examined as frequently as the common cold and its remedy has been equally as elusive. In various states, citizens' committees have totted together voluminous testimony about the paper curtain surrounding public welfare in a universal head shaking of disbelief. There usually are twin sources for this bureaucratic confetti: the federal welfare administration and the state welfare department, which—when the former is not watching the latter—are scrutinizing the local relief operation. Occasionally, an inventive soul on the precinct level will add a few more forms to keep short rein on the caseworker.

It took twenty-four separate pieces of paper to give one of my relief recipients her first check. These were extracted from a file cabinet that contained a stock of sixty-five different forms. They contributed to a numerical jargon that pervaded the office. For example, I had a client who neglected to sign the K-173. This was spotted by the accounting department and the clerk sent back the PA-14, the PA-16, the K-174 as well as the unsigned K-173, and a K-387 (a pink slip) telling me why the whole thing was rejected.

A California inquiry on relief produced these paragraphs under the title of "paper work":

Paper work in the Los Angeles County district welfare offices is costly and time-consuming. There are now over 1,000 forms to be filled out in various phases of the programs.

. . . One of the problems of cost (administrative) stems from the need, under present law and regulations, to make numerous changes of grant from month to month. Approximately 500,000 changes of grant were processed in Los Angeles County in fiscal 1959–60. A staff official comments: "Assuming the administrative cost of these actions to be $10 per change, it is readily apparent that upwards of $5,000,000 per year is consumed by a process which amounts to nothing more than increasing or decreasing recipients' grants by relatively nominal amounts."[9]

While the average wage-earner brings home a check and gives a portion of it to his wife to manage the week's affairs, not so with the caseworker. He itemizes and, consequently, figures the cost of a host of individual necessities. He adds 50 cents here (for castor oil) and 40 cents there (for school money). Each member of the family has a separate allowance down to the penny, depending on sex and age. A sample of my monthly budget schedule is listed below:

TABLE 13

Monthly Budget Schedule—Pre-Added Food, Clothing, Personal, and Household Incidentals, Erie County, New York, Department of Social Welfare: January 1960[10]

	Size of Household			
	1	*2*	*3*	*4+*
Age, Sex, and Activity	*Food Prepared in the Home*			
Birth through 3 yrs.		21.15	19.80	18.50 ea.
4–6 yrs.		24.25	22.65	21.10 ea.
7–9 yrs.		29.35	27.50	25.60 ea.
10–12 yrs.		33.80	31.55	29.35 ea.
13–17 yrs. (boy)		42.40	39.65	36.95 ea.
13–17 yrs. (girl)		36.50	34.20	31.90 ea.
Unemployed adults	35.95	32.35	30.20	28.00 ea.
Employed adults	41.55	37.75	35.45	33.10 ea.

If one or more members of the family happen to be in a different federal category of assistance, a separate budget schedule must be figured. This, of course, includes computing a portion of the rent, heat, light, and any other facility that might be shared with the entire group. If neither a man nor his wife has sufficient money to manage and need old age assistance, they are classified separately even though they live under the same roof.

In one such instance I had an elderly couple which was receiving welfare dollars to supplement a meager social security check. Each was receiving $25 from the welfare department. They told me they had moved two months earlier to an apartment where the rent was $8.80 higher. I had to change the address and give them $8.80 for two months because it was not included in their last two monthly grants. The changes required twenty-two pieces of paper. Four checks, two for each of them, went to the same address. The total, incidentally, does not include the regular monthly checks, four separate envelopes, and four stamps.

Since the slightest change in a family's circumstances—from Johnny going on summer vacation to baby no longer needing castor oil—the monthly check constantly needs adjusting. This continuous exercise in financial nitpicking leaves the door wide open for error. In one of my cases the previous worker had noted the recipient was receiving $42 weekly disability benefits. On the budget it showed up as a $42 monthly benefit and the client for almost a year was receiving $140 a month bonus she was not supposed to get.

This is not an isolated example. The national eligibility study of ADC families showed wholesale errors in many states.[11] In seven states more than half the families were getting the wrong amount of assistance.*

These costly exercises in basic mathematics and their accompanying frustrations have plagued caseworkers everywhere. For exam-

* These states were: Alabama, Illinois, Kansas, Massachusetts, North Carolina, Ohio, and Virginia. In North Carolina eight of ten families were receiving wrong amounts and in Kansas and Ohio it was seven of ten.

In many instances families were receiving less than they were supposed to. In Massachusetts, 26 per cent of the families were overpaid and an identical number were underpaid. In North Carolina, 61 per cent of the families were receiving less than they should. The highest overpayments (42 per cent) occurred in Alabama.

ple, Mrs. Richard C. Wright, a former caseworker in the Forsyth County Welfare Department, in Winston-Salem, North Carolina, told me:

> I filled out as many forms for mileage in using a county car as I did to get a client on ADC. To get a $2.00 roundtrip ticket for a child and her mother to an orthopedic clinic in Gastonia, North Carolina, I had to have typed six forms, signed by the superintendent, approved by the supervisor, paid by the county accountant whose office was in the court house downtown, before I could take the money to the bus station to buy the tickets and take them to the family. What could be a real calling is nothing but petty busy work.

The transportation forms in our welfare department were so cumbersome that caseworkers who had only an occasional trip sometimes chose to forego the money in order to avoid the accounting. The bus fares I used required a two-stage reporting procedure. This included a running tally on a "bus fare report" which required besides the date, the address and the number of fares used, and also the precise bus line engaged. At the end of the month the entries on the bus fare report (in duplicate) were recorded on the "bus fare claim" forms. These were signed by the caseworker under a 146-word statement that began: "I, the undersigned, hereby certify that the labor or services, merchandise, materials or articles charged in the within account or claim, payment of which is hereby acknowledged, actually have been performed, made or delivered for the County of Erie . . . ," etc.

The form-filled efforts that range from recording bus tokens to producing the wherewithal for a hungry relief recipient dominate a caseworker's time. My colleagues and I spent more than half of our working hours ensnared in these various accounting and reporting procedures. "You've got to make up your mind," I was told when I first started. "You're either going to be behind in your paper work or in your home calls."

For one month, officials of Luzerne County, Pennsylvania, examined the time a caseworker spent on various duties in a typical case load. The worker in the survey had 151 cases with total monthly grants of $11,655. "The worker," the report of the test noted, "went to her district on four different days of three, three, three, and four hours, for a total of 13 hours. In that time she interviewed in the homes of 18 active cases and traveled approximately 125 miles by personal auto and public transportation. . . . The above information indicates the extent of the worker's personal contacts with individuals during the course of her duties as a caseworker in this one-month period."[12]

The 50 per cent time estimate of desk-bound paper work has become a conservative rule of thumb in many welfare departments. The average worker spends about 220 days on the job during a year. Besides the time spent on forms, the caseworker devotes other hours to conferences, staff meetings, and refresher lectures. Therefore, any worker with 100 or more cases may average less than one day of personal contact per family per year.

The combined irritants of paper work, low salaries, and high caseloads act like sand in the machinery of public welfare. Their first contribution to breakdown is in the morale area. Greenleigh Associates of New York makes it a point to test morale in every survey. The consultants have developed an extensive test—an eight-page opinion sampler designed by a social psychologist. The tests are carefully administered without identifying those who take them. The results in three of the nation's largest welfare departments show that workers' attitudes about their jobs are largely negative. When the tests were given to a group of caseworkers in one of the major cities, the interviewer detailed their purpose: We want to find out the morale of the department. His introduction was interrupted by a chorus of laughs.

Generally more than half of the workers added written comments to the questionnaires. They ranged from polite dissatisfaction to curt demands for change. A review of these caseworker appraisals would startle even the most seasoned personnel officer in private industry or government. A few samples read like this:[13]

The needs of the client are taken in consideration more so than the needs of the staff. Feeling here is that because turnover is so great anyway, who cares if I leave also . . .

One never seems to get a feeling that something worthwhile

has been accomplished on this job . . .

Three-quarters of our day is spent with clerical work and answering telephones. One-quarter of the day, sometimes, is allotted to reading cases thoroughly. Most of my casework is done on overtime.

I have been with the department six years and can truthfully state I do not feel that my job has improved in the least. Most times I feel frustrated because it is more and more apparent families need more than financial assistance. I do not have time to handle families on individual basis, employing needed casework methods . . .

Whenever one speaks to another caseworker the one main thought is "When are you leaving?" or "How did you do on your last exam regarding another position?"

I am tired of surveys. Action is needed. You people are aware of the action needed.

Please help us.

But the attitude of workers need not be portrayed in such blunt slices. It can be gleaned from the day-to-day work of an individual. Sometimes they are stories told in anger. The child welfare worker in Connecticut whom I interviewed was cautious at first about his phrases. His background included ten years' experience and a graduate degree in social work. The tape recorder made him apprehensive. But midway through the conversation, hearing his own account gave him momentum. It built up to this:

I'm almost to the conclusion that we should do anything in the world—anything in the world that we can to get our program across. And this I don't even mean. I don't think the means justify the end—they don't. Yet we constantly seem to bombard the House and Senate Finance Committees with the same kind of very hard solid facts. We tell them, look, it costs the state of Connecticut anywhere in the neighborhood of $1,500 to $8,000 a year to care for one child, depending on his problems, what type of service he needs. We tell them that if we hired one social worker to return one child to his family successfully, or place one child in adoption, or plan for one child for his commitment to be revoked, we would say that's worth the salary. We document it. Now the legislators couldn't care less—they couldn't care less because they don't do anything about it. What other inference can you draw? I'm not so sure that they're interested in saving money. I think that they are interested in saving money, but in ways that are somehow politically effective.

If we place one child . . . You know, let me tell you—the day John Glenn was up in orbit going around the earth, the day he was there—you know what I was doing in my office? I knocked myself out for three hours trying to get a lousy $25 in order that a baby could be psychologically tested—developmentally tested—in order to go into adoption. So that the baby wouldn't be committed to our care.

Three hours I spent on the phone, dialing various people, agencies, trying to get 25 lousy dollars. At the same time that some nut down in Cape Canaveral twisted a bolt off and it delayed the whole deal three or four hours. How many thousands of dollars did that delay cost—thousands of dollars because some guy twisted a nut too hard and twisted it off.

The nose cone of that thing that sunk out there with the other [astronaut] cost between $4 and $6 million. The aircraft carrier that burned down here cost $75 million to repair it—and I'm sitting over there in the district office and I can't even get $25. . . . I finally got it and today that baby is in adoption.

If we hadn't been able to do this, this baby would have come under our care—it would have taken at least a year, well, let's say six months, everything going our way. It would have taken another three or four months to find the right home for this child. By this time the child's maybe a year old—been under care for a whole year. Fifteen bucks a week plus medical and clothing. This isn't the important thing. Everything in our adoption practice tells us that children that can move into adoption—even from the hospital—this is what should be done. This baby had been in the hospital because nobody knew what to do with it. You know, these are not isolated little cases.

In a book, as in a courtroom, there is danger in permitting a few witnesses to present the entire case. The cluttered administrative panorama of poverty has another side. For the man or woman viewing the casework job as a vocational rest home the morale question may be academic. Does it affect my co-worker, for example, who supposedly was making home calls when, actually, an hour before quitting time you could find him in his own living room? Or another who began building a business on the welfare department's time?

"I think everybody knows caseworkers who don't do anything," a welfare department union leader in a major city told me. "The excuse always is the caseload is so large and I have so much paper work to do. Instead of even doing a little bit, the result is that nothing is accomplished. Now, I don't think it's the caseworker's fault. I do believe that people become so overwhelmed by what's facing them or being told what's facing them so much, you know, that they never really can get motivated or activated to do anything."

If the phrases of the caseworkers are the measure of morale, the case records are the systematized documentation of its negative effect. Sometimes even the simple demands of the law are not carried out. For example, the welfare rule book in New York State requires that Home Relief and Aid to Dependent Children clients should be visited once every three months. Minimum requirements for the other categories is a home visit once every six months.

As a caseworker, I found that in one caseload alone, five recipients had not been visited in three years although they received their check every month. Ten had not been seen for at least two years, and in almost all the rest a caseworker had not rung their doorbell for six months to a year.

The same New York State rule book required that the eligibility of welfare recipients had to be rechecked once every six months if they were receiving ADC or Home Relief and at least once a year if they were in the other relief categories. In my caseload eighteen re-investigations were delinquent for three years, twenty-three for two years, and the majority for more than a year.

The rule books in welfare departments throughout the nation are now being expanded to shift the focus from simply finding out if a family is eligible, to providing help for its troubled members. A multitude of federal and state memoranda tell the caseworker about his new approach to the poor. But public welfare has yet to find a new approach to the caseworker and his task. Unless it does, the supplement of regulations will be as delinquent as the unfulfilled instructions of the past.

7

PAY TO THE ORDER OF . . .

In the waning hours of every weekday afternoon millions of Americans carefully wheel several hundred horsepower out of a parking space, creep through a few congested city blocks until they are on the gently curving arc that feeds into the superhighway. It is the daily exodus from work to leisure. It is the time when the six-lane asphalt ribbon leading to the suburbs becomes the guard rail that keeps most Americans from seeing what Jacob Riis called, "How the Other Half Lives."[1]

The need to go faster in the homeward-bound rush is obscuring the tenement, the rickety walk-up, the part of a city we call a slum. The cast-iron pattern of fire escapes and the flapping patchwork of laundry are only the blurred background for the 60 mph sign and the tail lights of the car ahead. The thruway, freeway, and expressway, named after a politician or war hero, have become the blindfold that shields the commuter from the places that urban decay calls home. The traffic flows under and over the fading neighborhoods. It no longer moves like the streetcar of yesterday—on an equal level; it no longer rubs shoulders with it.

Speed also means distance, and the new cloverleaf conduits annually serve to widen the boundary lines between the city and what is called the Greater Metropolitan Area. In the decade of the fifties, two-thirds of the population increase in the United States occurred in these suburbs, and the middle-class migrants are still coming in droves.

"One of the most encouraging features of suburban growth," a promotional article said, "is the high class of population that the suburb draws to itself. It seems to sift out the most desirable element in the city population, leaving the superficial and tawdry to continue its cooped-up life. . . . For the man who wants to put as many leagues as possible between his home and the tenderloin, to keep his wife and children apart from the contaminating sights and influences of a metropolis, to rear a family altar which shall be worthy of the sacred name of home, there can be no question but that the suburbs is the place."

This painted prose is the lure of the country realtor and it matters little that it happened to appear in 1905 in *The Suburbanite,* a monthly publication of the Central Railroad of New Jersey.[2]

What does matter, though, is that the inducement has changed from promise to fact. The tawdry and the tenderloin have been separated not only in distance but in thought as well. The suburbs and their express approaches—"not a stop light from here to downtown"—have insulated Americans from each other as never before. And amid crabgrass problems and lawn furniture to choose, it becomes difficult to breathe a sense of association into United States Census Bureau statistics like this:

Three million housing units in the United States are dilapidated.*

Another 8.3 million are deteriorating.

. . . And another 3.8 million lack a toilet, bath, or running water.

In the four-state area of Kentucky, Tennessee, Alabama, and Mississippi, 40 per cent of all housing was dilapidated. In Mississippi and Arkansas less than half of the housing was considered sound with all plumbing facilities. In some urban slum neighborhoods in other parts of the country the percentages of deteriorating

* All figures are from the 1960 Census Report made of 58,323,672 housing units in the United States.

and dilapidated housing are even higher.

In some of the blocks in which my welfare caseload was located in Buffalo, fewer than half of the houses were listed as sound in the latest census reports. In one, only ten of sixty-three housing units were sound; and in an entire census tract that contained a high incidence of welfare recipients, 2,023 units out of 5,741 were listed as deteriorating. The city block characteristics of the Newburgh, New York riverfront area—the focal point of that city's relief dispute—show some of the worst housing conditions in the nation. Six blocks, for example, reveal not a single sound housing unit, yet in 1960 a total of 684 persons lived in those deteriorating and dilapidated homes.

It is hard for most Americans to draw a uniform mental picture of what words like "deteriorated" and "dilapidated" mean. Is it a loose shingle or a hole in the screen door? Is it rain dripping through a roof onto the baby's crib, or is it a rat scurrying across the living room floor? The dilapidated house may mean a weathered shack seen on the back roads traveled during a summer vacation. It may be a recollection of literary images in John Steinbeck's *Grapes of Wrath* or in Erskine Caldwell's *Tobacco Road.* Rarely, for the city dweller, is it the neighborhood that is a lunch-hour stroll away from where he works.

"You can't judge these places in terms of what you are used to," was the admonition I received when I started as a welfare caseworker. "Because if you do, very few of them will look good to you. You've got to judge them against each other." Every caseworker has received such advice and many, like myself, probably have assumed they could not be shown much they had not seen before. Like most of the others who thought this way, I was wrong.

There is another world behind the brownstone tenements and the sagging farmhouse that shelters the poor. It becomes the working world of the caseworker, the rent collector, the meter reader, and occasionally of the detective and the truant officer. And it is a world not quite captured by such census adjectives as "deteriorated" and "dilapidated," and planners' words, as "blight" and "decay."

The words do not quite show the people living in blight and decay.

I remember two incidents that may help to bring that world out of the U.S. Census Reports. The first occurred a few months before this chapter was written. I was doing research in Chicago. A caseworker took me with her to check a complaint from a doctor who said the living conditions of this family were a threat to its health. I remember the drab dwelling on the city's South Side. When we entered the kitchen the first thing I saw was a large wire basket filled with five loaves of bread and hanging by a string from the ceiling.

"Why do you hang the bread from the ceiling?" I asked.

"On account of the rats. I can't leave nuthin' on the table. At night they gets right on that table."

"Have you tried to do something about them?"

"Yeah, he [the landlord] gave me a couple of traps and I got a couple. That one rat, he was so big he drug that trap right under that tank. I killed it with a stick. They goes all down and gets up on that stove."

"You see them actually go through here?"

"Yeah. You sit here for awhile and you'll see one. Them things will run right over your foot. They comes right through here. I am so nervous from those things I ain't sleepin'."

My second recollection comes from my own caseload. It was a home call on a cold and windy February day. The case was new to me and I had to hunt through the back alley for what I was told was a narrow stairway. At the top of the stairs was a lighted Christmas tree bulb and a piece of cardboard that said: "Can't speak—deaf—come in."

My relief family included a man and his wife in their fifties who had been both deaf and dumb since they were children. The man was not home, and I first saw the woman by the light of a single bulb dangling from the kitchen ceiling. She was hunched in a chair reading a newspaper.

"How are you?" I scribbled on a pad that I placed in front of her. I remember that I was a little bit embarrassed because it looked foolish when ordinary talk was written out like that. My pen had blue ink and hers, red. I have saved the slips of paper that were our conversation.

"You don't need anything?" the blue pen asked.

"Only broken panes. Three windows," the red pen answered. "I was told them several time every months with send a check for rent. They will fix them but never fix them since 4 years now."

I remember studying the jumbled grammar written by someone who never heard a sentence put together. She motioned me to follow. The window in the bathroom had a piece of shirt-laundry cardboard in the rectangle where the glass used to be. Several bent nails and strips of weakening tape kept it in place. The nails left their rust outline against the rain-splattered cardboard.

"Living room too. No glass," the red pen wrote.

The windows there were covered with plastic sheeting. Beneath them, carefully cut squares of cardboard fitted the sagging window frames. Nearby, a spring dangled from an overstuffed chair and a brown spread showed its frayed edges on the brown steel bed.

"Do you have a rent receipt so I can get the landlord's name and call him?" the blue pen asked. "Do you want me to talk to the landlord?"

"No. Afraid. Throw me out," the red pen answered.

"I'll see what I can do for finding another place to live. I'll look around," the blue pen said.

"In spring."

"Goodbye," the blue pen said.

The woman nodded, put down the pen, and pushed aside the tea kettle that had begun to whistle on the stove. It was the only sound in the room.

The two examples are but vignettes of how some welfare recipients live. There are no median characteristics, there is no statistical average or national composite of the slum dweller. As a matter of fact, nationwide information about housing for relief recipients is sparse. Too frequently relief housing has been a stepchild kept in the back room of the welfare field. In recent years it has been the subject on the agenda of an occasional national conference; sometimes it makes a few ripples in the newspapers when, for example, the New York City Welfare Department pays $260 a month to keep a relief family in a midtown hotel or when a local commissioner takes a swipe at the slumlords in his area.*

Behind these sporadic appearances is the fact that the landlord usually takes the biggest single slice out of the welfare check. In most communities this amount ranges from a third to a fourth of the total public assistance budget. In New York City in 1962 an estimated $67 million was spent for rent out of checks totaling $217,290,000. In the county where I was a caseworker the rent bill amounted to about $9 million out of $23,501,000. Probably more than one billion welfare dollars were paid to the order of landlords in the United States in 1962. This includes the largest unpublicized government subsidy in the nation. For, in too many instances, it quietly subsidizes slums. In part it constitutes the premium payments of a national housing shortage that is most acute among the poor.

While America has made gains in the housing field (substandard units in the last decade were reduced from 16.3 to 11 million), the new residential construction surge has skirted the inner cities and, particularly, the shabbier neighborhoods. In many cities new construction has not kept pace with the combination of need and demolition. Census figures show that 1.5 million occupied units were demolished in the last decade. One-fourth of these had been occupied by non-whites in 1950, and three-fifths of these were in

* Alvin E. Rose, executive director of the Chicago Housing Authority and for twenty years director of the Chicago Welfare Department, pointed to the void between the two government operations in a 1961 speech at the American Public Welfare Association national conference:

"When I was in public welfare, I must have read the phrase 'food, shelter and clothing' hundreds of times without it ever occurring to me that the word shelter was a mighty important word, and warranted a lot more attention than I was giving it, particularly as it applied to public housing."[3]

the central cities of this country. For the city relief recipient and the Negro, often the same, this has meant a scramble for fewer and fewer places to live.

While the housing market has opened up in many parts of a city, it has steadily contracted in the slums. In Trenton, New Jersey, for example, the 1960 census showed that 43 per cent of all occupied dwellings housed two persons or less—a 50 per cent increase since 1950—yet the number of overcrowded housing units increased by 20 per cent. In the middle-class neighborhoods the residents thinned out, while in the poor and predominantly Negro neighborhoods more and more families were jammed into inadequate apartments. The federal government's latest study of Aid to Dependent Children showed that more than half of the families lived in crowded housing and one-fourth of those faced serious overcrowding with one and one-half or more persons per room. Among all families in the nation, about 12 per cent had more than one person in a room.

Greenleigh Associates confirmed this in public welfare studies in both Chicago and New York State. In both, investigators found more persons in ADC families than rooms in their apartments. "ADC families live in generally substandard housing at high rentals," they reported in Chicago.[5] "The housing of public assistance recipients is generally miserable and inadequate, frequently rat-infested slums," they said about New York.[6] The investigators told of a mother and two children who "live in one 9 by 12 furnished room and share kitchen and bathroom facilities with seven other families. Their rental is $62 monthly. The family sleeps on folding cots. The three chairs are broken and held together by string."[7]

Another case was summed up in this six-sentence biography:

> The O family consists of a 42-year-old, full-time employed father, his wife and ten dependent children ranging in age from 2 to 17 years. The family lives in a four room shanty that the Department of Welfare found for them. The house is infested with rats and vermin. Peeling paint and plaster and defective plumbing

are in evidence. The windows are covered with worn sheeting, and the chairs had frames but no seats. The O family received special assistance from the Department of Welfare for medical care and utilities only.[8]

The Greenleigh investigators did not have to fish for isolated examples. The latest housing survey by the New York City Department of Welfare in August 1959 showed 14,057 welfare families—almost one-fifth of the total on relief—lived in single furnished rooms. This literally means *families* and does not count one person cases living in a furnished room. As many families lived this way as in public housing apartments. Rents for these single rooms averaged $63.03 a month. But eighty-four families paid between $180 and $200 a month for their furnished room.*[9]

But if welfare dollars pay a premium for a housing shortage, they also provide a down payment for prejudice. In many cities the color of the relief recipient can be determined by the size of the rent receipt. Negroes frequently pay anywhere from 10 to 30 per cent higher rent, often for quarters that are inferior to those occupied by whites. When I was a caseworker the tight Negro housing market—dictated in large measure by residential segregation—forced most of my Negro recipients to pay higher rents than the whites in my caseload. In one instance a Negro steelworker receiving partial welfare assistance, was paying $90 a month without heat or any other utility. Less than a mile away, a white recipient was paying $22.50 without utilities for a similar seven-room apartment.

If the Negro steelworker had been paying only twice the rent of the white man, his pay check could have supported his wife and seven children without any supplementary welfare help. Incidentally, two years earlier when his $90 apartment was still under

* Accommodations for welfare families in New York City are so scarce that since 1960 the Welfare Department has had to pay special fees to private agents for locating vacant space. In 1962 the amount paid for these "finders fees" more than doubled over the previous year. A total of $44,370 was paid in 250 cases for an average of $177.48 per "find."

rent control, the State Rent Commission set a $34.50 maximum on the place.

In New York State, Greenleigh found that taxpayers were charged $9 million a year extra just because the tenants were Negro and Puerto Rican.[10] In Chicago's Cook County alone, Greenleigh placed the rent prejudice check at $3.4 million a year. Negroes, he found, were paying private landlords a median rent of $82.77 a month, while whites were paying $64.84, a difference of 28 per cent.[11]

If these are some of the results of America's slum housing difficulties, what then are some of the causes? The traditional villain is the slumlord; he is to housing what the butler is to the detective story, except that he rarely gets it in the end. As the surface bad man he often distracts the casual observer from the fact that it is the community that permits him to exist. Furthermore, some federal programs originally designed to be his enemies, occasionally have wound up being his allies. These programs are urban renewal and public housing. Their gap between promise and performance is the fever chart of shelter for-the poor.

The phrase "urban renewal" is the public's shorthand for Title I of the 1949 Housing Act, a major federal step to help cities bulldoze away blight. The government agreed to pay for two-thirds of the slum property that would be torn down and the vacant land subsequently sold to private developers.* The result was to be new homes and factories on the soil that had become a depository for decay. In some parts of the nation this has happened; in many others, it has been an exercise in slow motion. At the beginning of 1963 the Urban Renewal Administration had 1,210 projects on its books—588 in execution and 536 in planning stages. Only eighty-six were completed. Eight years after the first urban renewal project was approved (March 1950), only 10 projects were finished.

* The 1961 Housing Act doubled cumulative authorization for urban renewal project grants from $2 billion to $4 billion, and the federal checkbook now underwrites three-fourths of the cost in cities with populations of 50,000 or less.

In January 1963, Pennsylvania led the list with 144 projects, and 19 completed. Four other states had this record: New York, 112 projects, 7 completed; Ohio, 40 projects, 1 completed; Michigan, 50 projects, 0 completed; Georgia, 48 projects, 0 completed.[12]

It is this lag time between plan, bulldozing, and building that has developed into a major problem, not only for the program but for public welfare as well. Urban renewal for a welfare department begins at the precise instant when the first public official mentions the two words about a neighborhood. If it was not classified as a slum before, it is now. Landlords try to get the most rent money while they can. Plans for needed repairs that might have been made are now discarded. Building, health, and fire department inspectors who might have issued a summons, now may be lenient because "City Hall says the damn stuff is going to be knocked down anyway." What was an integral part of a city has now become an island. It is an island that must be evacuated. And with the leaflets and the notices comes conflict.

My own caseload contained refugees from such an island. Many had moved to the fringe of the redevelopment area that slowly was turning into new slums. They had come from N.Y.-U.R. 1-1, the government's numerical label for the Ellicott District Redevelopment Project. It is a biography of frustration, difficulty, and delay.

Early in 1953, Buffalo's Mayor Steven Pankow talked about ripping down a twenty-nine-block area in the central city that was a tangle of overcrowded tenements principally occupied by Negroes. In April 1954 the Board of Redevelopment designated Ellicott as its first objective of study and that fall the Housing and Home Finance Agency approved a $3 million capital grant reservation. The city's Common Council approved Ellicott as a redevelopment area in June 1955, and a preliminary project report was submitted to the federal government the following January. For the next two years plans were altered, additions were made, property owners held mass meetings, and, at one point, the federal people felt the whole thing should be abandoned.

In December 1958, five years after Mayor Pankow's first pronouncements, the relocation of families began. There were about 2,200 families in the area, and the majority of them would have fitted under even the most stringent definitions of poverty. Twenty-nine per cent of them were on relief. There were 627 cases, and all but one street had from one to 89 welfare cases living on it. The Buffalo Municipal Housing Authority, in charge of the relocation, later reported that almost two-thirds of the displaced households were Negroes renting homes. They paid a median rent of $64.61 a month, while their median income was $3,214 a year per family. The minority whites in the area, meanwhile, paid median rents of $48.79 and their annual income was almost $1,000 higher.[13]

Most of the families found new quarters by themselves. It was apparent that formal relocation efforts were less than successful, because early in 1959 the Housing Authority asked the Community Welfare Council to hire a social worker to come to the assistance of the relocators. Again, the chronology shows difficulty and delay. It was not until fourteen months after the relocation office was opened that the social worker was on the job. By this time there were only two hundred families left on the site.

The social worker did a very brief random sample study of what happened to forty-six of these relocated families.

These are some of the things the worker found: Twenty-one families read in the newspapers that they had to move, twelve got the information through rumors, five from the landlord, and two realized they had to find other quarters when they saw demolition begin. The one who received assistance from the relocation office was the only one who asked for help. Only twenty-six knew that there was such help available.*

* Every urban renewal project must include a plan for the relocation of displaced families in new quarters that they can afford and are "decent, safe and sanitary dwellings." Frequently, as in Buffalo, many families fend for themselves, pay higher rents for their new homes, and wind up in buildings that are as shabby as those they left behind.

After the last two families moved out of the area in March 1961, the Board of Redevelopment rejected the bid of one private developer, and awarded the land to the only other bidder at the minimum price the government would allow. But the sound of new construction was yet to be heard. Early in 1962, Mayor Chester Kowal, the city's third chief executive in the Ellicott project, was dissatisfied with the plans and called for new ones. Nine new firms made proposals, and in the summer of 1963 city officials were in a wrangle over which one of the approved contractors should have the job. Ten years after urban renewal talk began, a motorist driving on the fringe of downtown Buffalo could see twenty-nine blocks lying vacant.

What has been the penalty for this bickering and delay? For the city it has meant the loss of vital new tax revenue, which is a major dividend of urban renewal. It has meant a more rapid rate of deterioration for the fringe neighborhoods because of prolonged overcrowding. For the welfare department it has meant keeping Negro recipients in these congested housing conditions at rents

---

But federal statistics disagree. In a relocation report of experiences through December 1961, the Urban Renewal Administration said: "During the past 13 years, more than 127,000 families have been displaced by urban renewal. Of this number, almost 80% moved to standard housing. The remaining 20% were almost evenly divided among those who moved out of the city, could not be located at their new address, or self-relocated in substandard housing and refused further offers of assistance from the Local Public Agency."[14]

Independent surveys are not that optimistic. The University of Southern California's School of Public Administration found that in twenty-six cities little relocation help was provided, and 70 per cent of those relocated moved to nearby housing "that was substandard and unsafe, with structural defects, lack of central heating or hot running water, shared toilets and overcrowding." The study, from 1955 to 1958, covered forty-one cities and 47,000 families. In the cities with poor relocation programs, 80 per cent of the families paid higher rents for their new quarters. In the fifteen cities which offered families full-time counseling from trained social workers, rent increases averaged lower and only 34 per cent moved to substandard housing.[15]

that have rapidly increased and continue to increase. As in other cities, the entire Negro housing market has worsened because expected new housing has failed to materialize.

The racial factor as an added problem is not peculiar to Buffalo. Up to June 1960 more than two-thirds of all families displaced by urban renewal were Negroes.

But what about public housing? While it has taken some heavy pressure off the straining slums, the key question is how much and how well. In 1962, the twenty-fifth anniversary of public housing, there were 520,000 low rent units in the United States—less than 1 per cent of the total housing supply. These were occupied by more than 2 million persons in 1,700 communities. Almost half (47.3 per cent) of the tenants were Negroes. Meanwhile, government housing officials reported that at the beginning of the decade 9 million other Americans with incomes below $4,000 a year still were living in substandard dwellings. Powerful real-estate interests and their high-paid lobbyists who still ask, "Can you afford to pay someone else's rent?" sometimes have left public housers fighting broomhandle skirmishes with the slums.

One-fourth of all public housing tenants are welfare recipients. In many instances they have neighbors who are only a few dollars away from the relief rolls. Many of this nation's public housing projects have become high rise containers of poverty. In too many areas they have become municipal sumps encased by new brick and adorned by old four-letter words. Even some of the proponents have become disenchanted. When Daniel Seligman wrote one of *Fortune* magazine's series on "The Exploding Metropolis," a student of New York's slums told him:

> Once upon a time we thought that if we could only get our problem families out of those dreadful slums, then Papa would stop taking dope, Mama would stop chasing around, and Junior would stop carrying a knife. Well, we got them into the nice new apartments with modern kitchens and a recreation center, and they're the same bunch of bastards they always were.[16]

This jaundiced summary for too many cities is a synopsis of public housing projects. For welfare departments it has major significance because, invariably, they are accused of being responsible for what the social worker more delicately calls "the multi-problem families." Conference after conference is held on how to bring middle-class standards to the tenants of these projects. In 1963 a federal task force of welfare and housing experts initiated experiments in several major housing projects.* The effort may be like trying to crawl up a glass wall—there's very little to hang on to. For while one part of government wants to provide uplifting services, other government rules and regulations are insuring that public housing remains not only low rent but low class as well. A major impetus of any community improvement is that drive to keep up with the Joneses. It has been successfully eliminated in public housing. There are very few Joneses, and when they do become pace-setters the income limit rules say they have to be thrown out. The best "social workers" in any project, the leaders who can set an example, consequently are banished. Low income limits not only guarantee that the projects will remain fortresses of poverty, but at the same time actively deny the welfare departments a free rehabilitation program in the form of the successful next-door neighbor.

At the beginning of 1962 the median income limit for admission to public housing was $3,200 per family, with a low of $2,100 in the Atlanta region and a high of $4,940 in the New York region. In 67 per cent of all the projects in the nation a family had to earn under $3,500 a year in order to qualify for an apartment. In the South, 49 per cent of the localities set the family income figure below $2,950.**

* The first of these programs occurred in the Pruitt-Igoe housing project, St. Louis, Missouri, and the Elm Haven housing project in New Haven, Connecticut.

** The maximum a family could earn and stay in public housing was 25 per cent above the median admission limit in all localities except New York, where it was 28 per cent. To remain in the projects, 44 per cent of the families had to earn less than $3,950 a year. The national median income limit for continued occupancy was $4,000, with a range

Former public housing tenants have described the effects of these poverty level income limits as well as anyone. In a 1958 federal study designed to find out why families move out of public housing, one of the most frequently mentioned complaints was social dissatisfaction. In the nine cities surveyed, this caused from 10 to 57 per cent of all the voluntary move-outs.* Some of the comments from former tenants included these:

"Nice at first but people tore it up; bad environment."

"All the nice families moved out."

"Wanted a neighborhood where you don't have people moving in and out."

"It is the opinion of people that a lower class of people live in the projects; we were ashamed to say we lived there."

"The neighbors were awful—crude and coarse; we wanted a location among better class of people."

"Friends and relatives looked down on us because we lived in a city project."[17]

It is this public housing policy—which has yet to meet the needs of the poor in either quantity or kind—and a lagging urban renewal program that have become the silent handmaidens of the slum profiteers. They can be found in every city in this nation. They have included prominent local businessmen and a member of Congress.

Usually a welfare department caseworker can name them individually and can provide a detailed list of their holdings. In some of the larger operations in New York and Chicago the real owners occasionally hide behind pleasant-sounding real estate companies or intricate corporate enterprises. The latter serve as a handy smokescreen for a building or health department inspector, who

---

of $2,600 for one locality in the Atlantic region to $7,020 for New York City.

* These moves are frequent and costly to the housing authorities. The 1958 study estimated that nearly 115,000 families would move from the projects that year. This meant a gross annual turnover cost of between $8.6 and $11.5 million.

may find that he needs the talents of a lawyer and a detective to deliver a summons to the owner of a ramshackle dwelling in his jurisdiction.

These purveyors of rotting real estate are the leeches of the city. They pay the least taxes on their holdings because their assessments are the lowest. Frequently, the return on their money is the highest in the real estate business. Their annual maintenance and repair bills are the smallest of any landlord, because often they do little or none. They operate quietly in back streets of the slums, with the aid of rent collectors whom they call agents. They are seen occasionally when a newspaper does a series of articles on a tawdry neighborhood, when a baby is chewed by a rat, or when an unvented space heater blows up and two or three youngsters are burned to death. The civic outrage and the inevitable investigations that result are part of the business risks of the slumlord.

The details of their operations are seldom unraveled. Rarely are they connected directly to the public welfare bill. But in 1961 and 1962, New Jersey State Senator Anthony J. Grossi devoted a substantial share of his legislative welfare investigation to relief housing. The committee reports its findings like this:

> Living conditions under which the average ADC recipient family lives were found inadequate and often lacking even elementary sanitation and health protection. Rents paid by ADC grants are unlimited and excessive. Evidence gathered by the committee substantially corroborates the fact that no control in rental payments exists, and that supervision and inspection of facilities rented by ADC recipients is almost non-existent. Many such facilities can best be described as hovels where rents are charged on a weekly basis, often exceeding $100 per month. Landlords consistently refuse to maintain minimum standards of decency and health. Unquestionably some specialize in buying slum properties at cheap prices and rent them exclusively to welfare clients at exorbitant rates.[18]

In one case, committee investigators who pieced together the holdings of a landlord in Hightstown found that he was getting an annual net return of 20 per cent on his investment and would have net income to fully amortize his property in four and a half years. Sound real estate investors, meanwhile, are satisfied with less than half such an annual return.

In another case in Paterson, detailed at a public hearing, Committee Counsel Grover C. Richman, Jr., questioned Passaic County Detective Vincent J. DiSimone, Jr., about his investigation of slum property. It produced some of the following testimony:*

Q. What was the condition of the inside of the apartment?

A. It was in an extremely overcrowded, filthy condition. The kitchen—incidentally, we took photographs of this apartment, which I believe you have in your possession. The kitchen was completely overcrowded. There was a gas burner that supplied the heat. The walls were in a state of disrepair. There was no covering on the floor. It appeared it hadn't been painted in many, many years. Adjoining that, separated by an archway, were these two bedrooms. The one bedroom was cluttered up with furniture so that there was only about a three-foot space running down the center of the room.

Q. What was the condition of the plumbing in this apartment?

A. It was in very poor condition.

Q. Was it workable?

A. At that time Mrs. —— told me the bathroom did not work and there was, if I remember correctly, a leak in the basin and she had a small hand basin in the back of the bedroom.

Q. In your opinion, detective, is this apartment fit for human habitation?

A. Definitely not.

The landlord who said he owned "about 10 or 12 or 15 properties," was shown pictures of this apartment renting for $60 a month without heat and utilities after he testified it was in "A-1 condition."

Q. Would you now say, after looking at those photographs, that is in A-1 condition?

* The deletions in this testimony involve the name of the relief recipient, the landlord, and the address of the property. The full testimony is in the official record of the second public hearing before the Welfare Investigating Committee of the New Jersey Legislature held January 5, 1961, at City Hall, Paterson.

A. The plumbing was in A-1 condition—the walls, in A-1 condition—and also the paint was in A-1 condition. Now it is dirty. I don't say no. In one week's time they dirty up the place.

Q. Would it surprise you to know . . . that as of January 4, 1961, the Department of Health made an inspection . . . and found 16 separate, substantial violations of the Health Code?

A. 1960.

Q. January the 4th, yesterday. Let me read you what the Department of Health found and see if you agree with this. (reading) "Improper ventilation of the toilet, exhaust fan broken." First floor front, this was. "Flush box on the toilet leaking. Bedroom ceiling plaster cracked. Broken window pane in bedroom. Paint peeling in the ceiling of the living room." First floor rear: "Side walls and toilet broken and dirty. Improper ventilation in toilet. Exhaust fan broken. Floor underneath bathtub faucets was broken. Ceiling and side walls dirty in kitchen. Plaster behind kitchen coal stove peeling. Defective grate in coal stove. Chimney flue loose, creating fire hazard. Defective hot water faucet in kitchen." Second floor rear: "Defective flush box in toilet. Trap on basin and toilet leaking. Premises completely infested with roaches."

Q. Now, do you still say it is in A-1 condition?

A. We have an exterminator who goes there and takes care of the roaches and rats. They never complain about it. And about the painting, it was A-1 when she moved in. She is only there six months and I went there the other day and I have never seen anything—seen any ceiling broken. The only thing that I saw was the bathroom wasn't flushing right.

Q. What was the other day? What do you mean by the other day?

A. Before yesterday.

Q. The day before yesterday?

A. Yes.

Q. In other words, all the things I just read to you must have happened sometime after you were there on Tuesday until the department got there yesterday?

A. The Board of Health man never gave me any notice that anything was wrong and I don't know unless somebody tells me.

Some of my welfare recipients lived in hovels like this. Throughout the nation other caseworkers have had to refer relief families to buildings that provided adequate housing not for the tenants, but only for the greed of the landlord. Because there was no other place to send homeless families, in some instances welfare departments have become unwilling assistants in these real estate operations. And the landlords know this. They send neatly typed vacancy lists to welfare district offices couched in euphemisms like "newly decorated," or "recently renovated." A memorandum from a district welfare office in Chicago analyzed one such listing of vacancies in fourteen different buildings all held by one realty company in Chicago's South Side. The letterhead carried the company's name against a background picture of the city's attractive lakefront loop where none of the property was located. This is what the memorandum said:

> I am attaching a notice from a realty company which from all appearances seems to be prospering with other slum holdings. I do not know whether a similar notice was sent to all offices. If so, I believe we should have some idea as to the condition of the flat before we advise a recipient of specific vacancies. For instance, the caseworker servicing the area in which the building at . . . is located, writes: "This building is in horrible condition and unfit for human habitation. The hallways are dark and dope addicts and drunks lurch in the hallways constantly, preying [on] service men, salesmen, and anyone who enters the building looking fairly prosperous. According to many clients five men have been found dead in the building due to misuse of dope addiction, and rats and other vermin run freely through the building, and the walls and ceilings are filthy and cracked. The apartments receive very little heat during the winter. Uncovered garbage cans are placed in the hallways outside the recipients' apartments."

Although these items occasionally become the springboard for a brief crusade, they are as temporary as they are repetitious. When the newspaper reporter approaches the political leadership of the city, the phrase most often heard is: "Give us enough inspectors and we will enforce the rules." The only thing these continuous platitudes provide is an indication that the blame for the slums and for the way in which some Americans force others to live goes far beyond the grimy hand that dispenses inflated rent receipts.

It goes to the basic questions: Does the city really want to spend the money to enforce the housing code, and where does this problem rest in the list of municipal priorities? And, too, it goes beyond the occasional inspector whose vision is affected by what is pressed into his palm.

The prosecution of slum landlords, even in the few instances where the case has reached the court, has been a failure in most American cities. Code enforcement has been sporadic and prosecution rare. The city of Buffalo, for example, for more than a decade has received special permission from the state legislature to ignore a multiple-dwelling law. In 1963 at least 7,500 multiple dwellings—many of them housing welfare recipients—had not been inspected to provide even a listing of violations.* "No one should minimize the problem of financing inspections in light of the city's critical budgetary needs," commented the *Buffalo Evening News,* "but the welfare of tenants and efforts to halt blight and decay cannot be served by endless state suspensions and a shameful lack of substantial community enforcement."[19]

The path from violation to punishment is a tortuous one indeed. In 1959, for example, Buffalo's County Health Department brought 438 cases to City Court. Many of these were adjourned repeatedly. As a result it required 1,110 separate court appearances. Sixteen persons paid fines.

Some communities have looked for better legal machinery to

* Enforcement activities in many cities are scattered among a variety of government departments. Some belong to the housing division, some to the buildings department, others to fire and to health. In New York City, for example, six departments have some jurisdiction over housing. Sometimes the hair is split depending upon the borough in which it grows. A housing violation in a one- or two-family home in Brooklyn is reported to the Department of Buildings, Non-Multiple Dwelling Section; if the same violation occurs in the Bronx it is reported to the Department of Health. If a welfare worker sees a rat it should be reported to the Housing Division of the Department of Buildings. However, if the rat bites somebody, then it is reported to the Department of Health.

take a swipe at the landlords. This has ranged from condemnation to refurbishing property and sending the bill to the owner. None of these methods has made any sizeable improvement in the slum situation.

Probably the most effective weapon against the landlords is a relatively new law in New York State that its drafter reports to be the first of its kind in the nation.* It strikes directly at the slumlord's only vulnerable area—his rent receipts. It permits a public welfare official to withhold rent payments in any case where a relief recipient is living in a building that contains violations that are "dangerous, hazardous or detrimental to life or health." The official obtains a list of these violations from the code enforcement agencies and then tells the relief recipient to ignore the landlord when he comes for his rent. A welfare department attorney is a participant in subsequent eviction proceedings against the tenant for non-payment of rent. The very existence of these major violations, the law says, is a valid defense for not paying the rent. This anti-slumlord legislation was first used in New York City and Binghamton, New York. In the latter city of 76,000, in the south-central part of the state, use of the law had a dramatic effect on the slums.

After the *Binghamton Sun-Bulletin* did a series—with the cooperation of the welfare department—"to point up the shocking conditions under which some Binghamtonians live," City Welfare Commissioner Rosemary Wilson withheld rents from recipients in substandard dwellings.[20] "Needless to say," she told me, "the pressure of the press played a part in our decision to throw caution to the wind and delete rent from the budgets of all recipients living in substandard housing. A list of all dwellings occupied by

* The new law is Section 143b of the New York State Social Welfare Law known as the "Spiegel Bill" enacted April 30, 1962, and effective July 1, 1962. Early in 1963 the constitutionality of the law was under question in the higher courts after it was found to be constitutional in New York City and unconstitutional in a Binghamton action.

welfare recipients was submitted to the Health Department which has the responsibility of housing code enforcement and within a few days we were presented a list of these dwellings that were known to be in violation. We immediately withheld rent in eighty-one cases."

Amid the headlines, the sound of carpenters, plumbers, and electricians was heard in the slum neighborhoods. The extent of their work is documented by Binghamton City Health Commissioner Dr. C. A. Sargent. In the two years before rents were withheld, an average of six dwellings came into compliance with the housing code every month. In the six months after the new law was used the monthly average jumped to forty-seven. "There is every reason to believe," Dr. Sargent reported, "that withholding the rent is the most effective way to bring about compliance. Of the buildings brought into compliance as a result of withholding the rent it has been necessary for us to make an average number of visits of 2 per building as against an average of 6.6 under the previous method."[21]

A law like this is a beginning. But it will remain only part of the prologue until communities adopt an aggressive code enforcement program that is coordinated with broad citywide planning, effective urban renewal, and adequate public housing. For most cities such a comprehensive anti-slum policy is tomorrow's ambition. For housing-troubled welfare departments, it is today's requirement. And for the ADC mother in Chicago, who stores her bread in a ceiling-suspended wire basket, and a speechless woman in Buffalo whose cardboard rectangles substitute for glass, it was yesterday's necessity.

8

A WHISPERED SOLUTION

This week I signed the death certificate of a 30 year old woman on relief who fatally ruptured her uterus in labor with her 17th pregnancy. She first became a mother at age 11. I never was able to ask her whether 17 pregnancies in 19 years was her voluntary goal. In so far as overfecundity is a major aspect of the problem of welfare families, then it seems apparent that birth control services can be a major factor in its solution and that to withhold these services, is to attempt to solve the welfare problem with your right hand tied behind your back.

DR. ALAN F. GUTTMACHER, *President*
Planned Parenthood Federation of America[1]

These are words of controversy. They swirl around a subject most Americans practice in the privacy of their bedrooms but are embarrassed and sometimes afraid to discuss outside of its doors. Like sex itself, it is debonair to whisper, but boorish to talk about out loud. Even the proponents of birth control have had to couch it in such euphemisms as "child spacing programs" and "family planning." In welfare circles, particularly those in the public sector, whatever the phrase used, it is most often as welcome as a witch doctor would be at an AMA convention. For many social workers the solution to the dilemma has been to ignore it. The luxury of this gambit is rapidly coming to a close.

With increasing frequency the birth control controversy is

spreading from a few militant clergymen, doctors, and zealous housewives to scientific and medical associations, powerful citizen groups, and large church organizations. The discussion is widening its circle of participants amid scientific warnings that, while it took 800,000 years to produce a world population of 3 billion, it will take less than half a century to double that number. The National Academy of Sciences, for example, made these predictions in an April 1963 report that urged the United States government to actively participate in international birth control studies. "Either the birth rate of the world must come down," the Academy warned, "or the death rate must go back up."[2]

In most of these areas, the debate has enjoyed neither calm, consistency, nor necessarily logic. In some parts of the nation where it has erupted, it has resembled the religious wars the twentieth century supposedly has left behind. In the political sector alone, the shadow of birth control has ranged over foreign aid, local elections, and even Presidential campaigns. In 1960, for example, Senator John F. Kennedy, aware of the voters' sensitivity to his Catholicism, outlined his birth control views in an interview with James Reston of the *New York Times* and again referred to it in his famous "religion speech" before the Houston ministers.*

* "Whatever issue may come before me as President—on birth control, divorce, censorship, gambling or any other subject—I will make my decision in accordance with these views, in accordance with what my conscience tells me to be the national interest, and without regard to outside religious pressures or dictates, and no power or threat of punishment could cause me to decide otherwise."

This was part of the speech given by the Presidential candidate on September 12, 1960, in the Rice Hotel, Houston, Texas, before the Greater Houston Ministerial Association.[3]

In a *New York Times* interview published November 27, 1959, Mr. Reston and Senator Kennedy included the following question and answer:

Question. The Bishops of the United States have said that U.S. Catholics "will not support any public assistance, either at home or abroad, to promote artificial birth prevention, abortion, or sterilization, whether

Twelve years earlier, a statewide birth control referendum in his home state of Massachusetts was blamed by some for the defeat of the Republican party. And more recently, after the Illinois Public Aid Commission voted 6 to 4 to provide contraceptives and information to Chicago relief recipients, George Tagge, *Chicago Tribune* political reporter, wrote on Dec. 9, 1962:

> The birth control controversy which has split the Illinois Public Aid Commission has set off reactions which may affect elections in Chicago next year and in the state in 1964. Echoes of the fight also are expected to sound thru the legislative session beginning in January.

In contrast, when the Dona Ana County Planned Parenthood Association opened a new center in Las Cruces, New Mexico, the same year, the mayor cut the ribbon.

The intent of this chapter is not to add new fury to this conflict, but rather to separate fact from myth in order to clarify the issue. The discussion is based on two major observations:

That most American couples obtain birth control information and make an active attempt to limit conception.

That many impoverished Americans, particularly those on relief, who depend on public rather than private medical care—are denied this information and, therefore, are unable to make a personal decision.

Fertility studies by sociologists provide significant data on how widely Americans use contraceptives. The major national study in the field was conducted in 1955 by a trio of researchers: Ronald

---

through direct aid or by means of international organizations." What is your position on this?

Answer. I think it would be a mistake for the U.S. Government to attempt to advocate the limitation of the population of underdeveloped countries. This problem involves important social and economic questions which must be solved by the people of those countries themselves. For the United States to intervene on this basis would involve a kind of mean patriotism, which I think they would find most objectionable.

(This "hands-off" policy was changed during the Kennedy administration.)

Freedman, professor of sociology, University of Michigan; Pascal K. Whelpton, director, Scripps Foundation for Research in Population Problems, Miami University; and Arthur A. Campbell, assistant professor, Scripps Foundation. After studying 2,713 white married women of child-bearing age, the authors concluded that "family limitation is now almost universally approved and is practiced widely and effectively by the white couples who need it."[4]

They found that of the 1,794 couples able to have children, 90 per cent deliberately attempted to prevent or intended to prevent conception. These were the variations according to religion:

TABLE 14

Percentage of Selected White Couples Practicing Birth Control, According to Religion: 1955

	Per Cent Prevented Conception[5]	*Per Cent Prevented & Intended to Prevent*
Total	83	90
Protestant	88	95
Catholic	71	80
Jewish	96	96

The study showed, too, that as the age of the child-bearing women rose so did their dependency on a contraceptive method. At the same time the gap between Protestant and Catholic women narrowed. For example, among the eighteen-to-twenty-four age group, 78 per cent of the Protestant wives used a contraceptive method while only 53 per cent of the Catholic wives did. Among wives in the thirty-five-to-thirty-nine age group, the users rose: Protestant, 93 per cent; Catholic, 85 per cent. The Protestants favored the appliance methods—condom, diaphragm, and douche—while the Catholics preferred the rhythm method (periodic continence) permitted by their church.

Most Catholics, the study showed, approved of family limitation and the majority used a method acceptable to the Church. However, of Catholic couples married at least ten years, 50 per cent used a method other than rhythm. "This figure," the authors observed, "indicates the extent of deviation from Church doctrine by Catholics who cannot depend on low fecundity to limit family size and who have been married long enough to face problems of a growing family."[6]

These and similar findings then should put to rest the suspicions that those who talk about birth control are proposing something foreign to present American sexual behavior.

Where, then, did this controversy begin?

The legal snarl started in 1873 when anti-sin crusader Anthony Comstock, a Protestant and president of the New York Watch and Ward Society, succeeded in prodding Congress to pass a bill that prohibited sending obscene literature through the mails. Included was a prohibition against articles "for preventing conception or producing abortion, or for any indecent or immoral purpose . . ." as well as literature about such devices. The Comstock law subsequently became the model for numerous state laws. But fourteen states exempted doctors, medical schools, and druggists. The federal courts later decided that the intent of the Forty-second Congress which heeded Anthony Comstock "was not to prevent the importation, sale, or carriage by mail of things which might be intelligently employed by conscientious and competent physicians for the purpose of saving life or promoting the well-being of their patients."[7]

Today forty-eight of fifty states consider birth-control legal. Two states—Connecticut and Massachusetts—have prohibitive statutes. In Massachusetts it is a crime to provide information and to sell "any drug, medicine, instrument or article whatever for the prevention of conception . . ." A salesman could be imprisoned for as much as five years and fined $1,000. In Connecticut any person using a contraceptive device commits a crime and, furthermore, the doctor who prescribes such use can be prosecuted as an accessory. "Late every night in Connecticut," *Time* magazine observed, "lights go out in the cities and towns, and citizens by tens of thousands proceed zestfully to break the law."[8] In both Connecticut and Massachusetts these laws have withstood repeated assaults by eminent physicians, clergymen, and citizen groups.* Attempts to modify the statutes have been defeated at the polls, in the courts, and before legislative committees. The defenders of the status quo no longer are the Anthony Comstocks but repeatedly are the spokesmen for the Catholic church. The zeal and frequency of their appearances have created a split among Catholic thinkers. "It is always a temptation for a religious organization, especially a powerful or dominant one, to impose through the clenched fist of the law its creedal viewpoint upon others," a Catholic priest, the Reverend John A. O'Brien, research professor of theology at the University of Notre Dame, wrote in a 1961 national magazine article. "Both Roman Catholics and Protestants have succumbed to this temptation in the past."[9]

In stating his opposition to clerical political pressure to maintain these laws, Father O'Brien cited several leading Catholic scholars who shared his viewpoint. Included was Norman St. John-Stevas, a Roman Catholic thinker who said:

Catholics in campaigning for the maintenance of such laws, gain

* Occasionally even a minor effort to dent the curtain may set off a major furor. This example, as detailed in the December 27, 1962, issue of the *Boston Globe,* borders on the comic:

"A Boston Redevelopment Authority employee has been reprimanded for allowing the Planned Parenthood Federation to give a lecture on birth control to the Washington Park, Roxbury, relocation staff.

"Treasurer James G. Colbert and board member Stephen McCloskey both expressed shock and indignation at the employee's action.

"Both Development Administrator Edward J. Logue and Kane Simonian, executive director who is in charge of relocation, disclaimed any knowledge of the lecture which took place in St. Richard's Catholic Church in Washington Park, where the B.R.A. has a site office.

"The employee who came under heavy criticism from the five-man board was identified as Walter Smart, a development specialist who recently was recommended for a promotion as assistant project director for Washington Park."

little for public morality. They do, however, increase the fear of Catholicism in the minds of non-Catholics and increase the likelihood that when Protestants visualize the Church the image will not be that of a religious body, but of a political power structure. This is a high price to pay for the maintenance of ineffectual statutes.[10]

Father O'Brien said this Catholic attitude is finding more adherents. "They [the scholars] are in substantial agreement with their Protestant and Jewish counterparts that the time has come to take the birth control issue out of politics, out of the field of civil legislation, and confine it to its legitimate domain of conscience and religion."[11]

But where do the religions stand?

In the last half-century the Protestant faiths have switched from opposition to endorsement of birth control. The last Lambeth Conference of the Anglican church, held in July 1958, and representing forty-six countries, passed a resolution that "the responsibility for deciding upon the number and frequency of children has been laid by God upon the consciences of parents everywhere . . ."[12] The Methodists have said that "planned parenthood, practiced in Christian conscience, fulfills rather than violates the will of God,"[13] and the United Presbyterians stated that "the proper use of medically approved contraceptives may contribute to the spiritual, emotional and economic welfare of the family . . ."[14]

The two large segments of the Jewish faith—Conservative and Reform—both have approved birth control. However, Orthodox Jews are forbidden to practice contraception, except when there is grave necessity.

Catholic doctrine will not sanction any mechanical or chemical device to prevent conception because, in the Church view, this would violate the natural law of God. The purpose of the conjugal act is primarily to have children, Church authorities have maintained. However, by expanding the dialogue on the rhythm method the Church has opened the door for acceptable family planning for its followers.

This method has been sanctioned by the Church's highest official.

As recently as 1951, Pope Pius XII, in an address to the Congress of the Italian Catholic Union of Midwives, said that a sexual union could take place without the intent of having children if there were medical, economic, and social reasons. The *Catholic Telegraph Register,* on November 9, 1951, reported parts of this speech as follows:

> To embrace the married state, therefore, continuously to make use of the faculty proper to it and lawful in it alone, and on the other hand to withdraw always and deliberately with no serious reason from its primary obligation, would be a sin against the very meaning of conjugal life. There are serious motives, such as those often mentioned in the so called medical, eugenic, economic, and social "indications" that can exempt for a long time, perhaps even the whole duration of the marriage, from the positive and obligatory carrying out of the act. From this it follows that observing the non-fertile periods alone can be lawful only under a moral aspect. Under the conditions mentioned it really is so.

This discussion within the Catholic church is hardly new. For example, on March 2, 1853, the Bishop of Amiens, France, asked the Sacred Penitentiary for guidance. The following exchange took place:

> The Bishop of Amiens, France, humbly requests of the Eminent Fathers of the Sacred Penitentiary, the solution of the following difficulty:
>
> Certain married people among the faithful, relying on the opinion of learned physicians, are convinced that in each month there are some days in which conception cannot take place in a woman. Are those to be disturbed who do not use marriage except on these days, at least if they have legitimate reasons for refraining from the conjugal act?
>
> The Sacred Penitentiary, having pondered the proposed case, replies to the Venerable Father in Christ, the Bishop of Amiens, that those mentioned in the petition should not be disturbed so long as they do nothing to prevent conception.[15]

The rhythm method today is taught in a few Catholic hospitals and in some Catholic women's colleges. In New York City, St. Vincent's Hospital has a sterility-fertility clinic and in Buffalo, St.

Luke's Hospital provides similar services. However, frequently the birth control taboo has been so strongly entrenched that a number of Catholics appear to be reluctant even to discuss this accepted method of family planning.

In a Pennsylvania county when the Planned Parenthood group sought the aid of a priest in opening a rhythm clinic "his initial reaction was one of violent anger," their memo said. "After further discussion [he] gave way to approval of instruction in the rhythm method . . . on later contact, he himself suggested opening of a rhythm clinic at a [Catholic] hospital."

In an upstate New York community a similar group reported plans to open a rhythm clinic and "attempting to enlist the services of a Catholic physician, but they are all afraid to participate . . ."

Physicians, through their professional organizations, repeatedly have said that birth control is part of the medical practice. As early as 1937 the House of Delegates of the American Medical Association said a doctor has the right to furnish information whether he is in the privacy of his office or in a dispensary.*[16] In the fall of 1959 the 13,000-member American Public Health Association, in urging greater research in human fertility and the effects of biological, psychological, and socio-economic factors on population change, said:

"Public and private programs concerned with population growth and family size should be integral parts of the health program . . ." and that "full freedom should be extended to all population groups for the selection and use of such methods for the regulation of family size as are consistent with the creed and mores of the individual concerned."[17]

* The statement, referring to the legal status of contraception, said: "Information concerning contraception is admittedly available to persons in favorable economic circumstances. There appears to be no law to prevent physicians who work in dispensaries from furnishing patients there with any information that may lawfully be furnished to patients in any other economic group. In all cases, the legal justification is the medical need of the patient."

Despite pronouncements like this, the legal, religious, and medical interpretations have yet to be translated into programs for "all population groups." The gap is wide among different social classes not only in the use of contraceptives, but in the knowledge of them. These class differences were noticed as early as the 1920's by Robert and Helen Lynd in their monumental American culture study, *Middletown.* The Lynds found that all twenty-seven business-class women who answered questions about contraception used some method of birth control. However, of the seventy-seven working-class wives fewer than half were found to use any birth control method. Among the majority who did not use anything, fifteen disapproved of contraception, fifteen approved but did not think they needed it, four were ignorant about any devices except those used by the husband, and nine wanted birth control help but did not know any method.

"The behavior of the community in this matter of the voluntary limitation of parenthood . . . presents the appearance of a pyramid," the Lynds said. "At the top, among most of the business group, the use of relatively efficacious contraceptive methods appears practically universal, while sloping down from this peak is a mixed array of knowledge and ignorance, until the base of ignorance is reached. Here fear and worry over pregnancy frequently walk hand in hand with discouragement as to the future of the husband's job and the dreaded lay-off."[18]

Almost four decades later a contradiction to the Lynds's findings is not in sight. Freedman, Whelpton, and Campbell found a direct relationship between income and use of contraceptives. Among couples able to have children when the husband earned $6,000 or more, 93 per cent of the wives did something to prevent conception. However, where the husband earned $3,000 or less, only 71 per cent of the wives tried to prevent conception. Working-class members also used contraceptives at a later stage in life and frequently were less successful at it than other groups.*

* Occasionally this gap is explained away with such theories that the poor have a higher fertility rate, that their sexual drive is greater,

This study, as well as Lee Rainwater's *And the Poor Get Children,* found that while the majority knew "something" about contraception, details about it and other sexual matters frequently were vague. "We thought about maybe three or four children would be nice; that is ideal I would say," one of Rainwater's study participants said. "What do you do about it?" she was asked. "We don't use anything; we just trust to luck."[19]

In Chicago when Greenleigh questioned welfare mothers whose youngest child was born out of wedlock, 90 per cent said they did not want a baby by the man they were going with, but "almost half the mothers in this group indicated that they had either no information about how to prevent conception or they used ineffective home remedies."[20]

Many ADC mothers with whom I talked about family planning were weary of trusting to luck or home remedies. Several were disturbed about the problems their large families presented. A Chicago ADC mother gave me this account of her pregnancies:

Me and my husband have seven children. My children were born —six of 'em was born every year—'45, '46, '47, '48—I missed

---

that they don't care how many children they bring into the world or, as one wag put it, that "procreation is the poor man's recreation." However, leading family sociologists have dismissed these arguments.

J. Mayone Stycos, director of the International Population Program at Cornell University, wrote in the February 1963 issue of *Marriage and Family Living*: "When asked to name the ideal number of children, or when asked whether or not they want more children, lower class women in societies as different as Peru, Lebanon, Puerto Rico, Jamaica and India do not regard the question as meaningless, and do not favor very large families. Three or four is generally seen as the ideal number and most women who have four children do not want any more."

In 1962 the Florida State Board of Health questioned 2,623 mothers in their public health clinics whose median number of children was four. Almost three-fourths said they wanted no more children. More Negro patients wanted no additional children than whites—a total of 78.3 per cent to 58.8 per cent.

'49—and '50, '51. Sometime I'd do housework and then I'd be pregnant and it wouldn't last long. Believe me when I tell you, mindin' seven children I'm a nervous wreck. What can I accumulate on aid with a house of kids. Now my kids is growin' up. We waited nine years and now I've got this 14-month-old baby. So I got stuck with this baby.

Q. How did it happen?

A. I had got disgusted. This particular time I had one kind of actin' up in school and I'd call my husband to come over. He'd always contribute to the kids when he's workin'. We never had no run in or nothin'. I'd call him when I'd be kind of stuck and disgusted and he'd come over and he'd talk to 'em and he'd also wup 'em. So this particular time me and him was talkin' and we did decide that we'd go back together and that's when I'd come up pregnant. I went out with him but I didn't want any more kids and with all I had he shouldn't want any more either. He's the type who doesn't like to use anything from havin' kids—a lot of men's like that. Well, after he did that, well, I figured it couldn't been no love. With all the kids we got we couldn't support 'em. We'd been on relief, different things on and off for the last years—nine, somewhere along there . . . off relief and on relief. I figured that if you couldn't support your family just don't get any more kids. But I never could show him the way. I just want two years of rest before I die. I've never been away from my kids in my life. I just want two years.

Q. When you said "he didn't want to use anything," did you use anything?

A. I want to tell you somethin'. When you is a country girl or a country boy you has to be in the city for quite a while before you gets the word that you should get hip. I didn't know nothin' about nothin' to use no more than just ordinary things men buy at the drug store, you know. But now I consider myself hip. I know what to use, but I didn't then because I was just a girl and I didn't know nothin' about goin' out and mixing with people. See, I never had that kind of time.

Q. There was no doctor who gave you that information?

A. No. See, my kids was born at the county [Cook County Hospital] most of 'em. At this particular time they didn't tell you nothin' about using nothin'. Now when I did begin to get hip to myself I ask the doctor if he could space my children for me or stop me from findin' kids. And he told me that if they would stop me from findin' kids I'd lose my health and findin' kids hadn't done anythin' to me and for that reason "we wouldn't stop you unless it was doin' something to your health." This was fifteen years ago, so in due time I just kept havin' 'em.

Whether this woman and tens of thousands like her will keep "havin' 'em" may depend frequently on the policies of public hospitals, clinics and welfare departments in all parts of the nation. These policies and their rationale are as varied as some of their phrasing is delicate. In Chicago, when Dr. Karl Meyer, administrator of Cook County Hospital, was confronted with demands to open a birth control clinic, he told reporters: "Birth control is a socio-economic problem, not a medical one."[21] In New York, when I asked the State Board of Social Welfare for its policy, I was told that it regards "birth control in public assistance solely on the basis of medical necessity." And this, according to another board rule, permits care "for conditions in a person that cause acute suffering, endanger life, result in illness or infirmity, interfere with [her] capacity for normal activities, or threaten some significant handicap."*[22]

When I was a caseworker in Buffalo, I mentioned to a supervisory employee that I had a woman in my caseload with eight children who might like to know about the possibilities of birth control. "That's not part of your job," I was told. A caseworker at a nearby desk who overheard the conversation, snickered. Later, I

* Dr. John Rock, a Roman Catholic who helped develop the oral contraceptive pill and is author of the book, *The Time Has Come,* commented about these policies during the CBS Reports television program, "Birth Control and the Law":

"It's interesting that influential medical bureaucrats involved are the ones to call contraception an economic matter, while the welfare officials define it as medical. This is at least suggestive of an inter-agency shell game, and if it weren't so tragic it would be amusing. The underlying reason for this sort of buck-passing, of course, is the real, or what is more likely, the imagined threat of Roman Catholic opposition and political reprisals. Medically, this situation is unquestionably unethical. Politically, I believe it is quite unnecessary."[23]

asked several of my coworkers what the policy was about this subject and no one knew of any official doctrine, but "that you just don't talk about it."

Today a handful of states provide tax-supported birth control services.* These are furnished by health departments in Alabama, Florida, Georgia, Mississippi, North Carolina, South Carolina, and Virginia. Most of these states offer contraceptive advice and devices through their maternity clinics. North Carolina's State Board of Health, for example, cooperates very closely with the Planned Parenthood Federation of America. "Most, but not all, of our county health departments have active contraceptive services available," Dr. James F. Donnelly, director of its Personal Health Division, wrote me. "We supply contraceptive services to 4,000-6,000 individuals a year."

Federal agencies in the health and welfare business have conducted a careful tippy-toe policy of non-involvement. The U.S. Public Health Service still refers to a 1942 policy memorandum that said, in part: "Should the State Department of Health decide on its own initiative to undertake a child-spacing program in accordance with the health laws of the State, the Public Health Service would give the proposal the same consideration as would be given to any other proposal in connection with the health program of the State."[24]

The Bureau of Family Services of the Federal Welfare Administration told me that it has received no material from any state which identified birth control services as part of its medical program. "The Bureau has no policy on either side of the issue. Where a state chooses to provide birth control information and/or devices as a

* The Illinois Public Aid Commission, in the fall of 1962, in the midst of its argument over birth control said that its survey of states showed that six state welfare agencies had provisions for referring to and paying for family planning services. These were New Hampshire, New Jersey, North Dakota, Virginia, West Virginia, and Wisconsin. Illinois State Auditor Michael J. Howlett, a member of the Public Aid Commission, subsequently challenged the validity of the survey.

part of its medical service to recipients of a federal-state assistance program, such services can be included for federal matching funds which are available for administrative costs and payments. States may define medical care as they wish so long as their definitions are reasonable."

Among local welfare departments these policies have the uniformity of a New England quilt. Many make no mention of the subject. Some departments say they have no policy on birth control, others quietly spell out policies in staff memos. A few tell caseworkers to advise on family planning, many say workers are not competent to do this. Several urge workers to refer their cases to Planned Parenthood clinics, many prohibit such referrals. Some will pay for private physicians to provide information, others will disallow such payments. While some permit caseworkers to discuss the subject, others will allow them to talk about it only if the recipient brings it up first. Here are some examples.

In California . . .

An April 13, 1962 office memorandum of the Sacramento County Welfare Department told caseworkers:

> Although this matter was commented on by your training supervisor, Harold Smith, during your training last fall, especially regarding the Agency's policy in this matter, much material is covered during the training period and it is possible that the significance of this was missed or misunderstood at the time. The Agency policy on this subject has been the same since the department was established in the 1930's. Each director has maintained this policy. The policy most recently stated by Mr. (John) Corey on Feb. 9, 1962 is as follows:
>
> If a client asks for birth control information such client is referred to a doctor or religious counselor. If the doctor sends Welfare his bill, Welfare does not pay it. We never refer to the subject unless the client mentions it specifically, at which time she is referred either to her doctor or religious counselor.

In Michigan . . .

The Detroit Public Welfare Commission on Dec. 16, 1958, acknowledged that relief recipients have the right to decide how large a family they should have and what "conception control" should be used. The caseworkers could not suggest families limit the number of children, but "when a recipient raised the question first," they could discuss it and refer them to a clergyman or private physician. The policy statement said "the Detroit Department of Public Welfare will approve payment for the office visit."

"No Department of Public Welfare employee," the statement continued, "may give information about, or refer a welfare family to any health clinic administered by the Detroit League for Planned Parenthood, Inc."*

In New York . . .

The New York City Department of Welfare, the largest in the nation, on Oct. 8, 1958, sent a memorandum to its staff that said:

> The dissemination of birth control information or therapy for non-medical reasons by staff of the Department or panel physicians is not a function of the Department of Welfare and is prohibited.
>
> When a panel physician is assigned by the Department to treat a recipient of public assistance and in his opinion such recipient medically requires birth control advice or the aid of contraceptive measures, he shall refer the client to the appropriate municipal hospital. Referral shall not be made to voluntary hospitals and voluntary hospitals will not be reimbursed for any contraceptive services given. The final determination of the medical need and the provision of contraceptive services by municipal hospitals will be determined by the particular hospital in accordance with the policies of the Department of Hospitals.

In Maryland . . .

* Prior to this statement the Detroit League for Planned Parenthood had pressed the city for an official birth control policy. Surprisingly, the League approved this statement that prohibited workers from referring welfare recipients to its clinic. On December 10, 1958, the president of the League wrote Daniel J. Ryan, superintendent of the Department of Welfare:

"I am glad to be able to report to you that the board of this agency believes that the present commission policy is basically sound and provides a good framework within which this question can be wisely resolved. . . ."

In an October 23, 1962, memorandum to all local welfare departments the State Board of Public Welfare's policy was announced. It said:

> Freedom from fear of unwanted pregnancy when the family cannot assume added responsibility can serve to promote the integrity and security of the family. The worker, in helping married parents understand and develop plans for the nurture of their children, upon recognizing the situation in which child-spacing becomes a desirable means of cultivating financial responsibility and independence and an instrument for protecting the mother's health and family security, or upon the request of the parent, shall make referral to a Planned Parenthood Clinic or to the family physician for child-spacing information as a normal resource made available by the community to married parents. The only exception to this policy is where the worker is made aware that planned child-spacing violates the religious or moral convictions of the parents.

In cities and counties that have restrictive policies, welfare department staff members have resorted to subterfuge in order to provide relief recipients with both birth control information and devices. For example, several counties in New York State have quiet "arrangements" to pay for the birth control pill if the prescription is routed through a drug store, but not if the pills come from Planned Parenthood centers. In one county this means that the physician at the Planned Parenthood clinic writes out a prescription for the pill to be filled at the local drug store. The prescription form carries the address of the center, but not the name "Planned Parenthood." The center would sell a month's supply of twenty pills at cost, for $1.60. At the drug store the same pills cost the welfare department between $3.00 and $3.50.

In Chicago, before the Illinois Public Aid Commission voted to provide birth control information and devices, a caseworker freely admitted to me that she violated a department rule that forbade referrals to planned parenthood clinics.

"I'm probably not the only one who has done it. Others have done it too. I've tried to get around the policy by directing them . . .

let's say to the center or to the immediate vicinity of the clinic for information."

"How will you do that?"

"By getting them as close as you can where the clinic is located."

"What would you do, for example, if I were your client?"

"Well, we'd talk about how hard it is to manage and how difficult it must be to have so many children and we might wonder if you wanted all the children. And by this time you probably would be telling me that you didn't know what to do and 'I would like to know something to do' and in this way I'd suggest the closest center and say 'Why don't you go over there and discuss this with the director?' "

Most welfare commissioners know that large numbers of their staff share these feelings and may follow the same surreptitous practices. They are uncomfortable with a problem that rarely has neat administrative guidelines and frequently is frayed with emotion at its borders. Some find themselves in a Jekyll and Hyde position: They are the chief spokesman for a department whose policy—either written or whispered—they personally and privately reject. A veteran welfare commissioner from a county in New York speaks for many of his colleagues in the nation in this tape-recorded interview. For reasons he explains, this conversation with me has to carry a guarantee of anonymity.

Q. Do you have a department policy about birth control?

A. Not a stated policy as such, but let me explain first. Our county is one made up of many religious groups. I would say the Catholic group is 50 per cent or more of the population. Of course, that is the group that has a very strong point of view about it. As a public official you realize you can do a certain amount of leading but you can't get too far ahead of the point of view of your community. And it is a hot issue any time it comes up. The idea that any public funds could derive partly from Catholic taxpayers could find their way to clinic work or anything that contributed to the knowledge of birth control is very repugnant to a part of the population. Of course, it's such a controversial issue—you know how the newspaper boys hop on it immediately—it's wonderful news if you can get your public official into controversy with any part of his community. So actually, I've got to say to you we shy away from it in spite of the fact that I . . . many of us in the department I think have a good deal of conviction that the day needs to come when people wouldn't be denied this information simply because they are poor and at the bottom of the heap. We never felt we dared have workers make it a policy just to refer people who needed this information to those places.

Q. Did any incident ever come up that helped formulate this policy so that you shied away from it?

A. Well, I'd say definitely so. Many years ago there was some question about our department as to whether we weren't in back of the scenes helping too many people to go to the right places to get this information, and this man made it very plain to me what the Church point of view would be and how they would view a public department that actively cooperated . . .

Q. Incidentally, what type of man was this? Was he a public official, a community leader . . .

A. No, this man was a man who had gone into the priesthood and rose very high in Catholic Charities of the archdiocese. He was interested in all social problems but here's one he just viewed differently because of his background.

Q. What did he say? Did he say it in so many words?

A. Well, it really was a friendly thing. He really did it as a friendly thing. He said, "There are rumors that you—through your department—are promoting the planned parenthood idea of contraception and for your own good, you had better realize what the view of the Church and a lot of your public is about this, you know.

Q. Was there some truth to these rumors?

A. On the part of individual workers and probably in the absence of very much guidance.

Q. For example, I understand now that in your county referrals are made but payments for the pills go through a drug store and are hidden that way because you cannot make payments directly to Planned Parenthood.

A. Yes. At the present time there could be no payments to Planned Parenthood. That would certainly stir up a terrific—well, it would be a regular cyclone in the different fiscal offices. In other words, at the present time, any official policy has to be in terms of people who for health reasons would need information or help. And like any other health thing with supplies, we would pay for it through the drug store. I don't think we're talking about anything unusual. You'll find it in all parts of the state exactly this way and perhaps your book will break some ground on it so that eventually public officials can do more of what they need to.

Q. Is there an unofficial policy too?

A. I wouldn't say so. I think there is knowledge that a good many people are interested. There are folks that need and are getting this information.

Q. And they are quietly referred to the Planned Parenthood centers by the case workers?

A. Yes.

Q. And you know of this?

A. Yes, sure.

Q. How do you feel about all this?

A. I would hope that the time would come pretty soon when the things that need to be done can be done without any particular surreptitious aspect to it, but we haven't arrived there yet.

Q. Do you feel that the issue is strong enough that you would lose your job?

A. Why, I think that in the past any commissioner in New York, in this state or neighboring states, would. At least there would have been such a controversial situation that the job wouldn't have been worth much as far as doing all the other things that needed to be done. It's a deep-rooted and, I'm sure, a very sincere belief on the part of the one religious group.

Q. Were you ever approached by the Planned Parenthood people to do something?

A. I wouldn't say so. I was approached to go to meetings.

Q. You would not go to a meeting of Planned Parenthood?

A. I never did. I was approached once by the president that the annual meeting was coming up and he was saying he would very much appreciate if I would attend, and so on.

Q. Why didn't you go?

A. Because I think I was trying to avoid this public issue over this thing which I didn't think was going to buy anything for anybody. The minute you go to an annual meeting you're asked to sit on the dais and all the rest of it . . . this is a type of sanction they probably sought and I wouldn't want to give. I was in accord with their cause although I wasn't as courageous as would be called for to become a part of it as a public official.

Q. Let's say all of these side issues were not present and this was a decision to be made by a welfare commissioner in the same way a decision is made whether to send someone to a hospital or not, what would your decision be?

A. My decision would be not to force such information on anybody but have workers explain that there is such information available and make it easy for them to get it if they wanted it. I would no longer limit it to cases of health hazard; I would take the whole social and economic situation of the family into account. On the other hand, I would never be a party to bulldozing anybody against their better judgment into going and getting this information. That I think would be my decision. It's simply that I don't see why it shouldn't be just as available to some unfortunate person without money as it is available to others, as it is available to me and my family as it is to most families. I would like to make it just as free as information about headache or anything else.

Q. But you can't?

A. No, I can't.

It is the gadfly of the controversy, the Planned Parenthood Federation of America, that has spent the past four decades trying to make the knowledge as available as information about headache. It traces its lineage back to 1921, when Margaret Sanger formed the American Birth Control League that provided the crusading zeal of an Anthony Comstock to remove part of the law he wrote. While still engaged in skirmishes against restrictive statutes and policies, Planned Parenthood operates 174 clinics throughout the nation that provide not only birth control services but help for childless couples as well. In the past five years—from 1958 through 1962—birth control patients increased 68 per cent. Of the total 187,000 patients served, about 20 per cent were welfare recipients and 66 per cent had incomes of less than $75 a week.

With the exception of the few state health departments that provide these services for the poor, Planned Parenthood is the only welfare group that serves some of the families who cannot afford a private physician. When its task is contrasted with need, Planned Parenthood is in the position of a lumberjack armed with a penknife. For example, the approximately 38,000 relief recipients served throughout the nation are fewer than half of the indigent families who could use birth control help in New York City alone. Dr. Donald J. Bogue, director of the University of Chicago's Community and Family Study Center, has estimated that 1 per cent of the population of any area represents the number of indigent families who would be in need of some kind of birth control services. His rule of thumb allows for mothers of child-bearing years, who have had two children, who have not yet started to practice birth control, or who are not practicing a reliable method of birth control.

In the effort to obtain help with this mammoth task, Planned Parenthood physicians and clergymen on many occasions have found themselves talking to each other. For example, in October 1962 the Federation held a symposium, "Public Welfare, Medical Care and Family Planning," in New York City for which more than 2,000 invitations were sent to officials of government and private health and welfare agencies. The lack of response was so noticeable that one of the speakers, William H. Robinson, a member of the Illinois General Assembly, closed his talk with a request: "I would like to see the hands of those in this audience who are not officially connected with Planned Parenthood." The stenographer's notes read: "About a dozen hands were raised."

But if Planned Parenthood frequently talks into an echo chamber, sometimes it provides information for the informed. "I think a lot of their publicity is directed for the middle classes," a public welfare caseworker told me. "They have difficulty reaching that part of the population which could best use it. I think this would be true of anyone with large families. They're just not getting the message. Because anybody in the middle class, they've all heard it."

Like other welfare agencies, Planned Parenthood has had difficulty penetrating the poverty culture and, in some cities, understanding it. A well-staffed clinic, for example, in one part of town may be empty of relief recipients for a reason as remote as one I observed in Chicago: A caseworker could not get a Negro mother to see an obstetrician simply because his office was in a white neighborhood and she did not want to risk potential insults.

It will take more than leaflets mailed or pushed under a doorway and clinics in private or public hospitals to make an impact in the slums of our cities. It will require scattered store-front offices, in the very neighborhoods where needy families live. This, of course, will cost money; far more than Planned Parenthood supporters can raise. In 1962 about three-fourths of its $4.3 million expenditures came from contributions from 70,418 individuals and 762 foundations. Although these gifts have been mounting, the organization is in a financial squeeze because its successes have been increasing at a faster rate than income. For example, in 1962 pill patients numbered 43,406, an increase of 200 per cent over the previous year. An annual supply of pills for one woman costs about $25. In a city of 50,000 population, with 400 women on relief using the pills, Planned Parenthood estimates the annual cost for complete birth control services to be about $20,000, or $50 per patient. The expensive pills and a far greater patient load require many affiliates to charge a fee. For an ADC mother even $2.00 a month plus transportation costs to visit a clinic in many states may literally mean that she has to deny food to the children she already has.

In short, no single private agency today can contribute to research and education and still provide services for a comprehensive family planning program in this nation. Government money will have to play a major role in the expensive areas of research and services. The first place to take significant action is in the research sector. This is one part of the birth control tangle where there is a growing accord among all religious groups. There is general agreement that government research funds have been woefully inadequate. In 1962 total federal research relevant to birth control amounted to $4.1 million, for 197 projects. Dr. John Rock, the Catholic physician who pleaded for an end to the fight in his book, *The Time Has Come,* revealed that one of the unannounced recommendations of a federal study group of which he was a member, included a request for a minimum of $16.6 million a year to develop new means of family planning.[25] These, of course, should include extensive research into the rhythm method, acceptable to the Catholic church.

Leading Catholics have made similar requests. Two years before Dr. Rock's book was published, Notre Dame's Father O'Brien urged Congress or the administration to direct the National Institute of Health to begin a "crash research program" to make the rhythm method 100 per cent effective.[26] When Dr. Rock's views were published, his spiritual leader, Massachusetts' Richard Cardinal Cushing, while disagreeing with the physician's interpretation of Catholic theology, significantly said: "He makes an eloquent, and much needed plea for federal grants to perfect the so-called rhythm system so that it might become a means of controlling births, which is not only morally acceptable but also scientifically accurate."[27]

But investigation into other potential chemical and mechanical birth control devices must be increased also. For today no total solution has been found. The expensive birth control pill, viewed by many as a major breakthrough in the field, is still too new to permit sweeping claims. Many physicians want to see more medical evidence about its safety and others want to have more information about its acceptability.* Meanwhile, a number of medical fertility specialists are urging stepped-up research for the intrauterine method which involves a plastic coil that a physician places in the womb which prevents pregnancy.

But before research and services can be expanded as they should, many Americans of all faiths will have to insist that their public officials cut through the emotional underbrush that surrounds birth control. The federal government is showing some cautious advances

* In Charlotte, North Carolina, where the single publicized "pill clinic" for public welfare recipients has been operating since November 1960, the effort has been called successful by Wallace H. Kuralt, director of the Mecklenburg County Department of Public Welfare. In the first twenty-two months, with welfare paying the bill and the county health department providing the service, 264 women were accepted. Twenty-eight were discharged, six for side reactions to the drug, eleven because they no longer needed it, and eight because they moved away. Nineteen were tardy in taking the pill leaving a total of 206 taking it regularly. No pregnancies were reported, even among those patients who have not returned regularly.[28]

in this area. For example, the hands-off policies of previous administrations were reversed in the spring of 1963, when it was revealed that the United States is now offering to help other nations with population growth problems if they request it. Furthermore, President Kennedy has said that we should know more about the whole reproduction cycle and that information about it should be made more available.*

The worn argument that tax dollars from Catholics cannot be spent for a service that is contrary to their belief is as valid as a Democrat refusing to pay taxes in a Republican administration or a Jew failing to file a return because the Army buys ham to feed its troops. At the same time, the few who want to use the birth control issue as a handy vehicle to pit Protestants against Catholics had better be expelled from the dispute.

The issue is not to have a Catholic doctor, nurse, or welfare worker advocate anything foreign to their personal convictions.

The issue is not to force on welfare recipients a birth control device that their conscience prohibits them to use.

The major issue is to make information about all methods of family planning easily available to all Americans. Welfare workers must be as free to suggest that a welfare recipient seek this advice as they are to suggest that an employment agency might help with a job problem or that night school might resolve illiteracy.

It is time for the leadership of every community—and this includes private and public welfare officials—to leave behind the

* On April 24, 1963, at his regular Washington news conference President Kennedy answered the following question: "Will you accept the recommendation of the National Academy that we should participate in international birth control studies, supply of funds . . . ?"

A. "Well, we are participating in the study of fertility and reproduction in the United Nations, which is an international study, at the present time. Now, if your question is: Can we do more should we know more, about the whole reproduction cycle, and should this information be made more available to the world so that everyone can make their own judgment, I would think that it would be a matter which we could certainly support."[29]

whispered conversation and talk about the issue out loud. The penalties of silence will be severe, for more strident voices will fill the void. In 1962 a bill was introduced into the Mississippi Senate that would have forced every mother of an illegitimate child to attend a birth control clinic under the penalty of a $500 fine, six months in jail, or both. With the continuing rise of welfare costs, radical spokesmen are bound to occupy more of the platform. They will argue not for the only valid issue in the dispute—the right to choose—but will shout for tax savings by making the poor have fewer children because they are too expensive. It will be a clamor Americans will regret.

9

THE WELFARE CURTAIN

In a nation that has 170 million radios, 1,763 daily newspapers, more than 55 million television sets, and an occasional communication satellite whirring in outer space, we have been unable to explain the pockets of poverty that exist a few miles from where most of us live. We have listed them, enumerated them, tallied their cost, and charted their rise, but we have failed to show why they persist. The have-nots today are foreigners to the haves, and the estrangement has grown amid suspicion, distrust, exaggeration, and distortion. The inability to understand poverty in the midst of a land of plenty has stalled the attack and thwarted a solution. It is one of the prime problems of public welfare.

What exists in the nation today is a welfare curtain that has been fashioned by a variety of contributors both from within and without the social work field. They include Americans who approach poverty as they do a cripple—they simply look the other way. They include those bombastic orators whose verbal strides long ago outraced the facts that should accompany their charges. They include some legislative bodies whose so-called welfare economies today require ever-larger expenditures tomorrow.

But they particularly include those who have accepted the responsibility to relieve poverty, if not to try and eliminate it. Americans have not been alerted to either the proportion or the significance of their task. They are dependent upon the public for support of difficult and costly programs which this public does not understand. Too many times—whether it be the private agency social worker or the public agency caseworker and administrator—they have failed to show the problems clearly, to actively battle for their solutions in the political arena, and to organize an informed citizen leadership whose help they must have.

Examples of this broad base of misunderstanding are neither isolated nor in short supply. Here are only a few:

". . . There is much ignorance and misunderstanding in regard to the basic purposes and provisions of social welfare programs," an executive of a group of New York City private welfare agencies told me. "The boards of our agencies with a few exceptions have remained silent during this period when these programs, particularly public assistance, have been under attack."

"I suppose the reason any exposé of the situation is frowned on, or considered unnewsworthy," the city editor of a large Texas newspaper told me, "is due to the fact that we think we're living in a rosy world and prefer to act like the ostrich and bury our heads in the sand and let the public welfare problem fade away."

In New Jersey, while I was discussing a welfare problem case with the local commissioner, he cautioned me not to use the details even though the family could not be identified. "You know, good casework is not to talk about a family's problems unless you can help them," he said.

And in a small New Hampshire town, a public welfare caseworker who wanted to campaign for housing reforms so that old age recipients would not have to live in roach-infested riverfront flats, said: "My state employers frown on us caseworkers becoming involved in community problems unless strictly within our limited work."

These attitudes and admonitions have contributed to a climate in which public welfare is freely translated into public distrust. These suspicions are voiced by most Americans when they talk about "that welfare mess." In the course of research for this book, I have asked a number of laymen what they think about public welfare today. A few sample interviews sound like this:

I don't think they should get any more. I have some opinions on that, and I think that all of the people on relief should be made to work because I think half of them are bums. And I can see them. I work in my father's diner . . . and I see them in there during the daytime. They drink up their checks. And that's that. I think they should take all these able-bodied men who are on relief and put them to work. If they are doing nothing else, they can pick up the papers in the city. I think it's a lot of baloney, all this relief stuff. There's jobs for them if they want to work, and they don't. Now, it makes it bad for the people who really need it. . . . I can see them every day sittin' in front of the library, walkin' around, half loaded.

• • •

There are some that don't deserve it. There are some that do deserve it. If I felt that someone really was in need of something, I would love to help them. So there are lots that don't deserve it and they are being helped. How do you figure it out?

Q. You have a feeling there may be lots that are getting help who should not be getting it?

A. I am sure . . . I'm sure there are . . . yes, sir. I am quite sure there are.

Q. Do you have any reason?

A. Yes, I would say, yes, because my husband is semi-retired now. Before he was in the restaurant business in New York and we had a lot of Puerto Ricans and they were getting relief and they were working, elevator operators, you know, working in factories, and we knew they were getting relief checks.

Q. Did you ever report any of them to the welfare department?

A. No . . . for that we would have to put ourselves on a spot. It was just one of those things. You know what I mean . . . It's a very hard question. . . . And then you see these people up in Newburgh and you feel that . . . Did you see that TV program . . . that one family? I felt like sending them a CARE package, knowing that his truck broke down . . . and no way of making a living. And we sit back . . . we're comfortable and we see all that's going on. . . . . We wonder why they couldn't have more investigation made about cases like that, to find out whether they really should get relief . . . if they went into the homes and found out whether a man is working . . . Now, lots of women work, I know. My brother's factory in New York . . . the women work . . . and a lot of them collect relief . . . and a lot of them probably don't even say they're working.

• • •

It seems a lot of people are getting it and don't deserve it. You see people drive up in Cadillacs to pick it up. Of course, there's the poor people.

Q. Have you seen anyone drive up in a Cadillac?

A. No, I read it in the paper. I assume they put things in the paper that are true. I don't know anybody that's getting relief, but I think the poor people should get it. Those who need it . . . the needy should get it. Everybody should have a decent living, a decent place to live. But they shouldn't be taking advantage of it.

Q. What do you think is wrong with it now?

A. They go in there and as soon as they go in, they get relief. We're paying for it and they don't belong there, those people.

These interviews underscore the observation of Elizabeth Wickenden in her report, *Public Welfare: Time for a Change,* that "People cannot be expected to support a program whose purpose they do not understand in any terms related to their own needs and values."[1] For most Americans it has been a program that has been explained in a tedious compendium of statistics or in the headline-making prose that reported a relief chisler with a moth-eaten mink coat, or a mother who neglected her illegitimate children. Frequently they have ignored the former and taken most of their impressions from the latter. Social workers, in the meantime, go off to big meetings crowded with seminars, where they tell each other how they are misunderstood. There is a miffed acceptance of the status quo, exemplified by an apologetic paragraph like this:

The tragedy is that we in public welfare have been unable to convey the true picture. There are reasons, of course, for this poor job of interpretation. The subject is unpopular, for normally the average man prefers to avert his gaze. It is hard to personalize but we cannot parade in print the hazards of individual persons on relief; they are entitled to this much privacy. Consequently we must fall back on barren figures, and our efforts at interpretation are dulled by statistics.

Behind rationalizations like this rests social work's perennial problem child called confidentiality—the need to keep a secret lawyer-client-like relationship. Interpretation ranges from the attitude that the identity of a relief recipient is none of anyone's business—which is as it should be—to such a broad blanket of secrecy that, for example, prevented "Candid Camera" from filming in the elevator of a New York City building simply because a welfare agency was one of the tenants.

The principle of the confidential relationship between the social worker and his client is traced back to the Hebraic command written in the Talmud: "If you are told something, do not repeat it unless you are given permission to do so." In some parts of the nation this principle has been observed so faithfully that not only has the identity of the individual been kept secret but his problems as well.

Victor Weingarten, a public relations consultant to several welfare agencies, documented this from his own experiences:

> In one Eastern city the shortage of public facilities for young children awaiting placement is so acute that many sleep two to a bed in a city shelter. It was a matter of public record, but the Department of Welfare would not allow photographers into the shelter to take pictures. Why? Confidentiality, naturally. Breach of social work ethics! Better to let the children sleep doubled up than use the most potent weapon possible to shame the public into providing more adequate facilities.[2]

In another instance Mr. Weingarten told of "an agency in the West that needed foster homes for 59 Negro children. It had just about given up hope when NBC's 'Home Show' offered to include some of the children in a program designed to help find homes for just such hard to place children. The agency turned NBC down flat on the ground that it would rather have no foster homes at all than have any of the children appear. And so the children remained in their institution, gloriously unpictured, but unwanted too."[3]

In contrast, in 1962, Don Edwards of WSYR-TV, Syracuse,

with the cooperation of the Onondaga County Welfare Department, told the foster home shortage story in a sensitive half-hour show. The television film was so popular that it was repeated. The television station and the welfare department received more than 600 letters, many of them with offers to take children. The foster home problem was solved.

In the few instances where television producers have surmounted the confidentiality barrier, social workers frequently have become the most enthusiastic part of the audience. Two such examples are NBC's nationally shown "The Battle of Newburgh" and a documentary called "Superfluous People," shown over New York City's WCBS-TV. Both programs used films of relief recipients telling some of their problems, and copies of both films have been shown at social work meetings. The Newburgh documentary won for its producer a 1963 National Conference on Social Welfare award. The New York local show received wide editorial praise.* Both programs shattered the dictum of confidentiality.

In my own research for this book, the degree of confidentiality has varied from city to city. In New York, I was denied case records and face-to-face interviews with relief recipients. In Chicago records and interviews were available for the asking. In other parts of the nation many welfare commissioners made all facilities

* *America,* the National Catholic Weekly, wrote an editorial about the program that said in part: "The cameras trundled through the streets of Harlem, up shabby tenement stairs, into rat-infested flats. New Yorkers learned that exorbitant rents are charged for the worst housing in their city—four and five families sharing the same bathroom, the same kitchen; ten and twelve people living in the same room. Welfare money pays the rent.

"Television opened the eyes of the city to the subsidized misery of welfare. Author Julius Horwitz appeared on the screen to denounce 'This underworld of public assistance.' He said the American attitude is: 'Pay the money; don't show us these people; don't tell us about them; we don't want to know.'

"WCBS-TV did its best to prevent New Yorkers from looking the other way. It was great television."[4]

available to me. Each instance, of course, was predicated on the valid agreement that no single recipient would be identified.

Occasionally, confidentiality is used not to hide the failure of the relief recipient from public view but rather to hide the failure of a welfare department. All-purpose confidentiality of this sort is simple censorship and is contrary to the public interest. I am still asked why, when I wrote my 1960 welfare series, I obtained a job as a caseworker without telling authorities I was a newspaper reporter. The answer is as unfortunate as it is simple: This was the only way I could obtain the truth. The *Buffalo Evening News* required no sensational headlines of an undercover caseworker to sell its newspaper. Most of the papers are home-delivered and sales do not depend on eye-catching black type shouting from a newsstand. The editors approved the undercover approach after reports provided by informants inside the department differed radically from information given by State Welfare Department officials.

For example, the state officials said the average caseworker carried about 75 cases, but the Buffalo caseworkers providing me with information proved that they were carrying anywhere from 160 to 200 cases each. The state officials were silent about the fact that some relief recipients had not been visited for several years, that case records were incomplete, that some caseloads were uncovered because there just were not enough workers, and that re-checking of eligibility was delinquent for many months. Also left unsaid were the causes of these difficulties—that caseworker turnover exceeded 50 per cent, that few had the training to do the job, and that salaries were too low to attract and hold those with talent and enthusiasm. The curtain of quiet successfully obscured the difficulties and equally as successfully prevented a solution.* Unfortu-

* The fourteen-part series, "Our Costly Dilemma," showed that newspaper articles can be productive to a welfare department even though they are critical of its operation.[5] After the series was published, Erie County Welfare Commissioner Paul F. Burke issued a thirty-four-point reform program. Subsequently he credited the newspaper articles

nately, this is not an isolated experience.

For example, less than seventy miles away, in the city of Rochester, the Gannett newspapers have a long record of community service journalism that has required neither the sensational nor the dramatic. Yet one day a headline announced: "Imprisoned in Filth, Squalor, Depravity." It was a story based on the information of a Rochester policewoman reporting about the diseased, dirty, underfed, and beaten children whose welfare was ignored by a number of agencies. At the 1959 Annual Meeting of the New York Public Welfare Association, Clifford E. Carpenter, editor of the *Democrat & Chronicle,* told of the "why" behind this story:

> There is no great criminal here, no bloated social welfare executive feeding at the public trough. The Society for the Prevention of Cruelty to Children boss, charged with failing to initiate sufficient referral proceedings, pointed out among other things that his staff turnover in that department was more than 90% . . . cases were bounced like evil rubber balls from one new worker to another with nobody getting started . . . legal difficulties prevented quick decisions by Children's Courts . . . Back came the Welfare Department with a retort that foster homes are jam-packed . . .
>
> But why did it happen? It happened because all levels of social welfare workers, public and volunteer, clung to the great philosophy and conspiracy of silence they have shared over the years. Nobody went to the newspapers to insist crisply that institutions were jammed with children and something must be done about it. Nobody complained that foster homes were full-up and there was a lack of foster parents . . . nobody came out with a plea to the Board of Supervisors or the County Manager or any source at all for aid in fighting a degrading and horrifying situation.[6]

---

with spurring a list of improvements that included: a 30 per cent increase in caseworker staff; new technical positions including personnel director and employment counselors; an increase in beginning salaries of caseworkers to $4,500 a year, and the opportunity to fill all casework positions for the first time in five years. Commissioner Burke said that the series "created a dramatic change in the public's understanding of some of the difficulties of this department, its employees and the individuals it assists."

In some communities and states public welfare boards and committees have contributed to the welfare curtain. They have conducted the public's business in private and, as a result, have helped keep the problems of the poor private.

For example, welfare services in New York are controlled by the policy-making State Board of Social Welfare, a group of fifteen lay citizens. Similar boards exist in twenty-one states.* Newspaper reporters and editors receive no official notification of when and where meetings are held. Only for a session at the height of the Newburgh controversy was press representation encouraged. Virtually all of the discussions over program and policies are conducted by the Committee of the Whole in executive session. The decisions are then put on the record at a meeting the following day. A private welfare agency executive who asked to attend a board meeting was told by a state official: "Sure, you can come but actually, you know, most of the work is done by committees in executive session." Occasionally, these meetings produce a news release that is distributed to reporters, which details a particular action that the board wants publicized.**

* Twenty-one states have policy-forming boards: Alabama, Arkansas, California, Colorado, Illinois, Indiana, Kansas, Louisiana, Mississippi, Montana, Nevada, New Mexico, New York, North Carolina, North Dakota, Ohio, Oklahoma, South Dakota, Texas, Virginia, Wyoming.

Eleven states have administrative boards: Arizona, Delaware, Florida, Iowa, Maryland, Michigan, New Jersey, Oregon, South Carolina, Utah, Washington.

Thirteen states have advisory boards: Connecticut, District of Columbia, Georgia, Hawaii, Maine, Massachusetts, New Hampshire, Pennsylvania, Rhode Island, Vermont, Virgin Islands, West Virginia, Wisconsin.

** Sometimes even the detailed accounting of annual expenditures has been made less than clear. For example, the New York State Department of Social Welfare's annual report for 1958 provided round figures of expenditures under a subtitle: "Protection against Fraud." The 1959 report made no mention whatsoever of the total spent that year. The figures subsequently appeared as a supplement to the monthly Social Statistics.

Such "private" meetings of public welfare bodies are by no means peculiar to New York State. Arnold H. Maremont, the controversial former chairman of the Illinois Public Aid Commission, told Chicago journalists in a post mortem review of the state's relief fight, that one thing he wanted to accept credit for was the commission's new policy of open meetings. In May 1963 he told members of the Headline Club of Chicago:

No commission spending $700 million in a biennium should meet in private to sweep controversy under a hotel rug. Yet some of you may recall the difficulties we had in establishing such a policy last August.

The policy was and is vital. It is the only way to really involve the general public. Without the complete editorial treatment in recent months, would people know anything about public aid? Would they think about the problems? Would they care?

We felt it was essential to bring this dialogue into the open, to carry the issues to the people. We knew that some would agree, some would disagree, and some would be complacent no matter what we did or said. But we also knew we'd have no chance to institute any positive measures or to accomplish more than just sitting on the lid without a real public debate. Do you think that we could have even discussed birth control without such a policy?[7]

In New York the State Department of Social Welfare periodically reviews the work of local welfare departments. These are the equivalent of report cards for the localities. No effort is made to publicize these performance ratings. Occasionally, deficiencies in welfare operations come to light because of an investigation by another agency. For example, early in 1963 the New York State Department of Audit and Control criticized one county for overdrafts in the Aid to Dependent Children program totaling more than $100,000, because some welfare checks had remained uncashed for as long as three years, and because its own bookkeeping errors cheated it of $7,000 of state funds for home relief. Presumably the state welfare investigators found similar discrepancies but their report was not publicized.

The State Welfare Department also inspects the activities of all private child-caring agencies in New York. Although these agencies campaign for charity contributions, most of their income is from tax dollars which purchase their services. In 1961, $57 million was spent in the state by private institutions for children and by private child-caring agencies. Of this, taxpayers provided $42 million. Some of these private agencies received more than 90 per cent of their budgets from government funds. Yet the state's review of their operations is not publicized.

Because these reports are confined to welfare officials and the agencies themselves, there is no accurate way for the contributing public to evaluate their performance. Some, however, are bound to fall short of their announced program. In 1962, for example, a State Welfare Department survey of one such private family and child-caring agency was critical of its child welfare services. The report said, in part:

> Agency policies are in accord with good child welfare practice, well defined and in a form acceptable to the State Department of Social Welfare. In view of this, these policies should be utilized by the staff as a guide for actual practice. A review of a selective sampling of case records indicated a lack of correlation between the administrative structure of the Agency and practices per se. Record reading did not reflect that the quality of work performed was in keeping with the good policies of the Agency and Board interests. The existing discrepancy between written policy and practice has had a weakening effect upon the Agency's total program. This poses a most difficult problem and is worthy of exploration if the Agency intends to continue its Child Welfare program.

This agency received tax dollars and private contributions for its work. Should not the taxpayers and the voluntary contributors be told that their money is not buying the services they expect?

If the public has received less information than it should, the states have had fewer specialists to give it than they should. Public information, a major activity of other state agencies, usually is assigned a stepchild role in the welfare department. A minority of state welfare departments have full-time public information specialists. In May 1963, when the federal Welfare Administration called together all state information personnel—the first such meeting ever held—a total of seventeen reported full-time jobs. In one state public relations is combined with rehabilitation, and in another it is wedded to the surplus food program.*

On the federal level, welfare information too often has been confined to lengthy statistical treatises. Until 1962, when Mrs. Ellen G. MacQuarrie, the highly skilled social welfare reporter of the *Milwaukee Journal,* came to the Bureau of Family Services as Public Information Officer, an orderly news policy and public relations program was non-existent. Requests for information formerly were handled by a social worker who was an assistant to the bureau's director. Mrs. MacQuarrie is the first person with journalism experience in the bureau's information job. Her professional staff of five now is responsible for all press relations, publications, and reports. There is a new emphasis on public information that is part of the expanded plans for rehabilitation.

However, an active information program sometimes is inhibited by federal fear of overstepping the vague boundary between telling and selling. A pair of Department of Health, Education, and Welfare policies outlines the restrictions. The first warns that "information issued by the Department must never advocate but always explain."[8] The second dictates that "information issued by the Department must be in response to specific requests."[9]

These edicts place a large responsibility on the press to ask questions. But the fact of the matter is that too few questions have been asked—both in Washington and in many of the states. In some newspapers public welfare ranks among the most poorly reported domestic issues. A few have given credence to press critic A. J. Liebling's twin charges: "The theme of the undeserving poor

* In New York State where the total welfare staff has doubled in the last twenty years because of expanded programs and increased responsibilities, the public information office has remained a two-man operation. The director is principally responsible for eighty publications that are produced under the supervision of his office, and any public relations has been forced into the role of a sideline activity.

recurs as often as Groundhog Sees His Shadow or Tommy Manville Takes Another Bride." And that the "crusade against the destitute is the favorite crusade of the newspaper publisher because it is the safest." Sometimes a collection of welfare tidbits strung together may look like a major revelation to both an editor and his readers.

In a 1962 issue of *Editor & Publisher,* the leading journalistic trade weekly, Henry B. Jameson, editor of the *Abilene* (Kansas) *Reflector-Chronicle,* reported breathlessly:

We shook hell out of the community! And it was done with a series of articles on two of the dullest subjects you can imagine—the county budget and the world is going to pot . . . In view of certain disclosures of scandal, graft and rising costs in general in the welfare field in other parts of the country, and following some chatty meetings with our own county officials, I decided 'to look into' the welfare situation in Dickinson County. I discovered, to my amazement, that over 40% of the entire Dickinson County budget for 1963 is earmarked for welfare. This amounts to a startling average of $31.22 for every man, woman and child in the county going for welfare . . .

Mr. Jameson pointed out that "the research required the equivalent of about a full day," and reported that "the first article on the $31.22 per head cost was a real blockbuster. I received many complimentary calls but the real impact did not come until after the series was completed. I am still getting calls and letters. In many years of newspapering in Abilene since the war, I do not recall any single such 'public service project' which has made such a profound impact on the community with such high praise for me personally and for the *Reflector-Chronicle.*"[10]

Mr. Jameson's "discovery" may not be as significant as the fact that *Editor & Publisher* devoted almost a full page to his tale of "public service" indicating that its editors thought that this information would be of value to other journalists in the nation.

I wrote to the editors of fifty of the nation's major newspapers in order to find out how they covered public welfare and what some of their problems in this field were. Their comments were candid and showed little of the welfare hostility that social workers sometimes attribute to them. Most admitted that they cover the subject only on a catch-as-catch-can basis.

Frank McCulloch, day managing editor of the *Los Angeles Times,* summarized the most frequently mentioned problem: "I think our principal difficulty in covering such news lies in the enormous complexity of the subject. There are at least four government jurisdictions—federal, state, county and city—involved in some degree, and aside from the statutes which affect all, they seem to share remarkably little in common. Overlapping, contradiction and confusion seem to be the inevitable accompaniments not only of the various public welfare programs but of the stories concerning them."

Norman E. Isaacs, executive editor of the *Louisville Courier-Journal,* said: "The big difficulty about the public attitude on welfare stems largely, I feel, from the fact that newspaper stories for the most part tend to center on the difficult and complex budgetary stories or on the extreme cases."

"From this desk," John W. Bloomer, managing editor of the *Birmingham News,* said, "I would tend to blame lack of enterprise and ingenuity on the part of the editorial staff rather than secretiveness on the part of welfare officials for inadequate coverage."

An editor who declined to be quoted provided a four-sentence summary that describes the press-welfare relationship in too many cities in the United States:

"We do not have a reporter assigned to the welfare offices. When things crop up we usually send someone by to check or call them on the phone. There are very few items to pursue. Our welfare department gets into the news only once in a while and it's usually when adverse publicity crops up."

Only a few newspapers have social welfare specialists on their staff. The number of reporters attending a national welfare conference from outside of the city in which it is held can be counted without exhausting the fingers of one hand. This includes the

National Conference on Social Welfare, which is the equivalent of the American Bar Association meeting and attracts anywhere from 5,000 to 7,000 social workers to a week-long session. Unlike other large professional meetings which generate news, little effort is made to provide the press with the major developments in the field.

Emma Harrison of the *New York Times* and Eve Edstrom of the *Washington Post* are the two best-known journalistic names in the welfare field. The *Post* probably has run more probing welfare stories than any other newspaper in the nation. These have ranged from detailed coverage of the local Aid to Dependent Children scandal to a series, "Social Welfare Soviet Style," based on Mrs. Edstrom's six-week tour of the Soviet Union. She and her newspaper have won about a dozen journalism awards for welfare articles.

The two major national wire services, the Associated Press and United Press International, are without any specialist in this field. A national conference is covered by a local bureau reporter, who frequently is lost in a sea of welfare terminology and technicalities. Because these conferences attract delegates from all over the nation, the order is to get "something on the wire," and that "something" usually is restricted to a few paragraphs from a prominent speaker or an isolated reference to a controversy. More subtle and possibly more important changes and trends in the welfare field frequently are lost to the general public because the wire service reporter simply does not have the background to piece such depth stories together.

The interlacing of inadequate press coverage with poor, if not sometimes near-secret, information practices provides the basic pattern in the curtain that separates most Americans from the problems of the poor. The effects of these shortcomings are felt far beyond the often-heard call of "the public's right to know." The leaders of a community, particularly those in the political sphere, frequently gauge public issues from a stack of press clippings, the content of a television program, and the words of a radio commentator. The political leader rarely forges ahead of the concern of those he represents. Most often he reflects that concern and because of this, today most politicians know little more about welfare problems than do their constituents.

The welfare field has given them far too little help to understand the complexities. Public and private welfare workers too often have avoided these very people on whose decisions their work depends. Frequently, like a prim maiden avoiding the puddles after a spring rain, they have sidestepped politics altogether. Individual participation has been lacking in most parts of the nation. When I searched through the biographies of the members of the Eighty-seventh Congress, I found a circus man, a smattering of professors, farmers, accountants, dentists, and doctors, but not a single social worker. In most state and local political bodies, social workers are equally prominent on the missing list.

Political participation has been largely confined to issuing position papers on a legislative proposal and reading a prepared text at a public hearing. "Social workers have been inconspicuous for much too long around the committee rooms, state legislatures and halls of Congress where the legal framework of our democratic society is built and mended," former Health, Education, and Welfare Secretary Abraham Ribicoff wrote in one of their professional journals.

"Your views should not be confined to dinner parties and membership meetings. They must reach your elected representatives. An annual statement of principles ground out by an organization's social action committee cannot be the whole answer. Most of these statements should be regarded as only a preliminary move in influencing welfare legislation. They are usually long and couched in generalities with strong moral overtones. They are not going to be much help to the lawmaker who has to decide immediately how to vote on a particular bill. . . . The men and women who write our laws need facts, not sermons," Mr. Ribicoff said.[11]

Those few social workers who have battled successfully in the political halls for their causes frequently are as irritated about their inarticulate brethren as is the outsider. Mrs. Sally E. McMahon, education and training program director of the Cook County Department of Public Aid, a professional social worker and part-time lobbyist in Illinois, told me:

Social workers always operate on the theory that politics are dirty and you just, as a professional person, do not get mixed up in it. You are not very nice if you do. Another thing, money to support welfare comes in great part from public funds. You get money through the legislative bodies. Legislative bodies have ways of reacting to the appeals of various departments. Now, who is better able to tell them how things ought to be than the social worker? Well, this would be fine if the legislator could understand the social worker, but they can't do so because the social worker hasn't learned how to talk to the legislator. You should hear these people when they testify—using that lingo of the profession. I've had legislators take me aside afterwards and ask me what they were talking about. "What's an acting-out child, Sally?" one of them said to me recently.

If vocabulary for the social worker has been a problem, a specific word has been an anathema. That word is "compromise." Too often it is non-existent in the social work lexicon. I have the feeling that some welfare workers consider it part of "the duty" to watch the flames of defeat consume their banners of perfection. This startles the politician whose pablum is compromise. All this has troubled him when he has had to respond to the public clamor to change "the welfare mess."

In a 1962 speech before the regional meeting of the American Public Welfare Association, Tom Adams, Florida Secretary of State, told his audience about the political evolution of his state's controversial Suitable Home Law that was to cut off children from the relief rolls. He said the legislators were under pressure "to do something," but most of them were not knowledgeable about public welfare.

Unfortunately, welfare people seem to have adopted a hands off policy. Thus the two groups most directly concerned—public welfare specialists and legislators—rather than working together through effective communication and engaging in a cooperative endeavor, acted as two separate groups each standing off from the other. Finally, a committee of legislators spent nearly two years studying the issues, as well as conferring with our welfare administrators, and made recommendations that culminated in the Suitable Home Law. The State Department of Public Welfare neither sponsored nor opposed the legislation. The law was not suggested by welfare people. As a matter of fact they did not offer a realistic legislative program that would eliminate the criticisms and at the same time protect the welfare of the dependent child. Rather, the law was imposed upon them. To me, this was almost tragic. The people involved in the day to day activities—the people most knowledgeable in the field, failed to suggest a proper program and seek enlightened public support for it.[12]

In a number of communities those who speak for welfare have confined themselves to converting the converted. They have brought their message to those who long ago have adopted it themselves, but they have shied away from the non-committed or the hostile audiences. Too few have sought invitations before such forums as the Rotary and Kiwanis clubs, the Chamber of Commerce, and the local Taxpayers League.

Occasionally, there is a dramatic exception. One of these occurred in welfare-famous Newburgh when a medical social worker in that city's welfare department enunciated her opposition to the city manager's restrictive policies in a voice that was clearly audible. At the height of the controversy Ann F. Power met with out-of-town newspapermen to provide "the other side of the story"; she denounced the Newburgh plan before public and private meetings, before her superiors, and her neighbors. She wrote letters to the local newspapers that quarreled not only with the city manager, the newspaper itself, but with the majority of the citizens in the community.

"Today's participation may leave us with no job tomorrow, but we believe in our profession," was the way Ann Power opened a speech before a group of New York state welfare workers. Her introduction was no exaggerated statement.

In mid-1961, Newburgh officials appealed to the State Civil Service Commission to eliminate the local Medical Social Worker position. After her speech before the welfare audience, Miss Power said she was prohibited from speaking to any other social work groups. "Some of the anonymous 3:00 and 4:00 A.M. phone calls were not so easily ignored," she told me, "nor could they be halted for some months." But two years after the controversy, the payroll sheets of the Newburgh City Welfare Department still carried the name of Ann F. Power.

It is this willingness for personal combat that must be adopted by welfare workers in hundreds of cities and towns in the nation. Wilbur F. Storey, a Chicago newspaper editor, once suggested that the function of a newspaper is to give the news and raise hell. Today part of the function of a social worker is to give the facts and raise hell. The communications media will have to transmit that hell-raising, and the leaders of each community—from bankers to politicians—will have to listen if the dilemma of the wasted Americans is to come into full view.

10

WHOSE WELFARE?

. . . The stark fact before us is that great numbers still remain unemployed. A large proportion of these unemployed and their dependents have been forced on the relief rolls. The burden on the federal government has grown with great rapidity . . . The lessons of history, confirmed by the evidence immediately before me, show conclusively that continued dependence upon relief induces a spiritual and moral disintegration fundamentally destructive to the national fiber. To dole out relief in this way is to administer a narcotic, a subtle destroyer of the human spirit. It is inimical to the dictates of sound policy. It is in violation of the traditions of America. Work must be found for able-bodied but destitute workers. The federal government must and shall quit this business of relief.

FRANKLIN D. ROOSEVELT
State of the Union Message to Congress, January 4, 1935

Today, in a year of relative prosperity and high employment, we are more concerned about the poverty that persists in the midst of abundance. The reasons are often more social than economic, more often subtle than simple . . . But merely responding with a "relief check" to complicated social or personal problems—such as ill health, faulty education, domestic discord, racial discrimination, or inadequate skills—is not likely to provide a lasting solution. Such a check must be supplemented, or in some cases made unnecessary, by positive services and solutions, offering the total resources of the community to meet the total needs of the family to help our less fortunate citizens help themselves.

JOHN F. KENNEDY
Special Message to Congress, February 1, 1962

These are excerpts from Presidential messages that voice a people's concern about poverty in a time of national deprivation and concern about poverty in a time of plenty. They span twenty-seven years in which public welfare has changed from the hoped-for temporary to the grudgingly acknowledged permanent. The words of two Presidents are the bench marks of two poverties.

Mr. Roosevelt's concern with the nation's first major welfare program came when 5 million unemployed were on relief. Its emphasis was on a government tide-me-over for an idle and stalled nation. Mr. Kennedy's complaint was that a tide-me-over is inadequate if it continues for several generations. It was an acknowledgment of a persistent poor among the affluent.

It is clear that today the public welfare department is no longer just a short-term government finance agency. It is the social seismograph of every community. It records the tremors of a faulty school system, the closing of a plant, the layoffs caused by automation, and the distinctions that are made between a face that is black and one that is white. Its difficulties are internal and external and their sum has made the big relief question both repetitious and louder:

What are we going to do about the welfare mess?

The agenda is long, and the answers are neither simple nor certain. They must come from a variety of sources. Some may be in the purview of the economist, the social worker, the educator, or the industrialist, the politician, and certainly the people he represents. How well each provides these answers will determine what happens not only to public welfare, but to much of the nation as well.

For the economists who have examined poverty, the key answer is within the nation's economic growth rate. And the analysis is that its forward progress has been mediocre at best. Leon H. Keyserling, in his poverty study for the Conference on Economic Progress, showed that from 1953 to 1961 the annual growth rate averaged only 2.5 per cent, while a 4.2 per cent rate was needed to fully use our labor and our plants. "For the period as a whole this caused us as a nation and a people to forfeit an estimated $344 billion in total national production and to forfeit almost 22½ million man-years of civilian employment opportunity," his report said.[1]

Furthermore, Mr. Keyserling tied these developments directly to poverty. When economic growth and employment were reasonably high from 1947 to 1953, poverty was dropping at an annual rate of 2.7 per cent. But in the next seven years Mr. Keyserling calculated that poverty was reduced at an annual rate of only 1.1 per cent. To speed this drop and raise the annual economic growth rate he and other economists have urged greatly increased government spending.*

There is little doubt that America's industrial system must expand at a faster rate than it has if the war babies grown to manhood and the widening shadow of automation are not to overtake it. The stubbornly high unemployment statistics make it more than a chance possibility that we will have a permanent, enforced leisure class at the economic bottom.

However, for the many-faceted problems that have accrued in the welfare departments of the United States, mere economic acceleration is not going to do the job.

And the major place to begin is in those welfare departments themselves. Some of the blueprint of reform was provided in the 1962 amendments to the federal body of public welfare laws. Some of the reforms, however, must be expanded and the tempo toward their goals vastly accelerated if the public charity bill spiral is to be halted.

Today the wonder word of welfare is rehabilitation. It rings through the halls of social work meetings. It is intoned in speeches of federal, state, and local relief officials. It has received its im-

* Among the recommendations of the Keyserling report were proposals to raise the federal budget by $16.5 billion by 1965 over what it was in 1963, to quadruple the federal per capita outlays for education, housing and community development, and to increase by two and one-half times the per capita expenditures for health services and research.

petus in mounting public dissatisfaction and it is spurred by those 1962 changes which emphasize that a variety of social work services must accompany every relief check. Public welfare amendments use the traditional government lever—money—in order to prod the states toward reforms. The key bait to progress is an increase in federal matching funds for services from 50 to 75 per cent.

New emphasis in rehabilitation is coming amid some impressive examples of successes in the past. Numerous demonstration projects have shown repeatedly what has become almost a worn truism: that if you reduce caseloads and provide skilled staff to counsel recipients, their chances toward self-sufficiency are increased. A parallel truism is that in most welfare departments the administrators and their workers have not been able to do what they know works. The Greenleigh report of the Cook County welfare department stated in one paragraph the difficulty that faces most welfare departments in the United States:

> The intensive study of the sample of 1010 active cases revealed that the problems of the families, other than financial need and medical care, are seldom identified by the caseworker. As a consequence, most are not remedied. The substantial potential for rehabilitation which exists in the ADC caseload is only partially realized, with the result that dependency is being prolonged and perpetuated, the future of the children is jeopardized and ADC expenditures continue to mount.[2]

The experimental projects to counteract such assessments have been conducted in small and large states alike. Only a partial list includes welfare departments in New York, California, Michigan, Virginia, Maryland, Florida, Pennsylvania, Texas, and the relief-troubled District of Columbia.

In a special review sponsored by the New York School of Social Work in 1961, Winifred Bell examined ten of these projects. Each contributed significant evidence to her statement that "substantial savings to the taxpayer could be secured by reducing caseloads of public assistance workers so that they have time to counsel actively the troubled families seeking financial assistance." Here are some excerpts from her summary of these projects:[3]

In Washington, D.C. . . .

The project involved 240 families with 900 children and was carried on from February 1953 to March 1954. Three skilled social workers were responsible for all of the counseling. They conclude that "the status" of the family was improved for 141 of the 240 families, as evidenced by increased financial support from 34 absent fathers, improved marital relationships in 32 families, improved health in 51 families, full-time employment in 18 cases, part-time employment in 9 cases, marked progress toward employment in 16 families, better housing for 23 families, and alleviation of school difficulties experienced by 9 children.

In Florida . . .

The project involved 505 families. After a fourteen-month period, about half of those families were no longer on public assistance. "By comparison, during that same period, about one-third of the cases carried by the regular staff were closed. Of the new applications handled by the experimental group, about 42 per cent were accepted for financial assistance while among the regular staff about 56 per cent were accepted."

In Pennsylvania . . .

"The economy of small caseloads (35 in the project of the Allegheny Board of Assistance) was demonstrated clearly . . . 98 cases, out of the project's 349 cases, were closed because of employment. Savings on assistance grants alone for these cases from the time they went off assistance until October, 1958, totalled more than $256,000."

In Indiana . . .

Lake County limited caseloads to 40 families for selected caseworkers in 1958 and referred only families who had been chronically dependent and showed signs of serious deterioration. Despite the gravity of these cases "it was found that the average rate of termination of grants for the total ADC caseload of the agency in 1958 was 19.4 per cent while the rate of termination for the 125 intensive cases was 28.8 per cent."

Many demonstration projects like this, however, never go beyond the demonstration stage although their results make it clear that they should. The check with officials of these and other projects conducted throughout the nation showed that often follow-up appropriations to provide staff to expand the projects were never made. For example, the Florida Department of Public Welfare told me: "The demonstration was never broadened, primarily because of lack of staff." Even more affluent welfare departments in New York counties, such as Westchester and Niagara, have had to abandon demonstrations because of lack of follow-up money.

The Washington, D.C., welfare department in July 1963 was beginning to adopt some of the methods learned from a project that started ten years earlier. "It is tragically significant," acting director Donald D. Brewer wrote me, "that ten years after the completion of this project, we are just now able to return to the basic concepts which the project firmly established."

One of the few demonstrations that has moved from the experimental to the operational stage is the family rehabilitation program devised by Community Research Associates of New York, a nonprofit welfare consultant agency. Instead of concentrating on the problems of the individual, this plan requires that the welfare worker attack the difficulties of the entire family. What began as an experiment in St. Paul, Minnesota, in 1947 is now operational in eighty-six Minnesota counties and in a smattering of welfare departments throughout the United States.*

The increasing activity in rehabilitation and prevention is an encouraging beginning. The demonstration projects, the isolated

* These include six counties in Pennsylvania, and one each in Connecticut, Nebraska, and California.

instances where some have become operational, the new federal impetus spurred by the President himself, all have provided public welfare with a new optimism that it can make a liar of the adage, "Ye have the poor with you always."

But the glitter of promise may be obscuring the ability to deliver. For rehabilitation to the taxpayer means simply: Back to work. To the welfare worker the same word may mean an ADC child receives a passing mark in a spelling course that it used to fail, or that its mother has learned how to buy groceries in quantity at the supermarket. The very word "rehabilitation," as it is used today, indicates an assumption that is often unwarranted. Like its popular companion word, "retraining," it assumes a starting point that is not there.

For many residents in America's troubled neighborhoods the social service words should be "habilitate" and "train." Many of the government's well-intentioned programs have shot over their heads. For example, far fewer welfare recipients than originally anticipated have qualified for retraining under the Manpower Development and Training Act. Fewer still have been enrolled in some of the technical adult vocational education classes. You cannot retrain a man to be a computer operator if he does not have basic arithmetic and reading skills. You cannot retrain a man for a machine-orientated industrial plant if he cannot read and comprehend a company manual and sometimes is unable to accurately fill out its personnel application blank.

If the task today is to habilitate and to train, then often the vocational courses have to be held in abeyance until the educational preliminaries have been satisfactorily completed. Basic literacy education that will include arithmetic and English at least up to the eighth-grade level should be the first requirement of any program designed to shed the shackles of relief. The Chicago survey of literacy which indicated that more than half of the adults could not perform at a fifth-grade level showed dramatically what is needed. In July 1963 almost 5,000 relief recipients were enrolled in the elementary school program and another 2,000 were taking high school courses. This program, scaled to the needs of the individual community, should be duplicated in most cities and counties in the United States. It should be mandatory for all recipients who need it.

But if the welfare recipients are to receive basic education that will represent the first step toward making a living, thousands more will have to receive another fundamental education that will show them how to make a life. There will be few immediate and clear dividends such as the Chicago man who learned to read and now earns his living as a taxicab driver. Frequently progress will be measurable only in succeeding generations—generations that now are consigned to follow the path of their predecessors as statistics on the relief rolls.

This basic education will mean teaching women such middle-class-take-for-granted items as cleaning a refrigerator, or washing dishes, or scrubbing a floor. It is these vital how-to-make-a-life courses that in the long run may prove more valuable than the training programs for the unemployed, but employable, relief recipient.

It will mean that home economic units will have to be organized in most welfare departments, and in the larger ones, in every high relief neighborhood. Model kitchens and living rooms will have to be provided as laboratories of housekeeping. They will have to be staffed with skilled home economists. The few welfare departments that have experimented with these housekeeping courses clearly have demonstrated the national need to expand them.

In Chicago, I had lunch with a group of ADC mothers who were students of Mrs. Lenora Collins, director of Cook County Welfare Department's Home Economics Training Center. During the luncheon, prepared by the mothers, we placed a tape recorder in the center of the table. The conversation showed what *habilitation* means:

MRS. A. When we first come, Mrs. Collins told us that the curtains was all made here, so I looked at the curtains, so I thought I'd make some and asked about material, how much you needed, and so I made some for the kitchen windows. I thought about it while in class, 'cause you know I never would have thought about making any curtains.

Q. How did they turn out?

MRS. A. Turned out nice, everybody around there likes the curtains.

Q. What do you mean by "around there"?

MRS. A. In the building. And now I'm supposed to make some for a lady downstairs for her kitchen window. It's a lot of fun. It takes a little time and attention. Like your kids going to bed and you sit down for a few minutes and you start sewing and it relaxes you.

Q. What else did you learn?

MRS. A. Like the "day system."

Q. What do you mean?

MRS. A. Well, it's like certain days you wash. I wash three times a week at least, and you iron once a week and I do wash Monday, Wednesday, and every Friday. You just got this system and it works out pretty certain and you have so much more time for the children, you go downstairs and watch them and you know what they're doin' and it's just pretty nice.

Q. How about this doing dishes before going to bed. Where does that idea come from?

MRS. B. Well, I used to say I'll have the boys wash the dishes in the morning. But after we discussed it here, I said maybe the kitchen would look better if I done 'em. And I thought I'd try and since then I'd have them [the children] wash dishes twice a day. And after dinner and at night I'd make sure there's no crumbs on the table. I notice it then and, you know, it's just a lot better than it used to be.

MRS. C. And another thing when you get up in the morning and you see the house is straight and you don't have to pick up behind children. When they take off their dirty clothes, they put 'em in the dirty clothes hamper, and after they get to bed I straighten out the living room. And in the morning when I get up, I don't have anything to do. Just make up the beds, dress them, and my house is clean. Before, I never had no time. But now I got time and I eats with the kids. When I fix their breakfast I sit down and have breakfast with them. And I fix their lunch—well, I hardly eat lunch—but I sit down with them. Before I tried coming here I didn't have time to do that.

Q. It really works?

A. (chorus) It really works.

MRS. B. Every week you learn something different and something interesting. I mean, you probably could have thought of these things, but you never tried 'em, you know. But with someone else around . . . well, a person say that "I know I can't do this with all these kids I got," but Mrs. Collins said "Let's try it for a week, let's try it for a week." After a couple of days, you know, you feel pretty good. You'd be surprised, the energy, the time, and how close you are to your children, that makes a lot of difference.

MRS. C. Like today when I was coming over here I got up, I washed, cleaned up the house, and made the kids breakfast, and washed, and had them clean up before I came here.

MRS. A. And I have everything planned what I'm going to fix for dinner.

Q. How about money? Has it saved you any money?

MRS. B. Before I came over here I wasn't usin' none of that non-fat dry milk at all. I know I didn't like it. I never tasted it, you know, how it go. I got quite a few suggestions and things about going to different stores and you can save a lot of money with that non-fat dry milk. You'd be surprised. The kids say they didn't like it, but now they like to make it. You know, sometime they put a little cocoa in it or different syrups like strawberries and now it go like hot cakes.

MRS. A. Mine didn't want any. And now all of 'em drink it.

Q. How many do you have?

MRS. A. I have five.

Q. Do the kids notice any difference?

MRS. A. Yes, they know that you have more time to sit down and listen to their problems, they notice that you have more time to sit down and play games, like mine they like to play "pitti-pat" and "war," you know. You sit down in the evening and take time to play with them, 'cause summer time they don't watch television too much. They stay outdoors 'til 8:30 or 9:00 o'clock. Well, we sit down and we have a little entertainment in the evening, or I have one that's pretty poor in spelling, one that's not too good. And I have these little books I bought and I try to help them, you know, even during the summer so by the time school starts again they wouldn't be so backwards, you know. Because a lot of 'em, all they want to do is play. So now I have this time and then when I go to bed I really don't feel as tired as I used to do.

Before programs like these and many others designed to habilitate millions of Americans can become operational, public welfare must remove its major difficulty. And this is the lack of personnel to do the job. In the past, when the major emphasis was just to get the checks out, many welfare departments have been unable to keep positions filled. Now, with the emphasis on service, the staff needs have become much more acute.

The federal goal is to change the proportion of fully trained social workers in public welfare from 4.5 per cent to 34 per cent by 1970. With the projected staff increase, this means a goal of 28,050 public welfare workers with graduate social work degrees. But the graduate schools cannot provide the manpower. Unless a major compromise plan is provided, the optimistic talk about giving necessary services to relief recipients will die in the social work meetings where they are discussed.

A national campaign to provide workers to assist our wasted Americans must be initiated at once. It must have the vocal support of the White House in order to give it prominence among America's list of domestic problems. Such a campaign should include two areas: a large-scale effort for a program of volunteers, and secondly, direct support with federal funds to train welfare workers.

The early enthusiasm that greeted suggestions for a domestic Peace Corps has been allowed to wane. The administration has failed to pursue the idea for a national service corps with the same urgency that was used to remit a campaign pledge for the original Peace Corps. It is unfortunate that most Americans today are more aware of the underdeveloped peoples in Ghana than in Georgia, and in Honduras than in Harlem.

The potential for alerting Americans about the difficulties of fellow citizens a few miles from where they live may be the most valuable contribution such a national corps of volunteers would provide. The argument that America's youth has been overwhelmed by materialism and is reluctant to provide service for the sake of serving has been shattered by the thousands who have streamed into the Peace Corps. It is time that some of the energy expanded in the jungles of South America also is allocated to the problem-filled underbrush of our big cities.

Secondly, the federal government must provide the money and the leadership that will make the turnstile guardians of relief more than transients, and the word "social worker" in public welfare more than a fiction. The emphasis must be placed on undergraduate training. Federal funds augmented by state tax dollars must be used to provide undergraduate facilities for welfare-oriented programs in all states that have major welfare staff problems. Some of the existing undergraduate programs in 133 colleges and universities across the nation must be strengthened. Others can be added at state universities and teachers colleges. In smaller states where demands for welfare workers are less, the federal government should support an undergraduate training program in a regional institution that serves several states. The present graduate schools of social work can provide the very necessary short-term courses for existing welfare staffs.*

To fill these classrooms, it will take a massive recruiting drive not only by the government but by local private and public welfare agencies as well. It will be a campaign that must begin in the high schools where today's sophomores and juniors are pressed by the councilors to make their career choices.

This recruiting drive is not only necessary for quantity, but for quality as well. Social work is not getting its share of the most talented American youth. Of the 1962 National Merit Scholars who are among the most able of the nation's high school graduates, only one of 1,041 students listed her career choice as social work. Furthermore, of 1,287 former Merit Scholars planning graduate work, only three indicated it would be in social work.

* Wayne Vasey, dean of the George Warren Brown School of Social Work of St. Louis University, already has provided such a tentative plan which calls for schools of social work in Missouri and Illinois to provide these courses.

For the professional social worker who takes rightful pride in the graduate training he, or she, has received, it will mean the need to compromise. In the past, too many social workers have been on the tail end of new educational approaches rather than in the vanguard. Too often the social worker's critical eye has centered on the potential loss of professional standing rather than on the potential gain of a strengthened public welfare system. It is time that the focus is shifted.

Any comprehensive effort to fill adequately the many public welfare jobs must be accompanied by a new look at the job itself. All the training will be to no avail so long as some caseworkers can calculate that their salary is only a few dollars different from that of the relief recipients whom they are serving. Salaries of caseworkers should be set by the states and should be pegged according to regions and responsibilities. If necessary, the federal government, which now can pay up to 75 per cent of these salaries, should raise even further its share if it means insuring an adequate wage for the worker. At the same time, the high caseloads obviously have to be drastically lowered.

As long as many county welfare departments have a caseworker turnover that ranges between 30 and 50 per cent annually, there is clearly more wrong with this job than just the weekly pay check. The Secretary of Health, Education, and Welfare should order a national job evaluation study of the caseworker's task to be conducted by a combination of welfare and top private management officials. They should produce a blueprint that would sweep away some of the paper work encumbrances and that could become operational and uniform in every welfare department in the nation.

Besides vigorously tackling the caseworker dilemma, the federal government must provide new and greater administrative leadership. The valid emphasis today is on the family. If this is to be effective, the tangle of existing relief categories will have to be reorganized. Federal law now permits welfare departments to combine the aged, blind, and disabled into a single category. This is insufficient.

The old-age assistance category is dwindling every year as more and more older Americans qualify for social security. Congress should consider moving these old age assistance recipients out of the welfare offices by blanketing them into the Social Security Act. However, to keep clear the definition between social security, which is an insurance program, and public welfare, which is government charity, such a move would have to be accompanied by annual tax revenues payable to the Social Security Administration for these old-age recipients. The money for their checks should not come from the insurance funds.

This means that the federal government would have to standardize eligibility requirements for old-age assistance under social security. The resources or lack of resources of a recipient would have to be checked when he applies, and subsequently he would have to be held responsible for reporting any changes in his financial circumstances. The success of such a transfer would hinge also on whether Congress provides a program of medical assistance for the aged under social security. The absence of this program has been a key reason for the relief needs of the elderly. If it is not approved, the old-age assistance rolls will be reduced at a far slower rate.

Because caseworkers would no longer visit aged relief recipients, individual communities would have to provide a mechanism to fill this breach. Loneliness, the disease that afflicts older Americans on and off the welfare rolls, would have to become a major community concern. A strong volunteer program that would center on visiting the aged could accomplish this task. The volunteer zeal in many communities has yet to be fully utilized, particularly at a time when many American housewives are becoming restive for lack of something to do.

Furthermore, the federal government should urge that states combine all other relief categories into a single family program in which eligibility rules and payments are standardized. Federal, state, and local welfare policies will have to be relaxed to permit experimentation. For example, welfare departments should be encouraged to permit working mothers in ADC families to retain a portion of their earnings if there is an indication that such vocational beginnings will lead to self-sufficiency.

At the same time all welfare authorities—with the Department of Health, Education, and Welfare hopefully providing the leadership—should brush away the taboos that now surround the birth control issue. All adult welfare recipients should have this information freely and easily available to them.

But these proposals concern only a portion of our national relief problem. They include some of the major difficulties that public welfare itself must correct. By themselves they will do little to lessen the social and financial cost of the wasted Americans unless they are accompanied by both shifts of ideas and policy far beyond the doors of the local public welfare office. The most skilled and dedicated caseworker will do little to reduce the relief rolls if he is walled in by the bricks of racial discrimination and the mortar of inferior education. These are the prime outside problems of public welfare today.

The nation can expect little more than high relief bills if the racial statistics in the preceding pages are going to be repeated. So long as 66 per cent of the high school graduates in a Negro neighborhood of Cleveland cannot find a job, so long as that Negro steel worker in Buffalo continues to pay more than double the rent of his white counterpart, and so long as Negro housing and income remain at the low water mark of any statistical chart, then the payroll of prejudice will continue to be tabulated in the local welfare department. The President of the United States in his 1963 Civil Rights message made integration a moral argument. Public welfare bluntly makes it a financial argument. Together they make integration a necessity.

Negroes will have to furnish more than civil rights demonstrations to make this "necessity" both obtainable and, more importantly, workable. The void of Negro leadership in the slums of many communities will have to be filled. There has been too little effort expended by Negroes for Negroes. "We have become so involved in trying to wipe out the institution of segregation, which certainly is a major cause of social problems among Negroes," the Reverend Martin Luther King, Jr. has acknowledged, "that we have neglected to push programs to raise the moral and cultural climate in our Negro neighborhoods."[4]

Integration does not stand alone with a "must" label. The reorganization of our educational thinking—particularly in the central city schools—is equally important. New job opportunities for the wasted Americans will hardly be of value if they do not have the skills to meet those opportunities. The sorry record of ADC youngsters in America's schools certainly should provide impetus for change. Dr. James Conant's analysis of these schools—which showed that city schools are far inferior to their suburban counterparts—is tantamount to an admission that public welfare tomorrow will pay exorbitant interest rates for education's failure today.* The emphasis must be shifted from the academic training that is meaningful for the few to the vocational training that is meaningful for the many. Education in work skills must be the paramount concern of these schools.

The poor cousin role that vocational training has played in the educational system must come to a halt.** Within the program itself the emphasis on agriculture and homemaking—which now

* Dr. Conant pointed out that expenditures per pupil in some of the wealthy suburban schools is as high as $1,000 a year while in big city schools it is less than half that amount. Furthermore, while some suburbs have as many as seventy professionals per 1,000 pupils, slum schools are staffed by forty or fewer professionals per 1,000 pupils.[5]

** Edward T. Chase in his *Harper's* article, "Learning to be Unemployed," made it clear in one paragraph how undernourished this segment of American education is:

"Ninety per cent of all U.S. schools offer no training for jobs in industry; 95% offer none in selling or merchandising although there are now more job opportunities in these fields than in production; only about 18% of high school students in the urban areas are getting any sort of preparation for work. Indeed the federal government spends ten times as much on the national school lunch program as on vocational education—which commands only 4% of all current expenditures on public education."[6]

enroll the majority of the 4 million teenage and adult "vo-ed" students—must be shifted to produce the technicians the economy needs. Local school systems must listen to the warnings expressed in 1962 by the vocational education consultants of the Secretary of Health, Education, and Welfare. "Investment in vocational education," they said, "is today grossly incommensurate with the national interest and federal responsibilities."[7]

Congress, heeding some of these warnings in the fall of 1963, began to bolster the skimpy vocational education appropriation which in the last fiscal year totaled $79.3 million under a series of different acts. The consultants urged the federal government to spend "at least $400 million."[8] This is an expenditure proposal that we can hardly afford to ignore.

The local welfare commissioner should press for expanded vocational training and be a participant in the planning of these programs. New training-for-work plans should be formulated and supervised by a separate board of vocational education composed of educators, welfare officials and leading local industrialists. The latter should be in a position to provide, with the help of state and federal employment services, detailed manpower projections for the area.

Further, local school officials must provide teachers and facilities that will permit welfare departments to organize classes for relief recipients who fail even basic tests of literacy and homemaking. They must become full partners in correcting earlier educational deficiencies.

In the past such cooperation between welfare departments and other community agencies whose efforts affect a relief recipient too often have been restricted to verbal pledges rather than practical performance. It is time that the heads of a variety of agencies, including housing, health, employment, and education, be welded into an effective team under the highest state and city leadership. This means that every governor and every mayor might organize state and city human renewal councils as vehicles for such teams.

These human renewal councils should not be restricted to

monthly meetings of top executives but should include liaison at the bottom as well. Caseworkers in local welfare departments should meet periodically with state employment councilors, with homemaking teachers, with housing inspectors, and health officers to plan for the individual families each of them serves. This could open the way for a task force approach to high incident welfare neighborhoods. Welfare, employment, housing, and health workers together might attack the problems of one family, then one house, and one street, at a time.

Many private welfare agencies will have to scrutinize their own caseloads and ask themselves a prime question: How many of the poor are they really serving? Those who largely have consigned the struggle against poverty to government will have to return to the fray or face the increasingly valid argument that too many charity dollars are subsidizing services for those who do not need charity.

But all of the reform efforts in and out of the welfare departments cannot be carried out until their purpose is understood. The difficulties and shortcomings of the relief recipients cannot be confined any more just to agency file cabinets. Newspaper, television, and radio editors will have to describe the issues in terms far more compelling than the annual welfare cost figure or the occasional arrest of a chiseler. The human ingredients of these needs will have to be provided by the local welfare departments with a candor that too often has been lacking in the past.

For public welfare there is no single beginning. There are a host of beginnings for it and the entire community. Too many of them have been postponed for too long. They will carry no bargain price tags. Any meaningful effort, whether it is providing technical training or raising the salary of a caseworker, will require money. Poverty, as the failures in these pages have shown, cannot be bought off with a minimum welfare check. It will have to be augmented by the tax appropriations for this list of reforms. Alleviating poverty may not have the glamour of the space program or the conquest of the moon, but it will require the same commitment from every American. It is a commitment that can no longer be deferred.

The boy who said:

"Guys say no work, no nothin' no work, and then you say 'to hell with it, let the job come to me.' "

The woman who wrote with a red pen:

"Only broken panes. Three windows. They will fix them but never fix them since four years now."

They and 7.5 million other wasted Americans are waiting.

NOTES

1. GO TO THE ANT, THOU SLUGGARD . . .

1 Leon H. Keyserling, *et al., Poverty and Deprivation in the United States,* Conference on Economic Progress (Washington, D.C.: April 1962), p. 2.
2 *Newburgh News* (June 1961).
3 Walter A. Friedlander, *Introduction to Social Welfare,* 2nd ed. (Englewood Cliffs, N. J.: Prentice-Hall, Inc., 1961), p. 11.
4 *Ibid.,* pp. 57, 62.
5 Quoted in Richard Hofstadter, *Social Darwinism in American Thought* (Boston: Beacon Press, 1955), p. 91.
6 N. Masterman, ed., *Chalmers on Charity* (Westminster, Eng.: Archibald Constable and Company, 1900), p. 20.
7 Quoted in Friedlander, *op. cit.,* p. 69.
8 Lewis B. Gunckel, *Charities Review* (November 1897).
9 Franklin Delano Roosevelt, Second Inaugural Address, January 20, 1937.
10 Jenkin Lloyd Jones, in an address, "Doctrine of Individual Responsibility" quoted in *Human Events* (November 24, 1961), p. 794.
11 John F. Kennedy, *Message from the President of the United States Relative to a Public Assistance and Welfare Program,* 87th Cong., 2nd Sess., House of Representatives, Document No. 325, February 1, 1962.
12 Peter Marris, "A Report on Urban Renewal in the United States," in *The Urban Condition,* Leonard J. Duhl, ed. (New York: Basic Books, 1963), p. 117.

13 Fred A. Ross, "Racial Amalgamation Propaganda versus Segregation and Racial Cooperation," address given at Edgewater Park, Miss., April 16, 1962.

2. NEWBURGH: THE CATALYST

1 "Committee to Report on Proposed Welfare Consolidation," Report to City Manager Albert J. Abrams, April 18, 1960.
2 Press release by Commissioner of Public Welfare, February 25, 1961.
3 Address before Newburgh Optimist Club, March 2, 1961, reported in *Newburgh News*.
4 "Trends in the Cost of Public Welfare and other Municipal Functions, City of Newburgh, New York, 1951–1961," prepared by Bureau of Research and Statistics, New York State Department of Social Welfare, January 30, 1962.
5 *Newburgh News* (May 2, 1961).
6 "Report of the Committee to Study Welfare Operations to City Manager Joseph McDowell Mitchell," May 8, 1961.
7 *Ibid.*, p. 15.
8 *Ibid.*, p. 16.
9 Official transcript, "In the Matter of Investigation of Administration of Public Welfare in the City of Newburgh," Buckley Reporting Service, Albany, New York, July 7, 1961, p. 51.
10 *Newburgh News* (May 23, 1961).
11 *Newburgh News* (June 13, 1961).
12 *Newburgh News* (June 19, 1961).
13 Statement by Newburgh City Manager Joseph McD. Mitchell, before the Moreland Commission, September 12, 1962, Hotel Roosevelt, New York, N.Y., p. 2.
14 The memorandum included the thirteen points that are in the official minutes of the Council of the City of Newburgh of June 19, 1961. The memorandum and press reports of the thirteen points deleted one word from the official record. In No. 10, ". . . who are not disabled, blind (ambulatory) or otherwise . . .", the word in parenthesis was eliminated.
15 *Newburgh News* (June 20, 1961).
16 Associated Press membership enterprise story (June 26, 1961).
17 Official transcript, Buckley Reporting Service, *op. cit.*, p. 58.
18 *Ibid.*, p. 100.
19 Letter dated July 5, 1961, reprinted in *Human Events* (July 21, 1961), p. 467.

20 *New York Herald Tribune* (July 19, 1961).
21 This poll later was used in "Public Welfare in the State of New York," Moreland Commission Report (New York: January 15, 1963), pp. 10, 11.
22 *Truth Seeker* (July 1961).
23 *Newburgh News* (June 26, 1961).
24 Quoted in "Newburgh: Evaporation of a Symbol," broadcast by Charles Collingwood, July 23, 1961, published in *Columbia Journalism Review,* Pilot Issue (Fall 1961), p. 29.
25 *Ibid.,* p. 29.
26 Press release, State Board of Social Welfare, Saranac Inn, July 18, 1961, p. 3.
27 Shown January 28, 1962.
28 Associated Press (August 18, 1961).
29 *Newburgh News* (September 12, 1961).
30 *New York Herald Tribune* (November 2, 1961).
31 *Columbia Journalism Review, op. cit.,* p. 30.
32 *San Francisco Sunday Chronicle* (August 27, 1961).

3. THE SHADOW CHILDREN

1 "Task Force Report—Summary Findings, Special Investigation, Aid to Dependent Children Cases" *Congressional Record,* Vol. 108, No. 176 (September 28, 1962), p. 20040.
2 Department of Health, Education, and Welfare, *Eligibility of Families Receiving Aid to Families with Dependent Children* (Washington, D.C.: U.S. Government Printing Office, July 1963).
3 Dr. Helen M. Hacker, "The Family Then and Now," mimeo. by Family Service Association of America (November 13, 1961), p. 6.
4 *Ibid.,* p. 10.
5 Clark E. Vincent, *Unmarried Mothers* (Glencoe, Ill.: The Free Press of Glencoe, Inc., 1961), p. 93.
6 Paul H. Jacobson, *American Marriage and Divorce* (New York: Rinehart and Company, Inc., 1959), quoted in Family Service *Highlights* (Fall 1960), p. 120.
7 Greenleigh Associates, Inc., *Facts, Fallacies and Future*—A Study of the Aid to Dependent Children Program of Cook County, Illinois (New York: 1960), p. 19.
8 Bureau of Family Services, Department of Health, Education, and Welfare, from preliminary reports of "Biennial Statistical Report on Characteristics of Families Receiving Aid to Dependent Chil-

dren, for a single month, November or December, 1961" (1963).

9 *Ibid.*

10 National Study Service, *Planning on Behalf of Troubled Children and Their Families,* General Report, Part I (Kansas City, Mo.: 1962), p. 7.

11 Greenleigh Associates, Inc., *Addenda to Facts, Fallacies and Future* (New York), p. 109.

12 Greenleigh, *op. cit.,* p. 19.

13 Prepared by Bureau of Public Assistance, *Illegitimacy and Its Impact on the Aid to Dependent Children Program* (Washington, D.C.: U.S. Government Printing Office, 1960).

14 Report on *Aid to Dependent Children Program, Monroe County Department of Social Welfare* (Rochester, N. Y.: June 1960).

15 *New York Times* (November 9, 1960).

16 W. L. Mitchell, Commissioner of Social Security, decision in the matter of the Conformity of the Louisiana Plan for Aid to Dependent Children under Title IV of the Social Security Act, Washington, January 16, 1961.

17 Mississippi Children's Code Commission, *What About These Children?,* a study of children removed from Aid to Dependent Children Rolls (Jackson, Miss.: 1958).

18 *Congressional Record, op. cit.,* p. 20047.

19 Moreland Commission Report (New York: January 15, 1963), p. 50.

20 M. Elaine Burgess and Daniel O. Price, *An American Dependency Challenge* (Chicago: American Public Welfare Association, 1963).

21 Gordon W. Blackwell and Raymond F. Gould, *Future Citizens All* (Chicago: American Public Welfare Association, 1952).

4. THE OBSOLETE YOUNG

1 *Wall Street Journal* (June 7, 1963).

2 Quoted in *Youth and Work,* Newsletter of National Committee on Employment of Youth (New York, June 1961).

3 *Ibid.*

4 From letter (November 21, 1962) submitting preliminary report of the Mayor's Task Force on Youth and Work, *Youth in New York City: Out-of-School and Out-of-Work.*

5 Bureau of Educational Research, Cleveland Public Schools, *Unemployed Out-of-School Youth Survey* (Cleveland, O.: 1962).

6 James Bryant Conant, *Slums and Suburbs* (New York: McGraw-Hill Book Company, Inc., 1961), p. 18.
7 Unpublished material provided author by Building Service Employees' International Union.
8 *Building Maintenance* (June 1960), p. 7.
9 All examples reported in *Automation Trends,* publication of Cook County Department of Public Aid (Chicago, Ill.).
10 Donald N. Michael, *Cybernation: The Silent Conquest,* a report to the Center for the Study of Democratic Institutions (Santa Barbara, Cal.: 1962), p. 15.
11 The author is indebted to the New York City Police Athletic League Youth and Work Program and its sponsor, the New York State Division for Youth, for making this interview and the one on page 81 available to him.
12 Harrison E. Salisbury, *The Shook-up Generation* (New York: Harper and Row, 1958).
13 Armour and Company and United Packinghouse Food and Allied Workers, AFL-CIO, and Amalgamated Meat Cutters and Butcher Workmen of North America AFL-CIO, *Progress Report Automation Committee* (Chicago: June 19, 1961), p. 7.
14 Cook County Department of Public Aid, *A Study to Determine the Literacy Level of Able-Bodied Persons Receiving Public Assistance* (Chicago: August 1, 1962).
15 *Ibid.,* p. 93.
16 *Ibid.,* p. 41.
17 *Ibid.,* p. 49.
18 *Ibid.,* p. 97.
19 Marguerite H. Coleman, in interview with author.
20 Footnote 11, *op. cit.*

5. 65 PLUS

1 President's Council on Aging, *The Older American,* first annual report (Washington, D.C.: U.S. Government Printing Office, May 14, 1963), p. 43.
2 Department of Health, Education, and Welfare, *Aging* (Washington, D.C.: U.S. Government Printing Office, February 1963), pp. 4, 5.
3 President's Council on Aging, *op. cit.,* pp. 5, 6.
4 Bureau of Public Assistance Report, No. 48, *Characteristics and Financial Circumstances of Recipients of Old-Age Assistance, 1960* (Washington, D.C., August 1961), pp. 3, 5.

5 Committee on Aging, Community Service Society of New York, *Medical Care for the Aged,* background material for review (New York: March 1962).
6 Bureau of Family Services, Department of Health, Education, and Welfare, advance release of statistics on public assistance, March 1963 (Washington, D.C.: May 10, 1963), Table 13.
7 John F. Kennedy, *Elderly Citizens of Our Nation,* Message from the President of the United States, 88th Cong., House of Representatives, Document No. 72, February 21, 1963, p. 2.
8 *Time* (August 3, 1962), p. 47.
9 *New York Times* (June 2, 1963), p. 12E.
10 Special Committee on Aging, U.S. Senate, "Background Facts on the Financing of the Health Care of the Aged" (Washington, D.C.: May 24, 1962), p. 8.
11 Harold N. Willard, "A Community Hospital and Its Neighboring Nursing Homes," summary of speech at Institute on Nursing Home Administration of American Hospital Association, Boston, Mass., October 3, 1962.
12 Barbara Callahan, "What About Kerr-Mills?", special report in *Hospital Progress* (St. Louis, Mo.: *Journal of the Catholic Hospital Association,* April 1963).
13 "Medical Assistance for the Aged in New York State," statements by the New York State Board of Social Welfare and the New York State Department of Social Welfare at the hearing of the State Legislature's Joint Legislative Committee on Health Insurance Plans, New York, November 16, 1962, p. 21.
14 American Medical Association, *The AMA News* (Chicago: April 15, 1963).
15 Walter M. Beattie, Jr., from a letter for the author.
16 Ollie Randall, interview with the author.

6. THE TURNSTILE GUARDIANS

1 Corinne H. Wolfe, Chief, Division of Technical Training, Bureau of Family Services, Department of Health, Education, and Welfare, "Staff Training for Public Assistance—A Bench Mark and a Projection," address at National Conference on Social Welfare, Cleveland, Ohio, May 1963.
2 Council on Social Work Education, *Social Work Education* (New York: February 1963), p. 24.
3 Prepared by Mrs. Mary Alice Flynn for the Subcommittee on Public

Welfare of the Temporary Commission on Coordination of State Activities of the New York State Legislature, Albany, New York, 1960.

4 Department of Public Welfare, Baltimore, Md., *Public Welfare—The Needy Under the Shadow of Guilt,* 26th annual report (1960), p. 10.

5 State of California Assembly Committee Reports, Vol. 21, No. 2, final report, *The Assembly Ways and Means Committee, Subcommittee on Welfare Costs* (November 21, 1960), p. 29.

6 Bureau of Family Services, Department of Health, Education, and Welfare, *Public Assistance Personnel, Fiscal 1962* (Washington, D.C.: April 1, 1963), Table 8.

7 Department of Welfare, Baltimore, Md., *Public Welfare, op. cit.,* p. 11.

8 The Welfare Investigating Committee of the New Jersey Legislature, *Legislative Report on the Aid to Dependent Children Program in New Jersey* (Trenton, N. J.: January 1963), p. 78.

9 State of California, *op. cit.,* p. 33.

10 Erie County Department of Social Welfare Monthly Allowances, budget schedule used while author was caseworker, Buffalo, N.Y., January, 1960.

11 Department of Health, Education, and Welfare, *Eligibility of Families Receiving Aid to Families with Dependent Children* (Washington, D.C.: U.S. Government Printing Office, July 1963), Table 4, p. 19.

12 R. J. Bartow, "Where Does the Caseworker's Time Go," *Public Welfare,* Journal of the American Public Welfare Association (Chicago: October 1961), p. 164.

13 From unpublished data, Greenleigh Associates, Inc.

7. *PAY TO THE ORDER OF . . .*

1 Jacob Riis, *How the Other Half Lives* (New York: Charles Scribner's Sons, 1897).

2 Quoted in Charles Abrams, *Forbidden Neighbors* (New York: Harper and Row, 1955), pp. 144, 145.

3 Alvin E. Rose, "A Public Houser Speaks," speech published in *Public Welfare,* Journal of the American Public Welfare Association (Chicago: April 1962), p. 91.

4 Bureau of Family Services, Department of Health, Education, and Welfare, from preliminary reports of "Biennial Statistical Report on

Characteristics of Families Receiving Aid to Dependent Children, for a single month, November or December, 1961" (1963).

5 Greenleigh Associates, Inc., *Facts, Fallacies and Future*—A Study of the Aid to Dependent Children Program of Cook County, Illinois (New York: 1960), p. 13.

6 Moreland Commission on Welfare, *Factual Data,* prepared by Greenleigh Associates (New York: November 1962), p. 21.

7 *Ibid.,* p. 21.

8 *Ibid.*

9 J. Anthony Panuch, "Building a Better New York," final report to Mayor Robert Wagner, New York, March 1, 1960.

10 Moreland Commission on Welfare, *op. cit.,* p. 22.

11 Greenleigh Associates, Inc., *Addenda to Facts, Fallacies and Future* (New York), p. 54.

12 Housing and Home Finance Agency, 16th annual report, "Urban Renewal Statistical Data" (Washington, D.C.: U.S. Government Printing Office, 1962), Table VII-1 (corrected), p. 294.

13 Buffalo Municipal Housing Authority, *Ellicott Relocation: Objectives, Experience and Appraisal* (November 1961), pp. 32, 34, 35.

14 Urban Renewal Administration, "Relocation from Urban Renewal Project Areas Through December, 1961" (Washington, D.C.), p. 7.

15 Harry W. Reynolds, "The Human Element in Urban Renewal," *Public Welfare,* Journal of the American Public Welfare Association (Chicago: April 1961), p. 72.

16 Daniel Seligman, "The Enduring Slums," *Fortune* (December 1957).

17 Public Housing Administration, Housing and Home Finance Agency, *Mobility and Motivations—Survey of Families Moving from Low-Rent Housing* (Washington, D.C.: April 1958), pp. 40, 43.

18 The Welfare Investigating Committee of the New Jersey Legislature, *Legislative Report on the Aid to Dependent Children Program in New Jersey* (Trenton, N.J.: January 1963), p. 64.

19 *Buffalo Evening News* (January 19, 1963).

20 *Binghamton Sun-Bulletin* (July 27, 1962).

21 C. A. Sargent, from memorandum prepared for the author.

8. A WHISPERED SOLUTION

1 Allan F. Guttmacher, "The Challenge for Family Planning," ad-

dress at the Planned Parenthood dinner, San Francisco, May 15, 1962.

2 National Academy of Sciences, "The Growth of World Population," Publication 1091 (Washington, D.C.: 1963), p. 9.

3 *Speeches of Senator John F. Kennedy, Presidential Campaign of 1960* (Washington, D.C.: U.S. Government Printing Office), p. 210.

4 Ronald Freedman, Pascal K. Whelpton, and Arthur A. Campbell, *Family Planning, Sterility and Population Growth* (New York: McGraw-Hill Book Company, Inc., 1959), p. 40.

5 *Ibid.*, Table 4-1, p. 105.

6 *Ibid.*, p. 183.

7 U.S. Circuit Court of Appeals (U.S. v. One Package, 13F. Supp, 334, S.D. N.Y., 1936).

8 *Time* (March 10, 1961), p. 49.

9 John A. O'Brien, "Let's Take Birth Control Out of Politics," *Look* (October 10, 1961).

10 *Ibid.*

11 *Ibid.*

12 "The Churches Speak Up on Birth Control," pamphlet of Planned Parenthood Federation of America.

13 *Ibid.*

14 *Ibid.*

15 Freedman, *op. cit.*, p. 416.

16 American Medical Association, Special Committee to Study Contraceptive Practices, House of Delegate approval, June 1937.

17 American Public Health Association, policy statement at annual meeting, Atlantic City, November 18, 1959.

18 Robert S. Lynd and Helen Merrell Lynd, *Middletown* (New York: Harcourt, Brace and Company, 1929), pp. 125, 126.

19 Lee Rainwater, *And the Poor Get Children* (Chicago: Quadrangle Books, 1960), p. 57.

20 Greenleigh Associates, Inc., *Addenda to Facts, Fallacies and Future* (New York), p. 36.

21 *Chicago's American* (February 17, 1960).

22 New York Department of Social Welfare, correspondence with author.

23 Transcript of "Birth Control and the Law," *CBS Reports* (May 10, 1962).

24 Confirmed as existing policy in letter to author by U.S. Public Health Service, May 31, 1963.

25 John Rock, *The Time Has Come* (New York: Alfred A. Knopf, 1963), p. 196.
26 John A. O'Brien, *op. cit.*
27 *New York Times* (April 20, 1963).
28 Wallace H. Kuralt and Elizabeth C. Corkey, report presented at symposium "Public Welfare, Medical Care and Family Planning," sponsored by Planned Parenthood Federation of America, Hotel Roosevelt, New York, October 23, 1962.
29 *New York Times* (April 25, 1963).

9. THE WELFARE CURTAIN

1 Elizabeth Wickenden and Winifred Bell, *Public Welfare: Time for a Change* (New York: Columbia University Office of University Publications, 1961), p. 12.
2 Victor Weingarten, "Breaking the Barrier of Confidentiality," address given at National Conference of United Community Campaigns and Councils, Cleveland, Ohio, February 25, 1958.
3 *Ibid.*
4 *America* (August 11, 1962).
5 Edgar May, "Our Costly Dilemma," *Buffalo Evening News* (June 7-22, 1960).
6 C. E. Carpenter, "Where You Goof!", address given at Annual Meeting of New York Public Welfare Association, June 23, 1959.
7 Arnold H. Maremont, in opening statement before a panel discussion, Headline Club of Chicago, Sheraton Blackstone Hotel, May 20, 1963.
8 Department of Health, Education, and Welfare, Manual Circular, Public Information (May 5, 1961).
9 *Ibid.*
10 *Editor & Publisher* (August 18, 1962).
11 Abraham Ribicoff, "Politics and Social Workers," *Social Work,* Journal of the National Association of Social Workers (April 1962).
12 Tom Adams, address before American Public Welfare Association, Americana Hotel, Miami Beach, Fla., September 7, 1962.

10. WHOSE WELFARE?

1 Leon H. Keyserling, *et al., Poverty and Deprivation in the United States,* Conference on Economic Progress (Washington, D.C.: April 1962), p. 75.

2 Greenleigh Associates, Inc., *Facts, Fallacies and Future*—A Study of the Aid to Dependent Children Program of Cook County, Illinois (New York: 1960), p. 60.
3 Winifred Bell, "The Practical Value of Social Work Service: Preliminary Report on Ten Demonstration Projects in Public Assistance," sponsored by the New York School of Social Work, Columbia University, April 20, 1961.
4 Charles E. Silberman, "The City and the Negro," *Fortune* (March 1962), p. 140.
5 James Bryant Conant, *Slums and Suburbs* (New York: McGraw-Hill Book Company, Inc., 1961), p. 3.
6 Edward T. Chase, "Learning to be Unemployed," *Harper's Magazine* (April 1963), p. 33.
7 Report, Panel of Consultants on Vocational Education, *Education for a Changing World of Work* (Washington, D.C.: U.S. Government Printing Office, 1963), p. 213.
8 *Ibid.*, summary of report, p. 20.

INDEX

Aaronson, David, The Reverend, 23
Abrams, Albert J., 30, 34
Adoption, 43, 44, 120
Aged: health, 86, 87; income, 87; life expectancy, 85; loneliness, 99-103; medical care, 94-98, 201, 202
Aid to Dependent Children: comparison with OAA, 90, 92; controversy, 38-40; cost, 40, 53, 56; dependency cause, 45; education, 44, 58, 59; eligibility study, 38, 39, 116; housing, 128, 137; father, 46-49; recipients, 39
Alabama, 40, 56, 92, 100, 112, 116, 123, 157, 178
Alabama Department of Pensions and Security, 112
Alger, Horatio, 14
Amend, Myles B., 30
American Birth Control League, 164
Arizona, 46, 178
Arkansas, 56, 92, 100, 112, 123, 178
Associated Press, 27, 54
Atlanta, Ga., 13
Atlantic County (N.J.), 113
Automation, 64-68, 72, 84

Baltimore, Md., 13, 49, 113
Bible, 2, 41
Binghamton, N.Y., 142
Birmingham, Ala., 13
Birmingham News, 183
Birth control: controversy, 144-146, 164; government supported, 157, 167; knowledge of, 153-156; legality of, 148; practice by religions, 147, 148; religious views, 149-152, 162; research, 167; welfare policies on, 157-161
Bishop of Amiens, France, The, 151
Bloomer, John W., 183
Bogue, Donald J., Dr., 165
Boyea, Ray, 22
Boston Globe, 149
Brewer, Donald D., 194
Brookings Institute, 94
Brooklyn, N.Y., 15
Brooks, Deton J., Jr., Dr., 72
Bruges, Flanders, 3
Buffalo Evening News, 176
Buffalo, N.Y., 6, 13, 105, 124, 132, 133, 134, 141, 143, 156, 176, 203
Building Service Employees' International Union, 65
Bureau of Family Services, Division of Program Statistics & Analysis, Department of Health, Education & Welfare, 13, 40, 44, 107

Burke, Paul F., 176-177
Burton, William D., The Reverend, 34
Byrd, Robert C., Senator, 38

Caldwell, Erskine, 124
California, 92, 93, 98, 109, 114, 158, 178, 192, 194
California State Department of Social Welfare, 93
Catholic Charities of the Archdiocese of New York, 24, 36
Catholic Telegraph Register, 151
Caseload, 112, 176; aged, 100
Caseworkers (public welfare): caseload, 112, 113; characteristics, 104-106; morale, 118-121; 201; responsibilities, 111; salaries, 113, 114, 201; shortage, 107, 109, 200; training, 107, 199, 200; training cost, 110; turnover, 108-111, 201
Chalmers, Thomas, 4
Charlotte, N.C., 167
Chicago, Ill., 1, 12, 13, 43, 49, 50, 52, 65, 72, 74, 75, 109, 125, 128, 130, 136, 140, 143, 146, 154, 156, 160, 165, 175, 179, 195, 196
Chicago Municipal Court, 46, 48
Child spacing. *See* Birth control
Chiselers, 5, 36, 38, 39
Christensen, Harold T., 42
Cincinnati, Ohio, 13
Civil Rights message (Presidential, 1963), 203
Clermont County (Ohio), 5
Cleveland, Ohio, 1, 13, 49, 63, 75, 203
Code enforcement, 141-143
Confidentiality, 171, 174-180
Cohen, Eli E., 62
Colbert, James G., 149
Collins, Lenora, Mrs., 196
Colorado, 178
Community Research Associates of New York, 194
Comstock, Anthony, 148, 149, 164
Congress of the Italian Catholic Union of Midwives, 151
Connecticut, 39, 46, 108, 119, 148, 149, 178, 194
Contraception, use of, 146, 147; *and see* Birth control
Cook County (Ill.), 43, 74, 130, 192
Cook County Department of Public Aid, 48, 81
Corey, John, 158
Cushing, Richard Cardinal, 167
Cybernation: The Silent Conquest (Michael), 68

Darwin, Charles, 3
Delaware, 39, 46, 178
Demonstration projects, 192-195
Denver, Colo., 13
Department of Health, Education & Welfare, 12, 17, 41, 203
Department of Health, Education & Welfare—Office on Aging, 86
Dependency: cause (ADC), 45; perpetuation, 57, 192
Descent of Man, The (Darwin), 3
Detroit, Mich., 13, 75
Detroit Department of Public Welfare, 159
Detroit League for Planned Parenthood, Inc., 159
Detroit Public Welfare Commission, 158
DiSimone, Vincent J., Jr., 138
Disraeli, Benjamin, 3
District of Columbia, 178, 192
Divorce, 43
Dona Ana County Planned Parenthood Association, 146
Donnelly, James F., Dr., 157
Donohue, John P., Judge, 32
Doulin, William E., Councilman, 23, 33
Drop-outs, 62-64, 79-81

Economy, growth rate, 190, 191
Education: achievement, 72-75, 83; ADC Children, 54, 55; ADC Mothers, 44; re-organization of, 204
Edwards, Don, 174
Elizabethan Poor Law of 1601, 3
Ellicott District Redevelopment Project, 131
Elm Haven Housing Project, 135
Eminent Fathers of the Sacred Penitentiary, 151
Employment of youth, 76, 77, 79-84
English Reformation Statute of 1536, 2

Essay on Population (Malthus), 3
Erie County (N.Y.), 6
Erie County Department of Social Welfare, 89-90, 109-117, 120-121, 176
Erie County (Buffalo) Health Department, 141
Erie County, welfare rents in, 127

Family planning. *See* Birth control
Federal Emergency Relief Act, 1933, 6
Federal Welfare Administration, Bureau of Family Services and, 157, 180
Florida, 15, 56, 157, 178, 192, 193
Florida Department of Public Welfare, 56, 194
Florida State Board of Health, 154
Forsyth County Welfare Department, N.C., 117
Foster homes, 54
Freud, Sigmund, 24

Gannett newspapers, 177
Gardner, Ralph R., 32
Georgia, 39, 131, 157, 178, 199
Goldwater, Barry, 28, 29
Grapes of Wrath (Steinbeck), 124
Greater Houston Ministerial Association, 145
Green, Councilman, 30
Greenleigh Associates of New York, 57, 118, 129; ADC Study of Cook County, 130
Grossi, Anthony J., Senator, 137
Guam, 56, 92

Hawaii, 46, 178
Hightstown, N.J., 137
Horwitz, Julius, 175
Housing: condition of, 123-130, 133, 137-141; cost, 127; inspections, 141; overcrowding, 128; violations, 141
Housing Act, 1949, 130
Housing Act, 1961, 130
Howlett, Michael J., 157

Illegitimacy, 42, 49-54
Illinois, 8, 14, 46, 49, 73, 74, 107, 109, 112, 116, 178, 200
Illinois Public Aid Commission, 96, 146, 157, 160
Illiteracy, 71, 195; functional, 72-75
Indiana, 178, 193
Indianapolis, Ind., 13
Infausto, Felix, 27, 28
Information policies: federal, 181; state, 175, 176, 178-180
International Association of City Managers, 33
Iowa, 178
Isaacs, Norman, 183

Jackson County (Miss.), 113
Jackson County (Mo.), 46
Jameson, Henry B., 182
Jersey City, N.J., 13
Juvenile delinquency, 69, 77, 78

Kahan, Norman, Rabbi, 23
Kansas, 116, 178
Kansas City, Mo., 13, 46
Karnak, Ill., 8
Kaufman, William H., 22, 23
Kennedy, John F., 37, 85, 168, 189, 190
Kentucky, 8, 39, 92, 123
Kerr-Mills Act, 97, 98
King, Martin Luther, Jr., The Reverend, 204
Kirschenbaum, Irving, 22, 23
Konysz, Frank, 22
Kowal, Chester, Mayor, 133

Labor: agricultural workers, 65; factory, 65; white collar, 65
Lambeth Conference of the Anglican Church, 150
Liberty Magazine, 88
Liebling, A.J., 181
Liebman Associates, Marvin, 30
Life Magazine, 28
Logue, Edward J., 149
Loneliness, 99-103
Los Angeles, Calif., 1, 75
Los Angeles County (Calif.), 114, 115
Los Angeles Times, 183
Louisiana, 14, 39, 54, 92, 100, 112, 178
Louisville Courier-Journal, 183

Louisville, Ky., 13
Luzerne County (Penn.), 117

MacQuarrie, Ellen G., Mrs., 181
Maine, 178
Malthus, Thomas, 3
Marriage, 42
Marriage and Family Living, 154
Marx, Karl, 24
Maryland, 46, 109, 159, 178, 192
Maryland State Board of Public Welfare, 160
Massachusetts, 46, 71, 98, 116, 146, 148, 149, 178
Massachusetts State Legislature, 5
Mecklenburg County Department of Public Welfare, 167
Medical Aid to Aged (under Social Security), 98, 201, 202
Medical Care: ADC and OAA comparison, 93; Aged, 92, 94-98
Memphis, Tenn., 13
Meyer, Karl, Dr., 156
Michigan, 67, 98, 131, 158, 178, 192
Miller, Walter A., 63
Milwaukee, Wisc., 13, 113
Minneapolis, Minn., 13
Mississippi, 14, 39, 54, 55, 56, 73, 74, 92, 100, 112, 123, 157, 178
Mississippi Senate, 169
Missouri, 200
Mitchell, Joseph McDowell, 3, 18, 19, 21, 22, 24, 25, 26, 27, 28, 30, 31, 32, 33, 34-35, 36, 37
Monroe County (N.Y.), 54
Montana, 178
Mounds, Ill., 8, 9
Mount City, Ill., 8
Mount Vernon, N.Y., 9
Mulder, Carel E.H., 93
Murray, Marie C., 32
McCarthy, Robert, 30
McCloskey, Stephen, 149
McCulloch, Frank, 183
McDonnell, James T., Monsignor, 23, 24
McIntyre, Councilman, 30-31, 33
McKneally, Martin B., 34
McKneally, George F., Councilman, 18, 23, 24, 32, 34
McNamara, Pat, Senator, 97
National Academy of Sciences, 168
National Broadcasting Company, 31
National Committee on Employment of Youth, 62, 65
National Institute of Health, 167
National Office of Vital Statistics, 41
National Urban League, 12
Nebraska, 194
Negro: adoptions, 43; divorce, 43; drop-outs, 63, 64; income, 12; percentage on relief, 12-14; population shift, 11; prejudice, 29, 43, 129, 130, 165, 203; public housing, 134; rent payments, 129; responsibilities of, 203, 204; unemployment, 47; urban renewal, 134
Nevada, 39, 178
New Poor Law of 1834, 3
New Hampshire, 157, 171, 178
New Haven, Conn., 135
New Jersey, 113, 157, 171, 178
New Jersey Legislature Welfare Investigating Committee, 137, 138
New Mexico, 178
New York (County), 49
New York City, 1, 9, 13, 36, 44, 63, 75, 99, 111, 127, 129, 136, 141, 142, 165, 171, 174, 175; welfare families living in single rooms, 129; welfare finders fees, 129; welfare rents, 127, 129
New York City Department of Welfare, 127, 129, 159
New York City Mayor's Task Force on Youth & Work, 62-63
New York City Youth Employment Service, 76, 77
New York Daily News, 30
New York Herald Tribune, 30
New York State, 9, 19, 29, 32, 40, 46, 57, 67, 92, 93, 98, 105, 107, 109, 112, 121, 128, 130, 131, 135, 142, 156, 159, 160, 178, 179, 180, 181, 192
New York State Board of Social Welfare, 28, 178
New York State Department of Audit & Control, 179
New York State Department of Social Welfare, 19, 20, 22, 27, 32, 36, 176, 178, 179, 180

New York State Legislature, 5, 32
New York State Social Welfare Law, 142
New York Times, 145
Newark, N.J., 13
Newburgh, N.Y., 3, 7, 14, 17-37, 88, 124, 175, 178, 187, 188; aged, 88; hearings, 23, 27, 28; housing, 18, 124; migrants, 22, 23; negroes, 29, 34, 35; news coverage, 26, 27, 30, 36, 175; police muster, 21; relief costs, 20; Thirteen Points, 25
Newburgh Area Protestant Men's League, 24
Newburgh Chamber of Commerce, 32
Newburgh City Council, 18, 22, 23, 26
Newburgh City Welfare Department, 19, 26, 188
Newburgh Ministerial Association, 23
Newburgh News, 21, 24, 25, 26, 27, 34
Newspapers, coverage of welfare and, 176, 182-184
Niagara County (N.Y.), 194
Norfolk, Va., 13
North Carolina, 19, 46, 116, 157, 178
North Carolina State Board of Health, 157
North Dakota, 157, 178
Nursing homes, 95-97

Odell Tuberculosis Sanitarium, 34
O'Donnell, John J., 19, 21, 26, 27, 28
Ohio, 5, 49, 92, 113, 116, 131, 178
Oklahoma, 46, 100, 112, 178
Oklahoma City, Okla., 13, 72
Oklahoma State Employment Service, 72
Old Age Assistance: caseload, 100; characteristics, 87; comparison with ADC, 92; cost, 90, 92; medical, 95; recipients, 90, 91
Old Age Survivors & Disability Insurance, 87
Olmsted, Ill., 8, 9
Omaha, Nebr., 13
Onondaga County Welfare Department, 175
Orange County (N.Y.), 19
Oregon, 46, 178

Pankow, Stephen, Mayor, 131, 132
Paperwork, 114-118
Parker, Sidney, The Reverend, 23
Paterson, N.J., 138
Peace Corps, 199-200
Peekskill, N.Y., 9
Pennsylvania, 4, 46, 67, 92, 98, 113, 131, 178, 192, 193, 194
Petrillo, Peter Z., Jr., 31, 33
Philadelphia (County), 49
Philadelphia, Penn., 13, 75
Pittsburgh, Penn., 1, 75
Planned Parenthood Federation of America, 42, 149, 152, 157, 158, 160, 164, 165, 166
Politics, social workers participation in, 185-187
Political Analysis Associates of Princeton, New Jersey, 29
Poor Laws, 2-6
Pope Pius XII, 151
Population shift, 41
Power, Ann F., 187-188
President's Council on Aging, 86
Press. *See* Newspapers
Private social agencies, 171, 179, 180, 206; Newburgh views on, 36
Pruitt-Igoe Housing Project, 135
Public housing: income limits, 135; number of, 134; opinions of, 136; percentage Negro in, 134; relation to welfare, 134, 135
Public Law 86-778, 97
Public opinions, 172, 173
Public relations, 174
Public welfare: amendments, 191, 192; cost, 2, 8-10; criticism, 7, 17, 19, 172, 173; persons receiving, 2; Presidential Message on, 189
Public Welfare, Medical Care & Family Planning (symposium), 165
Publicity. *See* Public relations
Puerto Rico, 56, 92
Pulaski County (Ill.), 8, 9, 10
Pulaski County Department of Public Aid, 9
Purchase, N.Y., 9
Puritans, 4

Rats, 125
Reflector-Chronicle, 182

Reforms, Erie County, 177
Rehabilitation, 191-199
Religion: birth control practice, 147, 148; birth control views, 149-152; de-emphasis, 41; Newburgh views, 23, 24, 36
Reston, James, 145
Rhode Island, 46, 178
Richman, Grover C., Jr., 138
Ritz, Joseph, 27
Robinson, William H., 165
Rochester, N.Y., 54
Rock, John, Dr., 156, 167
Rockefeller, Nelson A., Governor, 29
Roosevelt, Franklin Delano, 189, 190
Roosevelt, Teddy, 42
Rural poverty, 8, 9
Ryan, Daniel J., 159
Ryan, William, Mayor, 23, 24
Rhythm method, 151, 152, 167; *see also* Birth control

Sacramento County Welfare Department, 158
San Francisco, Calif., 15, 37
Sanger, Margaret, 164
Saturday Evening Post, 88
Saturday Review, 89
Scarsdale, N.Y., 9
Seattle, Wash., 13
Secrecy. *See* Confidentiality
Simonian, Kane, 149
Slumlords, 136-140; weapons against, 142, 143
Smart, Walter, 149
Smith, Charles, 29
Smith, Harold, 158
Social security: Amendments, 90; comparison with OAA, 91; history, 6
Social Security Act—1935, 6, 44, 87, 90, 202
Social Security Administration, 202
Social workers, 104; graduate, 107, 199-201; in public welfare, 107; *see also* Caseworkers
Social work education, 107
Social work schools, 107, 199, 200
South Carolina, 39, 56, 92, 157, 178
South Dakota, 178
Staff: training, 107; cost of, 110; turnover, 108-111
St. George, Katherine, Representative, 28
St. John-Stevas, Norman, 149
St. Louis, Mo., 13, 49, 135
St. Luke's Hospital, 151-152
St. Paul, Minn., 13, 194
St. Vincent's Hospital, 151
Steinbeck, John, 124
Stice, Glen., Dr., 62
Storey, Wilbur F., 188
Suburbs: ADC recipient rate, 10; growth of, 122, 123
Surburbanite, The, 123
Suitable home laws, 54
Sullivan, David, 65
Sumner, William Graham, 3
Stycos, J. Mayone, 154

Tagge, George, 146
Talmud, 174
Television, 175
Tennessee, 39, 123
Texas, 55, 92, 100, 112, 171 178, 192
Texas Legislature, 55
Thayer Hospital, 95
Time Has Come, The, (Rock), 156
Tobacco Road (Caldwell), 124
Training: caseworkers, 107, 199, 200; jobless workers, 72; youth, 204
Trenton, N.J., 128
Truth Seeker, The, 29
Tulsa Tribune (Okla.), 7

United Nations, 168
Ullin, Ill., 8
Undergraduate training, 199, 200
Unemployment, 191, 196; youth, 60-62
U.S. Bureau of the Census, 41, 68, 123, 125
U.S. Department of Agriculture, 56, 86
U.S. Department of Commerce, 86
U.S. Department of Labor—Bureau of Labor Statistics, 47, 61, 62, 65, 68
U.S. Department of Labor's Consumer Price Index, 94
U.S. Public Health Service, 86
U.S. Senate Committee on Appropriation, 39, 53
U.S. Senate's Special Committee on Aging, 86, 97, 98

University of Southern California's School of Public Administration, 133
Urban Renewal: statistics, 130; relation to welfare, 131; relocation, 133
Utah, 46, 178

Vasey, Wayne, 200
Vermont, 178
Virgin Islands, 56, 178
Virginia, 116, 157, 178, 192
Vives, Juan Luis, 3
Vocational education, 204, 205
Volunteers, 202

Washington, D.C., 12, 13, 38, 39, 49, 57, 193; Welfare Department, 194
Washington Nursing Center (Ill.), 95-96
Washington State, 46, 178
Weiner, Irving, Dr., 22
West Virginia, 8, 39, 46, 100, 157, 178
Westchester County (N.Y.), 9, 194
White Plains, N.Y., 9
Wichita, Kan., 13
Wiener, Norbert, 68
Wilson, Rosemary, 142
Wirtz, W. Willard, 61
Wisconsin, 157, 178
Work relief, 27, 30
World War II, 43, 62, 64
Wright, Richard C., Mrs., 117
Wyoming, 178

Yonkers, N.Y., 9
Young Americans for Freedom, 30
Youth: drop-outs, 62-64; employment, 76, 77, 79-84; unemployment, 60-62; unskilled, 68

About the Author

Pulitzer Prize-winning reporter EDGAR MAY was born in Switzerland in 1929 and came to New York City as a boy. He attended Columbia University Night School for three years while working as a file clerk for the *New York Times,* and received his B.S., *summa cum laude* in journalism, from the Medill School of Journalism at Northwestern.

As a reporter, his first job was with the *Bellows Falls* (Vt.) *Times.* He later worked as a reporter for the *Fitchburg* (Mass.) *Sentinel* and the *Buffalo Evening News.* He has also been an Army speechwriter and has done free lance reporting in Europe.

Mr. May's journalism awards include the 1961 Pulitzer Prize for local reporting for a fourteen-part public welfare series, "Our Costly Dilemma," in the *Buffalo Evening News;* the Walter A. Bingham Award of the Buffalo Newspaper Guild for outstanding journalism in Western New York; Page One Award, Buffalo Newspaper Guild; and Best News Story Award, Best Feature Award from the New England Weekly Press Association.

From 1962–1963, Mr. May worked as a public welfare consultant for the State Charities Aid Association in New York.